Legal Spaces

Sabine Müller-Mall

Legal Spaces

Towards a Topological Thinking of Law

Springer

Sabine Müller-Mall
Faculty of Law
Humboldt University Berlin
Berlin, Germany

ISBN 978-3-642-36729-8 ISBN 978-3-642-36730-4 (eBook)
DOI 10.1007/978-3-642-36730-4
Springer Heidelberg New York Dordrecht London

Library of Congress Control Number: 2013936436

Printed on acid-free paper

Springer is part of Springer Science+Business Media (www.springer.com)

For Marie and Joyce Kosley

Acknowledgments

I am grateful to *Nomos Verlagsgesellschaft* and to *Franz Steiner Verlag* for permission to include material from the following chapters of my own work: 'Verwaltungsrechtsraum Europa – Zur Möglichkeit seiner rechtswissenschaftlichen Erschließung', in: Debus et al. (eds.). Verwaltungsrechtsraum Europa, Baden-Baden: Nomos, pp. 9–31 and 'Rechtserzeugung als performativer Vorgang in der Sprache', in: Bäcker, Carsten/Ziemann, Sascha (eds.). *Junge Rechtsphilsophie. Archiv für Rechts- und Sozialphilosophie*, Beiheft 135, Stuttgart: Franz Steiner, pp. 117–126.

Several colleagues and friends have generously given their time and have read and commented on earlier versions of this research. I wish to thank all those who contributed in one way or another to the completion of this book, but in particular: Anja Breljak, Jochen Bung, Felix Creutzig, Thomas Hilgers, Anna-Bettina Kaiser, Ann-Katrin Kaufhold, Jan Philipp Kruse, Isabelle Ley, Anna Katharina Mangold, Nora Markard, Christoph Möllers, Reut Yael Paz, Cathrin Romeis, Franziska Schulte Ostermann, Ralf Seinecke, Chris Thomale, Luise Tremel, Tim Wihl, and Benjamin Wihstutz.

Contents

Chapter 1
Introduction

About 50 years ago, the legal cosmos seemed to have an unambiguous order. There were national states with their national legal orders, and there were a few international treaties to ensure rights that affected or involved more than one national state. If someone had a legal conflict, it did not seem to be too complicated to find the right court to which to turn. Of course this narrative could easily be called into question, because it is at best a very simplified description of the *Western* legal world; or because the picture shows the more complexities the closer we look at it; or because 50 years ago the world saw the height of the Cold War, for which reason it would be too simple to speak of an unambiguous situation. On the other hand, if we consider legal theory, it was at this time that *H. L. A. Hart* published his *Concept of Law* (1961)[1] and that *Lon L. Fuller* published his *Morality of Law* (1964)[2]—50 years ago, (Western) legal theory was in the middle of its great debates on positivism and morals. The questions were not so much about legal systems, but about law's normativity. We might assume the reason for this orientation to lie in the fact that it was not so much contested that there were national legal orders and international treaties at all, but that it was contested of what 'nature' these normative orders were. And the narrative of the unambiguous legal cosmos could be strengthened by comparing the situation to today's pressing questions concerning law. Even if we are a far cry from a definite solution to the problem of law's nature, the pressing questions seem to be more connected to the global legal situation than they were half a century ago: *how do we solve legal problems in a globalized world*, with both globalized and fragmented legal orders, with multi-level legal systems, with overlapping legal regimes, and with conflicts that involve more than one legal

[1] Hart, H. L. A. (1961). The Concept of Law. Oxford: Clarendon Press.

[2] Fuller, Lon (1964). *The Morality of Law*. New Haven: Yale University Press. In Germany, 50 years ago was the time that *Friedrich Müller* published his "Normstruktur und Normativität" (1966), and that the German edition *Duncker & Humblot* launched its famous series "Schriften zur Rechtstheorie" (1962): Müller, Friedrich (1966). *Normstruktur und Normativität. Zum Verhältnis von Recht und Wirklichkeit in der juristischen Hermeneutik, entwickelt an Fragen der Verfassungs-interpretation.* Berlin: Duncker und Humblot.

S. Müller-Mall, *Legal Spaces*, DOI 10.1007/978-3-642-36730-4_1,

order? Looking at discussions of legal pluralism,[3] or of constitutionalism,[4] of the globalization or internationalization of judicial systems,[5] we can state that one of the most important questions in legal theory today seems to be how to describe global law. This question is derived from the one of how to solve legal problems in a globalized world—because any answer to the latter question presupposes a consistent conceptual description of contemporary global law. The present (small) study tries to contribute to this (huge) issue in a very preliminary, nonetheless indispensable manner: we are going to reflect on the conditions of describing contemporary law in a theoretical way. The goal of this study is thereby twofold: to find an approach to contemporary law that renders possible a conceptual description *and* that can offer tools for a methodical investigation of contemporary law.

Such an investigation, of course, is not free of a central problem with which any theoretical investigation has to deal: an approach to contemporary law refers to an originally new phenomenon—the one of *contemporary* law. It is new in the sense that there does not yet exist a concept of description, or, to say it more precisely, there is not yet a commonly accepted concept of description for this phenomenon. Of course there are proposals in the theoretical world. The one of (global) legal pluralism is very important, for instance, as are those of network theory and systems theory. All of these proposals have many interesting features for describing contemporary law in a productive way. And still, they are not to be called commonly accepted concepts in this context. We shall have a closer look at the reasons for this in Chap. 2 of this book, but I might still indicate the general type of reasons that we will encounter: my assumption concerning these proposals is that their great impact lies in the sphere of description, but not in the one of methods for legal investigation. In positing a global legal pluralism, for example, we apply a possibly very appropriate concept to contemporary law, but we cannot deduce any solutions to concrete legal problems, e.g. collisions of different legal orders. Another difficulty that some of the existing approaches to contemporary law show is related to a more theoretical problem: typically, those approaches are not connected to a theoretical basis concerning the concept of law they apply. And here, we can close the circle to the problem of the object of this investigation being a *new* one. If there is not yet a common description of contemporary law on which we could base further investigation in a secure mode, then it will not be sufficient to describe the new aspects of the global legal constellation in contrast to former aspects of the global legal constellation, as if 'law' in 'earlier law' and 'contemporary law' had remained the same concept. The more, the assumption is that a concept of law that has been appropriate for describing national legal orders does not necessarily have to be

---

[3] *See below*, Chap. 2.

[4] *See* e.g. Klabbers, Jan & Peters, Anne & Ulfstein, Geir (eds.) (2009). *The Constitutionalization of International Law*. Oxford: Oxford University Press.

[5] *See* Marinez, Jenny S. (2003). Towards an International Judicial System. *Stanford Law Review 56*, 429-529; Slaughter, Anne-Marie (1999). Judicial Globalization. *Virginia Journal of International Law 40*, 1103-1124.

appropriate for describing a contemporary *globalized* law. New conceptual approaches might therefore be suitable. The course of this study, we can mention this here, will require the reader to engage with a concept that might be unfamiliar in this context: the one of *space*. This concept might provide us with a new perspective on contemporary global law: one that allows us to grasp these two types of approaches at the same time—a conceptual, descriptive one as well as a methodological one. However, we should not anticipate the result of the present investigation at this point.

If we are embarked here for an approach to contemporary law that might offer a conceptual description as well as methodical tools for investigating law, then we have to include several aspects in our considerations:

(1) We have to devote attention to the concept of law we are presupposing, because it is impossible to approach contemporary law without at least assuming a certain concept of law.
(2) We have to extract specific characteristics of contemporary law to make visible starting points for our approach. And since we are not set out for a historical study, we will not try to extract these characteristics from comparisons with descriptions of previous legal phenomena, but we shall gain these characteristics by analyzing other concepts of description referring to contemporary law, such as legal pluralism or network theory.
(3) We have to make explicit the presuppositions we have, because any application of the term 'contemporary law' contains presuppositions.

Following these tasks, the present study integrates three main chapters. Chap. 2 elaborates the presuppositions on which further considerations are based. As indicated above, these presuppositions include two main aspects belonging to the object of this study, contemporary law. One aspect relates to contemporary law's characteristic as a complex order, as a structure, while the other relates to its normativity—the concept of law that is included in the term 'contemporary law'. In other words, assuming that we discuss law as a phenomenon of normative order, of normative complexity, in Chap. 2 we will have a look at both sides of this expression—law's normativity and law's complexity. In attempting to make explicit the major prerequisites and to define what a perspective on contemporary law could be, we will encounter contemporary law as *hybrid, relational, and dynamic law*; and we will reformulate law's normativity setting out from the assumption that it is best explained by the notion of *performativity*.

Based on these two conceptual backgrounds, we will then encircle a conceptual idea to describe contemporary law: the one of *thinking law spatially*. In Chap. 3, we therefore have to develop a *concept of space* that might be fruitful in this context. As we will see, referring to the concept of space does not necessarily mean employing the notion of a three-dimensional container, to resemble natural space. Rather, we can learn from other disciplines (such as cultural studies, philosophy, but also mathematics) that *space* is a concept with the capacity to capture relationality, dynamics, and hybridity. In analyzing *Michel de Certeau*'s performative conception of space, we shall find a way to apply the concept of space to our approach to law. With these theoretical considerations, Chap. 3 is the core of our investigation.

Chap. 4, then, tries to point out different advantages that thinking law spatially might have: we shall see three different possible ways of applying the concept. These cover legal theory as well as methods of exploring law, and might indicate where further considerations could take up the concept of space.

In this sense, the character of the present book is preliminary: it approximates a perspective on law that is not fixed from the beginning, but instead is to be developed in the process of this study. While in Chap. 2 we have to filter out slowly (and from time to time even arduously) some presuppositions concerning the object of the perspective to be developed, the investigation will pick up speed in encircling the spatial perspective in Chaps. 3 and 4. At the end of such an attempt, there will in the best case be a starting point: a perspective on law we can assume for undertaking further investigations.

Chapter 2
Taking a Perspective on Contemporary Law: Complexity and Normativity

2.1 Looking for a Perspective I

To investigate contemporary law means to take a perspective on it. And 'taking a perspective' is a far more complicated procedure than it might at first sound. Indeed, if we think of a photographer taking a picture of a landscape it seems to be very clear what it means to take a perspective: the detail of the landscape can be defined well using a topographical scale, the focal length, the zoom, even the quadrangular frame of the picture—all these aspects constitute the 'perspective'.[1] *How can we take a perspective on contemporary law?* This is the central question of this present chapter, and this question is necessarily connected to the more general one of how we can take a perspective on something that is hardly perceivable sensually. There are many differences between landscape and law, certainly, but among them the differing capacities to be observed by us might display best where it is that the problems of taking a perspective on contemporary law have their origins: even if we can hear a judge pass sentence, if we can touch a copy of the Constitution, we do not sensually perceive law by the act of listening to the judge or touching the copy. The pure sensation might resemble the one of hearing the words 'the sky is blue' uttered by just any person, or the one of touching a copy of some novel. Law cannot be found through the physical sensation—the grounds from which law grows are different ones than the grounds of landscapes, they are *conceptual* grounds.

If we do not have any capacity to perceive conceptual objects of investigation in a sensual way, we have to look for alternative methods of investigation. The most obvious alternative would be to investigate these objects *conceptually*. We shall therefore try in this chapter to approximate a conceptual investigation of law. And

[1] Of course, in this case, too, the concept of a perspective becomes a very difficult one as soon as we 'take a closer look', cf. e. g. Elkins, James (1994). The *poetics of perspective*. Ithaca: Cornell University Press.

S. Müller-Mall, *Legal Spaces*, DOI 10.1007/978-3-642-36730-4_2,

still, the question remains: how can we take a perspective on contemporary law that is grounded conceptually?

The idea for the present study is based on the assumption that we have to make explicit the presuppositions that we carry with us in thinking of contemporary law and thus to develop a perspective that is shaped by these presuppositions. Concerning these presuppositions, though, it is illusive to provide them with a definite article. This is the case because presuppositions cannot be objective; to the contrary, they are originally subjective, just as any perspective is subjective. Even more complicated is the problem that also from a subjective point of view it is impossible to make explicit all the conceptual presuppositions we make. The only chance of getting out of this regressive situation is to select some presuppositions and to construct a perspective based on the ones chosen. My starting point for taking a perspective on contemporary law, therefore, will be the attempt to describe as precisely as possible presuppositions I make when I think of contemporary law. Of course, as I have to make a selection in any case, I am going to choose presuppositions that might suit the conceptual idea I want to develop and to propose later in this book. It is obvious now—this study will not try to deduce any concept or any hypothesis. The more, it should be read as an attempt to capture a procedure of developing, we could even say constructing, a theoretical proposal. And because this procedure does not necessarily take place at the exact same time as these lines are written, one should read it as the *simulation* of such a procedure.

The presuppositions on which I choose to base a conceptual and descriptive approach to contemporary law are connected to the reduced scale of the perspective for which I am looking: looking at 'contemporary law', and at no more than that, means to use a highly reduced scale. It means, in other words, to look at the 'whole' of law. Of course, looking at the whole does not mean having a megalomaniacal attitude; it just means focusing on different aspects than we would, for instance, if we were to take a micro-perspective. In the case of contemporary law, taking a macro-perspective involves the systematic level of law, the structure and the shapes of law as a whole. In other words, we have to negotiate law's complexity, which we shall treat in Sect. 2.2 of this chapter. In addition, we have to look at what we could call the quality structure of law—in legal language: 'normativity' (Sect. 2.3). Since we shall focus on the macro-perspective, we have to describe the normative order of law rather than law's ontology.

With all these difficulties of taking a perspective in mind, we are now embarking for a conceptual and descriptive approach in taking a perspective that integrates law's complexity as well as law's normativity.

2.2 The Complexity of Law: Hybrid, Relational, Dynamic

2.2.1 *Presuppositions*

As we have already mentioned, our presuppositions can neither be enumerated exactly, nor can they be found at any place in a precise formulation that we only need to pick up. We are therefore starting here with two assumptions, on both of which we will work throughout this chapter. The two assumptions are connected to each other, but we shall use them to explore different spheres: one, *the concept of plural law*, indicates some characteristics of law to us that will become more important in Chaps. 3 and 4—hybridity, relationality, and dynamics of law; the other one, *the pluralism of forms of legal normativity*, is a necessary condition for the approach to legal normativity that we will take in Sect. 2.3 of this chapter.

2.2.1.1 Pluralism of Laws: Plural Law

The first central presupposition of this approach lies in the assumption that *contemporary law is plural law*. Law's pluralism is neither a new observation[2] nor a much-contested thesis (any more). On the contrary, even though 'legal pluralism' was a quite controversial concept for a while, it now seems to be a more or less common concept to describe contemporary law[3]—*Boaventura de Sousa Santos* eventually

[2] As a fact, a pluralism of legal orders has been almost typical for a premodern legal world, *see* Seinecke, Ralf (2013). Rechtspluralismus als Kampf für das Recht – historisch, theoretisch, normativ, in: Estermann, Josef (ed.). *Der Kampf ums Recht*. Beckendried: Orlux, pp. 121–136 (123), referring to Stolleis, Michael (2008). Vormodernes und postmodernes Recht. Quarderni Fiorentini 37, 543–551 (547);, and *see* Medieval European Law as an example in Tamanaha, Brian Z. (2008). Understanding Legal Pluralism. Past to Present, Local to Global, *Sydney Law Review 30*, 375–411 (pp. 377). There have been conceptual debates on pluralism also regarding situations of conflict between state and non-state authority, such as church authority, *see* e.g. Figgis, John Neville (1913). *Churches in the Modern State*. London: Longmans, Green, pp. 54, and *Paul Schiff Berman* referring to this discourse, Berman, Paul Schiff (2009). The New Legal Pluralism. *Annual Review of Law and Social Science*, 5, 225–242 (226). In addition, colonial and post-colonial settings undergoing conflicts of indigenous (non-state) law and law set by the colonizing authority have been discussed in terms of pluralism, cf. Michaels, Ralf (2009). Global Legal Pluralism. *Duke Law School Faculty Scholarship Series*. Paper 185. (http://lsr.nellco.org/duke_fs/185; accessed 12 december 2012) p. 4, and Merry, Sally Engle (1988). Legal Pluralism. *Law and Society Review 22*, 869–896 (872–874) considering this phase as "Classical Legal Pluralism". For an example *see* Pospisil, Leopold (1981). Modern and Traditional Administration of Justice in New Guinea. *Journal of Legal Pluralism 19* (93–116).

[3] Qualifying legal pluralism as part of the mainstream legal discourse, *see* Michaels, Ralf (2009). Global Legal Pluralism. *Duke Law School Faculty Scholarship Series*. Paper 185. (http://lsr.nellco.org/duke_fs/185; accessed 12 December 2012), p. 1.

called it a *key concept,*[4] and that already in 1987. Today this concept is even shared in many fields of legal scholarship. It is to be found not only in socio-legal studies, which probably are the field the most suspicious of using the concept,[5] or in legal anthropology. Especially in diverse works dealing with the globalization or transnationalization of law, the concept of legal pluralism has become outright ubiquitous: in terms of "global legal pluralism".[6]

Legal pluralism "is when in a social field more than one source of 'law', more than one 'legal order', is observable".[7] Since its key aspects—the plurality of legal orders, the coexistence of domestic state law with other legal orders, the absence of a linear hierarchical order—"reappear in the global sphere" today,[8] the concept of global legal pluralism has become a descriptive tool for both (socio-)legal pluralists and international lawyers. And still, maybe just because the options of applying this concept are (at least) two-fold, it is used very broadly, in different contexts. For this reason, it is helpful here, too, to use the concept in a very broad sense, (at least in the first step), because any rash concretization would lead to confusion.

To say it with the words of *Brian Z. Tamanaha*: "Legal pluralism is everywhere. There is, in every social arena one examines, a seeming multiplicity of legal orders, from the lowest local level to the most expansive global level. There are village, town, or municipal laws of various types; there are state, district or regional laws of various types; there are national, transnational, and international laws of various types. In addition to these familiar bodies of law, in many societies there are more

[4] *See* de Sousa Santos, Boaventura (1987). Law: A Map of Misreading. Toward a Postmodern Conception of Law. *Journal of Law and Society, 14*(3), 279–302 (297): "*Legal pluralism* is the key concept in a postmodern view of law."

[5] *See* e.g. Merry, Sally Engle (1988). Legal Pluralism. *Law and Society Review 22*, 869–896; Teubner, Gunther (1996). Global Bukowina. Legal Pluralism in the World Society, in: G. Teubner (Ed.), *Global Law Without A State*, Aldershot: Dartmouth, pp. 3–28; Griffiths, John (1986). What is Legal Pluralism? *Journal of Legal Pluralism 24*, 1–55; Riles, Annelise (1994). Representing the In-Between: Law, Anthropology, and the Rhetoric of Interdisciplinarity. *Illinois Law Review*, 597–653 (641); Tamanaha, Brian Z. (2000). A Non-Essentialist Version of Legal Pluralism. *Journal of Law and Society 27*(2), 296–321.

[6] *See* e.g. Berman, Paul Schiff (2007). Global Legal Pluralism. *Southern California Law Review 80*, 1155–1237; Koskenniemi, Martti (2005). *Global Legal Pluralism: Multiple Regimes and Multiple Modes of Thought.* http://www.helsinki.fi/eci/Publications/Koskenniemi/MKPluralism-Harvard-05d[1].pdf. Accessed 12 December 2012; Rajagopal, Balakrishnan. (2005). The Role of Law in Counter-Hegemonic Globalization and Global Legal Pluralism: Lessons from the Narmada Valley Struggle in India. *Leiden Journal of International Law 18*, 345–387; Michaels, Ralf (2005). The Re-*State*-ment of Non-state Law: the State, Choice of Law, and the Challenge from Global Legal Pluralism. *Wayne Law Review 51*, 1209–1259; Teubner, Gunther (1996). Global Bukowina. Legal Pluralism in the World Society, in: G. Teubner (Ed.), *Global Law Without A State*, Aldershot: Dartmouth, pp. 3–28; Merry, Sally Engle (2005), Human Rights and Global Legal Pluralism: Reciprocity and Disjuncture, In: F. v. Benda-Beckmann, K. v. Benda-Beckmann & A. Griffiths (Eds.). *Mobile People, Mobile Law. Expanding Legal Relations in a Contracting World.* Aldershot: Ashgate,pp. 215–232.

[7] Griffith, John (1986). What is Legal Pluralism? *Journal of Legal Pluralism 24*, 1–55 (38).

[8] *See* for citation and enumeration of topics Michaels, Ralf (2009). Global Legal Pluralism. *Duke Law School Faculty Scholarship Series.* Paper 185. (http://lsr.nellco.org/duke_fs/185; accessed 12 december 2012), p. 1.

exotic forms of law, like customary law, indigenous law, religious law, or law connected to distinct ethnic or cultural groups within a society. There is also an evident increase in quasi-legal activities, from private policing and judging, to privately run prisons, to the on-going creation of the new *lex mercatoria*, a body of transnational commercial law that is almost entirely the product of private law making activities."[9]

If we state that contemporary law is plural law, this is at first not more than a description referring to multiple orders and regimes[10] that float around in the normative cosmos[11] at the same time.[12] On the way towards a conceptual approach this description is a necessary and helpful foundation providing a far developed vocabulary from which we can borrow in different ways. But there is an important incompleteness that prevents the concept of legal pluralism from offering more features than only descriptive ones, for it to be the foundation of a comprehensive legal theory: its silence concerning the question of legal normativity. It could be irritating to use the term silence in this context, as numerous attempts have been made by legal pluralists to draw the distinction between law and non-law.[13] The results of these attempts consist in different definitions of the distinction, ranging from 'all social orders can be legal orders'[14] to a certain hopelessness of finding a criterion to differentiate social norms from legal norms.[15] However, there is no definite connection of the concept of legal pluralism and the one of legal normativity. Instead of regretting this deficiency of legal pluralism as a concept, we should put this observation into relation with the aim of the concept: initially, it was not the result of a search for a comprehensive theory of law, but for a conceptual tool that could make possible an appropriate description of overlapping and parallel normative orders in a globalized world. Therefore it is already methodologically impossible to create a definition of law that is deduced from such a

[9] Tamanaha, Brian Z. (2008). Understanding Legal Pluralism. Past to Present, Local to Global, *Sydney Law Review 30*, 375–411 (375).

[10] Speaking of "regimes": Fischer-Lescano, Andreas & Teubner, Gunther (2006). Regime-Kollisionen. Zur Fragmentierung des globalen Rechts. Frankfurt am Main: Suhrkamp; Fischer-Lescano, Andreas & Teubner, Gunther (2004). Regime-Collisions: The Vain Search for Legal Unitiy in the Fragmentation of Global Law. *Michigan Journal of International Law* 25, 999–1046.

[11] In the words of *Robert M. Cover*: "We inhabit a *nomos* – a normative Universe", Cover, Robert M. (1983). The Supreme Court 1982 Term. Foreword: Nomos and Narrative. *Harvard Law Review 97*, 4–68 (4).

[12] And yet, there are global legal pluralists who are developing a normative impact of the concept of 'global legal pluralism', e.g. *Paul Schiff Berman*. *See* Berman, Paul Schiff (2007). Global Legal Pluralism. *Southern California Law Review 80*, 1155–1237 (1156): "(…)pluralism offers not only a more comprehensive descriptive account of the world we live in, but also suggests a potentially useful alternative approach to the design of procedural mechanisms, institutions, and practices."

[13] *See* with further acknowledgements Tamanaha, Brian Z. (2000). A Non-Essentialist Version of Legal Pluralism. *Journal of Law and Society 27*(2), 296-321(297).

[14] *See* Macdonald, Roderick & Kleinhans, Martha-Marie (1997). What is Critical Legal Pluralism? *Canadian Journal of Law and Society (12)*, 25–46 (40).

[15] Teubner, Gunther (1996). Global Bukowina. Legal Pluralism in the World Society, in: G. Teubner (Ed.), *Global Law Without A State*, Aldershot: Dartmouth, pp. 3–28 (13).

concept. Looking at an isolated characteristic of an object will never grant us the opportunity to conclude a general theory of the object. There is only one possible exception to this assumption: the case that we can add another presupposition—that the characteristic is a necessary part of every possible kind of the object in question. For legal pluralism it is simply not possible to show such a conceptual necessity, because we have very well-developed models of purely linear-hierarchic law, e. g. *Kelsen's Pure Theory of Law*,[16] functioning as counterexamples.

2.2.1.2 Pluralism of Forms of Legal Normativity

Since we are embarked here for the search of a theoretical approach to contemporary *law*, for us at least the presupposition of pluralism is not sufficient. Rather, we have to presuppose a second central assumption, this time concerning the concept of law: legal normativity can be found not only in positive laws and constitutions, but also in judicial decisions, administrative acts, legal doctrine and even legal theory. This might not be a very surprising remark, it is not even a much-contested presupposition, and still it is extremely important. This is the case because this simple observation mirrors legal pluralism as a global *pluralism of laws* in a *pluralism of forms* of legal normativity. We will have to come back to this assumption in Sect. 2.3 of this chapter.

2.2.2 *Looking for a Perspective II*

Looking for a perspective on this law that is pluralized in two senses involves a certain complication I already mentioned at the beginning of this chapter[17]: how can we take a perspective on this entire arrangement of law without already having determined a perspective? The answer is as simple as it is disappointing: there is no way of doing so. As soon as we define a point of view on law, we reduce the angle of observation and thus lose the option of looking at law as a whole. Every observation requires such a reduction of perspective by taking a perspective. But, and here we find a chance to escape the observation problem, the great capacity of concepts lies in their possibility to be applied to other concepts. Hence, we can conceptualize the way we use certain concepts for description, for taking perspectives on law.[18] For

[16] *See* Kelsen, Hans (1967). *Pure Theory of Law*. Berkeley and Los Angeles: University of California Press (Translation from the 2nd German Edition); Kelsen, Hans (1960). *Reine Rechtslehre*. 2nd Edition. Wien: Deuticke.

[17] *See above* Sect. 2.1.

[18] The task of any descriptive approach to law does not have to refer necessarily either to natural kinds or functional kinds (*see* for analyzing this thesis: Rodriguez Blanco, Veronica (2006). The Methodological Problem in Legal Theory: Normative and Descriptive Jurisprudence Revisited. *Ratio Juris 19* (1), 26–54 (26)), as e.g. *Brian Leiter* or *Michael Moore* argue, *cf.* Leiter, Brian

example, classifying perspectives along sizes of territoriality, we get a certain concept of territorial order—a distinction between global, continental, regional and local perspectives on law. For plural law in both of the dimensions described above, there are numerous, maybe an infinite number of such concepts of description thinkable: not only territorially scaled perspectives, but also such that are arranged temporally, or along possible actors, along institutions,[19] etc. Even the nation state would be nothing more than one of the thinkable (and not exactly rarely used) concepts for describing pluralized law in a certain conceptual framework. Considering these reflections on different perspectives and the concepts leading to them, the way our approach will avoid fixing one special perspective becomes more obvious: it has to *conceptualize the totality of possible perspectives on contemporary, pluralized law by analyzing the implications following from the presuppositions described above.* And this is the aim of the present study: to conceptualize how we can look at pluralized law in order to receive both, concepts of description *and* methods of taking perspective.

On the one hand concepts of description are necessary[20] for both understanding and explaining law. They are not the only access to legal theory, but they are a helpful tool for building models of law. And only by way of models are we able to generate an imagination of the world that can be different from the perspective we take on anyway. These different imaginations are the precondition for both, satisfying what we could call scientific curiosity and improving the world by inventing better tools. Therefore, we need concepts of description as a first step.[21]

And on the other hand methods of taking perspective are important; for it is by delivering such methods that our approach could maintain the hope of also providing applicable tools to help solve concrete problems that occur in this pluralized law.

Therefore, the conceptual approach for which we are looking should be descriptive and a method at the same time. Of course, this is not an easy job—the ideal result of this study could not be more than an attempt, and still, we will be confronted with the possibility of failure all the long of this stretch of road. We will dare it, though.

(1997), Rethinking Legal Realism: Toward a Naturalized Jurisprudence. *Texas Law Review 76*, 267–315, Moore, Michael (1987). Metaphysics, Epistemology and Legal Theory. *Southern California Law Review 60*, 453–506.

[19] As an example, *see Neil MacCormick's* institutional pluralism – e. g. MacCormick, Neil (1993). Beyond the Sovereign State. *The Modern Law Review 56*/1, 1–18 or MacCormick, Neil (1999). *Questioning Sovereignty. Oxford: Oxford University Press.*

[20] By no means do I argue that they are more important or even fully distinguishable from normative approaches to law (concerning this debate, *see* Rodriguez Blanco, Veronica (2006). The Methodological Problem in Legal Theory: Normative and Descriptive Jurisprudence Revisited. *Ratio Juris 19* (1), 26–54).

[21] Of course these concepts of description will never exempt us from previous notions we already have while looking at what we seek to describe. But although we are not able to escape our conceptual surroundings, there is still a chance of comprehension.

The first steps toward a conceptual and descriptive approach on contemporary law will now consist in outlining characteristics of the totality of perspectives that could be taken on pluralized law. Furthermore, such characteristics will be our basis for *conceptualizing* perspectives on pluralized law. Since our presuppositions alone can offer clues for the beginning of the search, we have to look at them and their implications.[22] We are reducing the scope of this study to the limits of the presuppositions, but on the other side we gain a starting point.

2.2.3 *Hybridity*

2.2.3.1 Hybridity and/or Pluralism

One characteristic, one quality to be found in pluralized law can be called its *hybridity*. This originally botanical concept[23] refers to the simultaneous existence of different legal (and non-legal or quasi-legal) regimes, traditions, doctrines, and discourses. It does not describe the *coexistence* of at least two legal regimes, nor does it capture a pure overlap (without transferring at least one of the regimes into another sphere)—instead, "hybridity describes, in a somewhat generic way, situations in which laws overlap without fully supplanting each other".[24] Hybridity is more about supplementing than supplanting,[25] more about a product than a sum. The term 'hybrid law' describes different laws, supplementing each other as well as interacting with each other.[26] Thus, the concept of hybridity is in a certain sense at odds with the one of pluralism: pluralism contains the notion of a parallelism where different regimes, different laws merely coexist.[27] Pluralism for example can

---

[22] *See* Sects. 2.2.3, 2.2.4, and 2.2.5.

[23] It entails the crossing of at least two different species.

[24] Michaels, Ralf (2009). Global Legal Pluralism. *Duke Law School Faculty Scholarship Series*. Paper 185. (http://lsr.nellco.org/duke_fs/185; accessed at 12 December 2012), p. 19.

[25] Similarly *Michael Wilkinson* describes the way *De Burca* & Scott use the concept of hybridity; *see* his review of De Burca, Graìnne & Scott, Joanne (Eds.) (2006). *Law and New Governance in the EU and the U. S.* Oxford: Hart. – Wilkinson, Michael (2007). Between Constitutionalism and Democratic Experimentalism? New Governance in the EU and the U. S. *Modern Law Review 70*/4, 680–700 (690).

[26] There is also a well-established use of the concept of hybridity referring to internationalized courts and tribunals in post-conflict situations that often integrate international and domestic legal authority: *see* e.g. Dickinson, Laura A (2003). The Promise of Hybrid Courts. *American Journal of International Law 97*, 295–310; Cohen, David (2007). "Hybrid" Justice in East Timor, Sierra Leone, and Cambodia: "Lessons Learned" and Prospects for the Future. *Stanford Journal of International Law 43*, 1–38; Bruch, Elisabeth M. (2010). Hybrid Courts: Examining Hybridity through a Post-Colonial Lens. *Boston University International Law Journal 28*/1, 1–38.

[27] For considering this problem from a normative point of view, *see* Woodman, Gordon R. (2007). Social and Religious Diversity, Legal Pluralism: Can State Law Survive? *IIUM Law Journal 15*, 154–70 (165, 166).

sufficiently describe two linear, hierarchical legal orders which exist in two neighbour states, but which neither interact nor overlap. Those can never be called 'hybrid', though. Therefore, the use of the concept of hybridity by some legal pluralists is somewhat problematic—I would not argue that it is deficient to use the term hybridity in the contexts they do,[28] but rather that the notion of pluralism has received a different appearance by this use: legal pluralism may describe hybrid laws as well as coexisting laws, and probably it even refers to a legal web of both kinds of simultaneity. Or, to turn it around, it is a question of perspective: the concept of plurality implies looking at the multiplicity of legal regimes that can take an either coexisting or overlapping and interacting form, while the concept of hybridity applies to the whole of 'law', which can either be qualified as a unified system or as hybrid. And since we are approaching the whole of law, we shall consider the concept of hybridity better suited than the one of plurality.

One might wonder about the nature of the relationship between the concepts of pluralism and hybridity, given that I called hybridity a characteristic of legal pluralism at the beginning of this section. In now supplanting *plural law* by *hybrid law* as the object of this examination, we are not playing the concept of hybridity off against the one of plurality. Rather, in doing so we are narrowing the focus to the aspect of hybridity.

2.2.3.2 From Plural Law to Hybrid Law

Hence, we shall make a fresh start here with respect to the term we are applying: our aim is to conceptualize the perspective on *hybrid law* rather than *pluralized law*. Thus, "legal pluralism as a concept or even as an empirical phenomenon juxtaposed

[28] *Berman* for example explores a 'jurisprudence of hybridity', looking at the interaction of state and non-state lawmaking, *see* Berman, Paul Schiff (2010). Towards A Jurisprudence of Hybridity. *Utah Law Review*, 11–29 and defining legal hybridity as "spheres of complex overlapping legal authority", Berman, Paul Schiff (2007). Global Legal Pluralism. *Southern California Law Review 80*, 1155–1237 (1162). *Santos* refers to a similar phenomenon, the "intersection of different legal orders", not calling it Hybridity, but 'interlegality', and he qualifies 'interlegality' as the "second key concept of a postmodern conception of law" (while 'legal pluralism' was the first one, cf. above, footnote 5), *see* e.g. de Sousa Santos, Boaventura (1987). Law: A Map of Misreading. Toward a Postmodern Conception of Law. *Journal of Law and Society, 14*(3), 279–302 (298). And finally, some relevant governance approaches conceptualize hybridity also as a legal concept, e.g. the New Governance approach, formulating hybrid models of integrating multiple actors, institutions, and laws, focuses on 'orchestration'—"rather than direct promulgation and enforcement of rules" (*see* Abbott, Kenneth W. & Snidal, Duncan (2009). Strengthening International Regulation Transnational New Governance: Overcoming the Orchestration Deficit. *Vanderbilt Journal of Transnational Law 42*, 501–578 (509)); *see* also Trubek, David M. & Trubek, Louise G. (2006). New Governance & Legal Regulation: Complementarity, Rivalry, and Transformation. *Columbia Journal of European Law 13*, 539–564 (543–544), Alexander, Lisa T. (2010). Wisconsin Law Review Symposium Afterword. Part III. *Wisconsin Law Review*, 737–748 (744–746) and Osofsky, Hari M. (2011). Multidimensional Governance and the BP Deepwater Horizon Oil Spill. *Florida Law Review 63*, 1077–1137 (1117).

to legal monism disappears".[29] By applying the concept of hybridity to law, we avoid concentrating on the question of how multiple legal regimes might coexist or overlap or interact. Instead, in a first step we admit that there is a multiplicity of legal and quasi-legal regimes that constitute the law. In a second step, then, we take a new look at law, which is a look at *hybrid law*: this includes the multiplicity and the whole of law at the same time, and *both are not even separable*. This way the concept of hybridity makes it impossible for us to do a backward roll: hybrid law cannot be examined by examining its different ingredients because they are no longer thinkable as discrete entities.[30] Apples may serve as an (nevertheless simplifying) example: if an apple cultivator crosses an apple of the kind *a* and one of the kind *b*, obtaining a result that consists in an apple of the new kind *c*, we will not be able to understand this new kind as the sum of apple *a* and apple *b*, nor will it be an apple that is *completely* different from both original kinds. Probably molecular biologists will be able to extract some DNA sequences of this new apple *c* that are identical to the ones to be found in apples of the kinds *a* or *b*. But they will also find parts of the DNA that are neither identical to the DNA of apple *a*, nor to apple *b*. Therefore, a description of apple *c* that draws only on the characteristics of apple *a* and apple *b* will never be sufficient. But neither will a description of apple *c* be complete without referring to apples *a* and *b*, or at least it will ignore important parts of the apple's genesis that are interesting not only from a historical point of view, but also concerning its characteristics. The same is true for hybrid law. And, to name the problem using traditional concepts—neither a dualistic (or pluralistic) perspective nor a monistic one is sufficient to describe hybrid law. Hence, we have to look at it from both perspectives at once; the concept of hybridity offers the conceptual tool for this enterprise while simultaneously obliging us to do so.

2.2.3.3 Pluralism of Forms and Hybridity

But there is possibly a second level of hybridity in law to be exposed, a level that I already indicated in making a second presupposition of this approach: I assumed a pluralism of forms of legal normativity.[31] Law consists in a multiplicity of forms that its normativity can adopt. But in this case we cannot replace the term plural with the term hybrid. Indeed, these different forms do not only coexist, but they merge into each other. We can imagine this as follows: every single time one of these forms is applied,[32] other forms get involved and transformed by the

[29] Michaels, Ralf (2009). Global Legal Pluralism. *Duke Law School Faculty Scholarship Series*. Paper 185. (http://lsr.nellco.org/duke_fs/185; accessed at 12 December 2012), p. 20.

[30] Concerning the question of how to describe the interrelations of these non-discrete elements of law, *see below*, Sect. 2.2.4.

[31] *See above*, Sect. 2.2.1.2.

[32] Later we will see that the concept of application is better replaced by the one of perception. *See* below, Sects. 2.2.4.2, 2.3.1 and 2.3.2.

procedure of application. For example (simplifying a little[33]), a judge decides a case. In doing so, she applies a specific interpretation of a norm and/or a precedent. These interpretations fall back upon the norm text, the precedent text and case, and they probably also fall back upon legal doctrine as well as legal theory; and these are only the very simplest of settings (it is not very useful here to already explain the whole of theoretical presuppositions that lead to this thesis, since we will expose those later on[34]). In any case, the merging thesis consists in the idea that by applying a norm, a norm text, and/or a doctrine to a certain case, in a certain interpretation, we transform them, we add one meaning that is able to do both: to influence and transform the arrangement of the applied norm with respect to other norms, but also to change the content of the norm by adding another application. This is why the concept of hybridity is not appropriate for the description of this phenomenon—it tells more about the process of transformation itself than about its result that could be called hybrid. Therefore we shall abstain from the idea of examining the presupposition of a plurality of forms as a special field of hybridity. Instead, we shall revisit this phenomenon below, discussing transformations in and dynamics of law.[35]

2.2.3.4 Example: European Administrative Law I

For a better understanding of hybridity it could be illuminating at this point to apply the concept to an example. Therefore we shall have a short look at European administrative law: In a very rough definition, it can be understood as "the body of law governing administration by EU institutions and bodies as well as Member States administrations acting within the Sphere of EU law, i.e., when they act either to implement EU law or when they are bound in their activity by general principles of EU law".[36,37] Sources of this 'mixed system'[38] are to be found in the European Treaties,[39] but also in treaties concluded between the (former) EC and accession

[33] Again, I have to postpone a more exact look on the application of law, or better, its practice, for a few sections, *see below*, Sects. 2.2.4.2 and 2.3.1.

[34] *See* Sect. 2.3 of this chapter.

[35] *See below*, Sect. 2.2.5, but also Chap. 4, Sect. 4.1.2.3.

[36] Hofmann, Herwig C.H. (2009). Decisionmaking in EU Administrative Law – the Problem of Composite Procedures. *Administrative Law Review 61*, 199–222 (203, note 13).

[37] For a different evaluation—not considering Member States' acting and laws as constituting European administrative law—*see* Craig, Paul (2006). *EU Administrative Law*. Oxford: Oxford University Press, and Schwarze, Jürgen (2005^2), *Europäisches Verwaltungsrecht, Entstehung und Entwicklung im Rahmen der Europäischen Gemeinschaft*. Baden-Baden: Nomos.

[38] Örücü, Esin (2001). Public Law in Mixed Legal Systems and Public Law as a „Mixed System". *Electronic Journal of Comparative Law 5/2*; *see* also Raducu, Ioana & Levrat, Nicolas (2007). Le métissage des ordres juridiques européens. *Cahiers de Droit Européen*, 111–148.

[39] The former EU and EC Treaties are substituted now by the new „Treaty of the European Union" (TEU) and the Treaty on the Functioning of the European Union (TFEU). It was the Treaty of Lisbon (in force since 1 December 2009) that brought on this transformation.

states,[40] as well as in EU secondary law, and in the respective Member States' administrative law. Accordingly, decisions of the CJEU as well as those from national courts can be added to European administrative law, provided they deal with administrative issues. Of course this list could be extended (to contain multiple kinds of administrative acts for example) and differentiated, but this is not the task of this study—what should be noted instead is that European administrative law is not sufficiently described by the terms pluralism or coexistence. For example, member states that put a European Union directive into national legislation establish both, national law and national law as European law. This form of simultaneous change would not be sufficiently described by the term 'coexistence', because the whole process involves a special connection. To explain it in other words: a directive put into 27 different national legislations with all their peculiarities is not the same as 27 different national legislations treating a similar object. Nor does this set-up resemble that of a EU regulation being valid in all 27 member states. Rather, the different national legislations relate to each other by a prefiguration consisting in the same directive *and* differ from each other due to different national legal traditions influencing the concrete embodiment of the directive. In return, the national law will be transformed by the new legislation in every member state, and the directive itself will also be enriched by this.

From a perspective on the whole, including the directive as well as the different national legislations and the several connections in between them, the structure appears to be *hybrid*. An important marker for hybridity is to be found in its *irreversibility*—once a process has occurred as described above, the legislations thus combined cannot be divided out again, since they are no longer independent of one another. With regard to the hybridity of law it is impossible to describe any part of the law as an autonomous, discrete, or closed order. Referring to the example of European Administrative Law, this means that it is not possible to adopt a point of view on European Administrative Law by looking at a single national legislation apart from the others, or at the European directive in the description.

So far, the implications of the concept of hybridity do not sound very surprising nor do they seem to be very far-reaching. And still they are, since they are not limited to this first little observation. The description's further implications can be illuminated by the counter-concepts of hybridity, concepts that cannot be applied at the same time as hybridity: if law is hybrid, this implies that it does not conform to a linear hierarchy, nor is it to be described by the concepts of verticality or horizontality. To the contrary, hybrid law is a multidimensional and non-linear law. Following this, the perspective on pluralized law as hybrid law has to be extended by two concepts linked to hybridity: these are *dynamics* and *relationality*, both to be exposed in the upcoming sections.

[40] So Hofmann, Herwig & Rowe, Gerard C. & Türk, Alexander (2011). *Administrative Law and Policy of the European Union*. Oxford: Oxford University Press, p. 68.

2.2.4 *Relationality*

2.2.4.1 Hierarchy and Hybridity

In a consequently linear legal system, every legal norm and every legal act is derived from another legal norm. At the top or the bottom of the whole (depending on the perspective taken on the system) has to be either a *Basic Norm*[41] or a *Rule of Recognition,*[42] then, as traditional legal theory pointed out.[43] Thus, law can be described in terms of a norm pyramid,[44] for example. For any hybrid law, the arrangement cannot possibly be described in such a manner: for its generic mix of origins is the very aspect of hybridity that constitutes the concept. In addition, whereas hierarchical law presupposes the ideal of a certain consistency, or a certain unity of the normative order, this is not the case with hybrid law: the latter might show these characteristics in some constellations, but the opposite might be true for other constellations.—Even a fully fragmented law with elements, e.g. norms, that contradict each other is to be described as a whole, a hybrid law.

It is evident that the concepts of hierarchy and hybridity draw on very different perspectives on law. While the notion of a hierarchical normative order of law excludes all occurrences of law that challenge a hierarchical order[45] already conceptually, the one of hybridity refers precisely to multiple and different origins of law—which certainly does not exclude hierarchical parts of law (e.g. parallel hierarchies of legal orders can be part of hybrid law).[46] Thus, the concept of

---

[41] As *Kelsen* conceptualizes it, *see* Kelsen, Hans (1967). *Pure Theory of Law*. Berkeley and Los Angeles: University of California Press (Translation from the 2nd German Edition), pp. 193. For analyzing Kelsen's Theory, *see* e.g. Raz, Joseph (1998). The Purity of the Pure Theory, in: Paulson, Stanley & Lischnewski-Paulson, Bonnie (1998). *Normativity and Norms: Critical Perspectives on Kelsenian Themes*. Oxford: Oxford University Press, pp. 237–252, and introducing a periodization analysis Paulson, Stanley (1998). Four Phases in Kelsen's Legal Theory? Reflections on a Periodization. *Oxford Journal of Legal Studies 18*, 153–166.

[42] *See* Hart, H. L. A. (^{2}1994). *The Concept of Law*. Oxford: Oxford University Press, pp. 100 and Hart, H. L. A. (1994). Postscript, in: Hart, H. L. A. *The Concept of Law*. Oxford: Oxford University Press, pp. 238–276.

[43] For a comparative approach to the conception of normativity of both theories, *see* Delacroix, Sylvie (2004). Hart's and Kelsen's Concepts of Normativity Contrasted. *Ratio Juris 17*, 501–520. Outlining a "classic statement of the hierarchy of precepts and their pattern of nested consistency" (*see* Cover, Robert M. (1983). The Supreme Court 1982 Term. Foreword: Nomos and Narrative. *Harvard Law Review 97*, 4–68 (17, note 44)), Gray, John Chipman (1909). *The Nature and Sources of the Law*. New York: Columbia University Press.

[44] *See* Merkl, Adolf (1923). *Die Lehre von der Rechtskraft. Entwickelt aus dem Rechtsbegriff.* Leipzig: Deuticke, pp. 201

[45] In the most severe version to be found in *Kelsen's* Theory, where the derivation of the basic or a higher norm is a necessary condition for the validity of a norm, *see* Kelsen, Hans (1967). *Pure Theory of Law*. Berkeley and Los Angeles: University of California Press (Translation from the 2nd German Edition), pp.193.

[46] The only case that cannot be called a hybrid law is a strict and only hierarchical legal order.

hybridity broadens the perspective on law by not laying down any qualified requirements regarding the interrelations between the elements that compose the hybrid law. Then, of course, the question to be answered is: what can be understood by the notion of *non-qualified interrelations between the elements of law*?

2.2.4.2 Normative Perceptions and a Radically Different Perspective on Law

There are several problems implied in this question.—What are the elements of law at all? What are their interrelations, and why are they 'non-qualified'? The conceptual answer to all these questions has to be called *relationality*, and this section aims to explain this suggestion.

The relationships between legal norms, decisions, acts and discourses are what makes up (hybrid) law as a whole, as a normative order. In this perspective, the constituting aspects of law, then, are not its elements, but the relations in between them. And here, at this inconspicuous point, we are making the move to a *radically different perspective on law*: towards the interrelations inside law, away from the sources, elements, or, in other words: texts of law. There is no necessity for doing so, except for the promise of an interesting and hopefully productive description of law, which this move brings about. And obviously, it is the notion of hybridity itself that suggests making this move by not allowing hierarchy or unity to be reasons for law's coherence—even if there were hierarchical structures observed in law, the totality of hybrid law could not be founded on them. On the other hand, the hybridity of law can be founded on its relationality. Without entering into the complicated sphere of ontological reflections by asking the question of law's form of *existence*, we can proceed from the assumption that law is observable as an accumulation[47] of what I call *normative perceptions*.[48] This has to be the case because the central action of any agent in law, the common aspect of any legal action, is a normative perception. If we think, for example, of the application[49] of legal norms by way of a judicial decision or an administrative act, or of an act of legislation; if we think of the jurisprudential critique of a court decision, or if we think of the deduction or invention of legal doctrine—it is impossible to imagine any of these acts as legal acts without the normative perception of at least one other element of the law. Whether we think about a judgment as proportionalization of a case and one or more norms, whether we think about a legislation act as generating a new norm that refers to procedural norms as well as the already existing norms, whether we think of a development of legal doctrine by a legal scholar, all of these examples can be understood as normative perceptions of the various elements of

[47] I prefer the term accumulation in this passage, because I would like to reserve the question of how this accumulation is arranged (e.g. as web, system or rhizome, or: space) for a later chapter. *See* Chap. 3 *below*.

[48] For a further conceptualization of '*normative perception*', *see* Sect. 2.3 *below*.

[49] Concerning the problems of the application of legal norms, *see* Sect. 2.3.1 *below*.

law. And we can in turn identify all *objects* of these perceptions of law as further perceptions. Even if for each of these acts the moment of perception is not the most characteristic aspect, it is what connects all of them on a formal level. Thus, we can describe law as a whole context of perceptions, or rather a *web* of perceptions.

The concept of perception always includes two inseparable aspects: on the one hand there is this (formal) external moment of connection—perceptions connect an object of perception to the act of perception; and on the other hand normative perceptions always refer to content, to a meaning. We can describe normative perceptions on both levels, formally e.g. as citations, and as referring to the content. So far, the concept bears great similarity to how we can talk about legal acts: them, too, we can describe on a purely formal level, e.g. a judgment as application of a norm, as well as on a content level, e.g. freedom of speech is applied in one or the other sense, with one or the other meaning. And this similarity, I suppose, is not a pure accident; we will come back to this below.[50]

But there is another aspect to the concept of normative perception that we have already used implicitly: perception can be understood as event, as process, as something we *do*, and at the same time it can be an object, as a special perception to which we can refer again. When I say that we already used this two-fold understanding of perceptions, I am referring to the description of law as a web of perceptions, where the interrelations between the elements are formed by perceptions, while the elements themselves can also be considered as normative perceptions. Thus, by the concept of normative perception, we describe both, law's elements and their formal interconnectivity.

The reason for this manner of description is to be found in the fact that law is necessarily connected to language: we can imagine all kinds of written or oral laws and legal actions, but none that does not fall back upon language.[51] And since communication by language can be understood as a context of perceptions of language expressions, this must be true for law as well.[52] In this way, we focus on law as a context of normative perceptions. These perceptions constitute the relationships that build the law, and their peculiarity lies in the fact that perceptions are not stable entities but actions, or in other words: events.[53]

[50] *See below*, Sect. 2.3.1.

[51] Even if we count non-verbal symbolic actions as part of the sphere of law, these symbolic actions have the same function as verbal language, only that the signs are different ones.

[52] For a better description of this model of communication and legal action, *see below* Sect. 2.3.1.

[53] For the concept of an event in this context, *see below*, Sect. 2.3.1.

2.2.4.3 Delimitations: Web of Citations and Networks

This perceptional approach is neither new[54] nor very rare—there is quite a significant amount of legal literature that examines law as a *web of citations*, not only, but often focussing on jurisdiction networks.[55] And of course *network theory*[56] as well

---

[54] *Chandler* for example refers to the „seamless web", „to which the law is often analogized", *see* Chandler, Seth S. (2005). The Network Structure of Supreme Court Jurisprudence. *University of Houston Public Law and Legal Theory Series* 2005-W-01, p. 23.

[55] *Smith* devotes a paper called "The Web of Law" to this topic; *see* Smith, Thomas A. (2007). The Web of Law. *San Diego Law Review 44*, 309–354. Further examples of studies on 'webs of citation' that deal with Supreme Courts' Jurisdiction are for example: Merryman, John H. (1954). The authority of authority: What the California Supreme Court cited in 1950. *Stanford Law Review* 6, 613–673; Merryman, John H. (1977). Toward a Theory of Citations: An Empirical Study of the Citation Practice of the California Supreme Court in 1950, 1960, and *1970. Southern California Law Review 50*, 381–428; Friedman, Lawrence M. & Kagan, Robert A. & Cartwright, Bliss & Wheeler, Stanton (1981). State Supreme Courts: A Century of Style and Citation. *Stanford Law Review 33*, 773–818; Landes, William M. & Lessig, Lawrence & Solimine, Michael E. (1998). Judicial influence: A Citation Analysis of Federal Courts and Appeals Judges. *Journal of Legal Studies* 27, 271–332; Fowler, James H. & Jeon Sangick (2008). The Authority of Supreme Court Precedent. *Social networks 30*, 16–30; Chandler, Seth S. (2005). The Network Structure of Supreme Court Jurisprudence. *University of Houston Public Law and Legal Theory Series* 2005-W-01; Kosma, Montgomery N. (1998). Measuring the Influence of Supreme Court Justices. *Journal of Legal Studies 27*, 333–372; Caldeira, Gregory (1988). Legal Precedent: Structures of Communication Between State Supreme Courts. *Social networks 10*, 29–55; Caldeira, Gregory (1985). The Transmission of Legal Precedent: A Study of State Supreme Courts. *American Political Science Review 79*, 178–194; Johnson, Charles A. (1986). Follow-Up Citations in the U. S. Supreme Court. *Western Political Quarterly 39*, 538–547; Landes, William M. & Posner, Richard A. (1976). Legal Precedent: A Theoretical and Empirical Analysis. *Journal of Law & Economics 19*, 249–307. For the analysis of citing Law Reviews resp. Law Journals, *see* Sirico, Louis J. Jr. (2000). The Citing of Law Reviews by the Supreme Court: 1971–1999. *Indiana Law Journal 75*, 1009–1039 and Shapiro, Fred R. (1991). The Most-Cited Articles from The Yale Law Journal. *Yale Law Journal 100*, 1449–1514. For a more general approach, *see* Post, David G. & Eisen, Michael B. (2000). How Long is the Coastline of the Law? Thoughts on the Fractal Nature of Legal Systems. *Journal of Legal Studies 29*, 545–584.

[56] Networks are currently still undergoing a 'conceptual boom' in many disciplines (see Barabási, Albert László (2005). Taming Complexity. *Nature physics 1*, 68–70 (68)), which was triggered by a mathematical paper on so-called 'random networks' (networks of which the nodes are linked in pairs through a connection of probability) published in 1959: Erdös, Paul & Rényi, Alfréd (1959). On Random Graphs. *Publicationes Mathematicae 6*, 290–291. Especially in the social sciences, network theory has a long tradition, e.g. the early works of *Moreno* and *Lewin*: Moreno, Jacob (1934). *Who Shall Survive?* Washington, D.C.: Nervous and Mental Desease Publishing and Lewin, Kurt (1951). *Field Theory in Social Science*. New York: Harper & Row,, both trying to model sociality by tools that stem from mathematics (analytical geometry, topology, and graph theory). Legal discourses, too, are discussing networks (*see* e.g. *Ost*, Francois & Van de Kerchove, Michel (2002). *De la pyramide au reseau? Pour une théorie dialéctique du droit*. Brussels: Publications des Facultés universitaires St. Louis Bruxelles), but they describe those networks that are connected to government (*see* e.g. Slaughter, Anne-Marie (2000/2001). The Accountability of Government Networks. *Indiana Journal of Global Legal Studies 8*, 347–367; Slaughter, Anne-Marie (2004). *A New World Order*. Princeton: Princeton University Press, pp. 36 and pp. 152) or judicial networks (see e.g. Chandler, Seth S. (2005). The Network Structure of Supreme

as *system theory*[57] both describe law in very similar ways.[58] All of these yield important perspectives on law, for which reason we shall consider them while developing our conceptual approach to law. However, for a global perspective on law, these approaches are not sufficient—because they lack concepts that would make it possible *to scale* these networks. Webs and networks (and systems in a *luhmannian* sense) are well-developed concepts for the description of relationality, but in general they are subject to two fundamental defects, neither of which is negligible for the here sought-after perspective on law: (a) they are originally non-dimensional, i.e. their structure and form result from the relations between their elements only. Therefore webs and networks do not permit us to scale them, nor to define frames of reference. This circumstance feature could be an advantage for description, in fact (because it allows far-reaching views on law without requiring exact definitions of the different connections), but such a description necessarily has to remain on a structural level. As soon as we look for a more differentiated picture of *how* different perceptional webs of law are connected to each other, scales and reference frames necessarily have to be components of the perspective, or, at least, such a perspective has to include the option of defining scales and frames of reference. In line with this consideration, we do not reject the web/network analogy. Rather, the concept of relationality is to be interpreted as emphasizing the web/network analogy. And still we have seen that it is only one constituent on the way to our perspective on law—others have to be added.

A second insufficiency of the web and network perspective is to be found (b) in its differentiation between stable entities of law and legal action on the one hand and procedures such as citation or perception on the other. This can be explained as follows: network approaches to law mostly are concerned with judicial, institutional or personal interconnections.[59] But even if they do not place the emphasis on persons or institutions as acting instances, they are built on a distinction of entities

Court Jurisprudence. *University of Houston Public Law and Legal Theory Series* 2005-W-01; Slaughter, Anne-Marie (2004). *A New World Order*. Princeton: Princeton University Press, pp. 65; Katz, Daniel M. & Stafford, Derek K. & Provins, Eric (2008). Social Architecture, Judicial Peer Effects and the "Evolution" of the Law: Toward a Positive Theory of Judicial Social Structure. *Georgia State University Law Review 24*/4, 975–999; Fischer-Lescano, Andreas & Teubner, Gunther (2006). Regime-Kollisionen. Zur Fragmentierung des globalen Rechts. Frankfurt am Main: Suhrkamp, pp. 57).

[57] *See* for a general version Luhmann, Niklas (1987). Soziale Systeme. Grundriss einer allgemeinen Theorie. Frankfurt am Main: Suhrkamp. For a legal system theory, *see* e.g. Luhmann, Niklas (1995). *Das Recht der Gesellschaft*. Frankfurt am Main: Suhrkamp (English publications: Luhmann, Niklas (1995). Social Systems. Stanford: Stanford University Press; Luhmann, Niklas (2004). Law as a Social System. Oxford: Oxford University Press.).

[58] System theory after *Luhmann* can be understood as a special network theory, more or less as a dynamic version of network theory, *see* Vesting, Thomas (2007). *Rechtstheorie*. München: C. H. Beck, pp. 67.

[59] *See* Fischer-Lescano, Andreas & Teubner, Gunther (2006). Regime-Kollisionen. Zur Fragmentierung des globalen Rechts. Frankfurt am Main: Suhrkamp, pp. 58. Examples are Slaughter, Anne-Marie (2004). *A New World Order*. Princeton: Princeton University Press; Katz, Daniel M. & Gubler, Joshua R. & Zelner, Jon & Bommarito II, Michael J. & Provins,

that either act themselves (e.g. if a court is such an entity) or that are subject to actions of other agents (e.g. if a legal norm is seen as a stable entity in a web of law, wherein courts *apply* such norms). In both versions, stable entities are to be distinguished from the procedures that constitute the relations of a network.[60] A probable reason for this typical two-fold consideration is to be found in the picture of a network itself: it consists of nodes and links (relationships between these nodes).[61] Such an arrangement then, suggests looking for these two different levels in law. Of course, the differentiation fits into a traditional notion of positive law, where we can distinguish between (positive) legal norms and their application. But this metaphor presupposes that any citation, any legal action, any established interconnection between two nodes does not change the nodes, but only their position or location within the network. And here, suddenly, there is a problem—it does not seem very fruitful to distinguish between a stable entity and a legal action, between nodes and links. The reasons for this are connected to our description of legal procedures as *normative perceptions*: we have said that every legal action *is* a perception, and that the perception of norms, decisions, or concepts consists in the legal action perceiving other legal actions (themselves being perceptions again). If this were true and if at the same time we tried to distinguish between a stable legal entity and a legal action (or: between nodes and links), then we would be conceptually renouncing a core characteristic of law: to arise, to be observable only in its application and not as a stable entity. Therefore, looking for a global perspective on law, it is favourable not to divide into nodes and links from the beginning (while a network analysis might be a productive procedure for different approaches, of course) and rather start with the less presupposing concept of *relationality*.

The term relationality refers to the interconnectedness of every legal action, and still it does not need to fall back upon a dubious distinction between stable law and procedures. On the contrary, the concept of relationality can either be thought to refer to a stable and only a stable web, such as a perfect spider's web (where it makes sense to talk about nodes and links). Or, it can be thought exclusively to refer to dynamic interrelations, as take place in an on-going Scrabble game. However, it is not possible to talk about relationality to refer to a mixed system of stable and dynamic entities. And since it is not possible to think law without its applications or

---

Eric & Ingall, Eitan (2011). Reproduction of Hierarchy? A Social Network Analysis of the American Law Professoriate. *Journal of Legal Education 61*, 1–28.

[60] *See* e.g. *Fowler et al.*, who "consider Supreme Court opinions as nodes in a legal network. These case nodes are linked to other case nodes through citations to existing precend." (Fowler, James H. & Johnson, Timothy R. & Spriggs II, James F. & Jeon, Sangick & Wahlbeck, Paul J. (2007). *Political Analysis 15*, 324–346 (325).) Supreme Court opinions are the stable entities here, to which something occurs.

[61] *See* e.g. Smith, Thomas A. (2007). The Web of Law. *San Diego Law Review 44*, 309–354 (316): "A network is just a set of items, termed *nodes* or *vertices*, with connections among them, termed *links* or *edges*."

without its procedures[62]—shortly, without dynamics[63]—the concept of relationality, when referring to law, is clearly defined as dynamic relationality. The concept of relationality therefore makes it possible to describe law as a set of dynamic interconnections—which is a possibility strengthened by the description of law as perception-constituted, as has been introduced above.

2.2.4.4 Multidimensionality

In addition, there is another important implication of relationality as concept, and here we are coming back to a characteristic qualified above as a deficiency of the network approach: the lack of scaling possibilities, the lack of a coordinate system that allows measuring certain relational constellations. The concept of network does not include the one of scale, although it is not impossible to lay scales next to networks—but, and this is important since we are embarked for a conceptual approach, scales are not implied in the network concept. So maybe deficiency is not the right term for this lack, it is more a disadvantage. And still, as long as we are looking for a perspective on law that makes it possible at the same time to define a global or general view on law as well as a concrete, a special perspective, that is, a method of walking through law, as long as we are following this trace, we should not give up the idea of scaling law too early. And the concept of relationality is equipped to make both possible: emphasizing the interconnections of law (as normative perceptions) *and* its scaling.

First of all, the concept of relationality does not qualify the interconnections constituting it in any sense; so far, it does not describe anything more than interconnectivity. The relationships within the relational system[64] might be of any proximity, of any number, and of any direction. This means that the system's topology[65] is not defined by the concept of relationality. This consideration implies that especially the number of dimensions, i.e. directions of expansion, is not determined if we are dealing with a relational system without further definitions.[66]

---

[62] One might object to this assumption that it is very easily possible to think law as a system of stable positive norms, though. This objection is true, if we choose a sectional perspective on law, therefore of course it is permissible and sometimes even very productive to look at the part of law that may be described as consisting in positive norms. But since we are looking for a global perspective on law here, this way is cut off.

[63] *See below*, Sect. 2.2.5.

[64] I use the term here in a very weak sense—this system is characterized by the term 'relational'.

[65] For the concept of topology, *see below* Chap. 3, Sects. 3.3.2 and 3.3.3.

[66] We can imagine further defined relational systems, of course. E.g. if we describe a certain (very small) law system as a cube, consisting of eight elements (perceptions) and twelve interrelations, i.e. eight edges and twelve lines between them, where each edge has exactly three lines going out or in, and all lines touching each other do so in a 90-degree angle. In this only imaginable case, we have three dimensions, not more and not less. For law, this is a quite extraordinary case and one that can hardly be imagined—because in almost any case of an agglomeration of law perceptions we can imagine adding yet another perception of a perception.

And this is what I meant above, talking about non-qualified interconnections of law.[67]

Following this, the relationality of law includes a non-definite number of dimensions that hybrid law can take. In addition, there is an aspect which we can deduce from the hybridity of law and which is linked to this aspect of relationality: hybrid law, this is described by different authors, is *multidimensional*.[68] This is the case because neither the dimension of *verticality* (e.g. in the sense of a hierarchic law), nor the one of *horizontality* (e.g. in the sense of multiple, same-level laws) is sufficient to describe hybrid law. If we think back to the example of European Administrative Law, we could at the very least distinguish European laws and jurisdiction and the Member States' respective laws and jurisdictions, each with their own versions and forms of laws, legal acting and traditions, not to speak about the public international law connections—one can easily see that there is a certain necessity to talk about multidimensionality in this context.

Given the multidimensionality of hybrid law, another aspect concerning the perspective of which we are in search appears on the scene: dimensionality allows *scaling*. This is the case because the capacity of extracting dimensions of a relational web alone gives us the opportunity to compare lengths and distances, or to measure constellations. And scales are the tools for measuring. It is not yet time to go deeper into detail regarding this matter of scaling—this topic will occupy

---

[67] *See above*, Sect. 2.2.4.2.

[68] *Osofsky* for example investigates the multidimensionality in an actor-oriented and thus governance perspective—describing multidimensional governance as follows: "(...) governance that involves a wide range of governmental and non-governmental actors in substantively crosscutting issues at local, state, national, and international levels", *see* Osofsky, Hari M. (2011). Multidimensional Governance and the BP Deepwater Horizon Oil Spill. *Florida Law Review 63*, 1077–1137 (1079). Within the analysis, *Osofsky* distinguishes at least five dimensions of applicable law in the case of an example (pp. 1081); further, *Osofsky* sees her multidimensional governance model founded in legal hybridity (1117). *Teubner* and *Korth* qualify global legal pluralism as multidimensional (*see* Teubner, Gunther & Korth, Peter (2012). Two Kinds of Legal Pluralism: Collision of Transnational Regimes in the Double Fragmentation of World Society, in: Young, Margaret A. (ed.). Regime Interaction in International Law. Facing Fragmentation. Cambridge: Cambridge University Press, pp. 23–54

Holding on what I would call the 'content-level' of perceptions, *Bruch* for example theorizes law as "multidimensional", making explicit as dimensions violence, bureaucracy, and governance, *see* Bruch, Elizabeth M. (2011). Is International Law Really Law? Theorizing the Multi-Dimensionality of Law. *Akron Law Review 44*, 333–373 (334); even *Hart* refers to the concept of multidimensionality, writing about the "multidimensional generalities of a constitution", *see* Hart, H. L. A. (1958). Positivism and the Separation of Law and Morals. *Harvard Law Review 71*/4, 593–629 (607). As for a special legal context, *Dinwoodie* writes "about an increasingly multidimensional nature of international intellectual property litigation", *see* Dinwoodie, Graeme B. (2001). International Intellectual Property Litigation: A Vehicle For Resurgent Comparativist Thought. *American Journal of Comparative Law 49*, 429–453 (441). As a random notice has to be mentioned, that *Fishman* and *Law* expose a whole concept of the "multidimensionality of judicial ideology", *see* Fischman, Joshua B. & Law, David S. (2009).What Is Judicial Ideology, and How Should We Measure It? *Journal of Law & Policy 29*, 1–82 (pp.18).

us in greater detail below.[69] For the moment, what is important is the assumption that the relationality of hybrid law yields not only a description perspective, but also a method of scaling, or at least its possibility.

2.2.5 *Dynamics*

One further aspect of this perception-based approach on hybrid law has already been mentioned[70]: its dynamic character. Law's relationality is necessarily a dynamic relationality, because its interrelations are constituted by normative perceptions, which for their part are again thinkable as events.[71] The concept of an event, further, falls back on temporality. For the moment, for a large-meshed outline of the perspective on law that I am going to develop in the following chapters, it might be sufficient to mention that this event character of the normative perceptions produces the dynamics that characterize law: *the* law will never be the same in two different moments of time; dynamics does not mean any more than changes over time. This is probably not a very surprising assumption; maybe it is even trivial. Nevertheless, it has to be emphasized here, because it causes certain problems concerning the perspective for which we are looking: If hybrid, relational law is dynamic, a description perspective as well as a method constructing perspective on law will have to take this into account, which is less trivial. This is necessary, though, because it will not be sufficient to draw a picture of law as one would draw a construction plan. Rather, the perspective to be found has to make both possible: describing the whole of law including its dynamics, and giving a tool for taking a point of view on law at a certain moment in time. Such a perspective, then, does not provide a specific, well-defined point of view; it should allow us to take on *any* point of view. Therefore it necessarily has to be a conceptual perspective on law, and the concept has to be able to deal with all of the presupposed characteristics of law: hybridity, relationality, and dynamics.

2.2.6 *Dealing with Law's Complexity*

Having outlined in the previous section the characteristics on which the perspective on law we are searching has to focus, we should take the opportunity here to reconsider both, the status and the impact of these characteristics within a conceptual approach to law.

[69] *See below* Chap. 4, Sect. 4.2.2.

[70] *See above*, Sects. 2.2.3.3 and 2.2.4.3.

[71] *See below*, Sect. 2.3.1.

The preliminary findings of these first sections basically consist in the idea that looking for a conceptual and descriptive approach on contemporary law essentially means attempting to describe law as a hybrid, relational and dynamic system. The concept of 'system', though, is not a much elaborated one.[72] Even if it is extremely common to write about 'the legal system', the term is not very well defined in legal literature.[73] But since our aim here is not to investigate the concept of a system, we will not follow up on this; instead, we clarify that we are using the term 'system' as a provisional variable indicating that we are (at this point) not examining the concept or the nature of law but the phenomenon of a multiplicity of laws, jurisdictions, legal theories, legal institutions as a whole.

After a process of narrowing the scope of perspective in the first step, we have dissected some aspects that will direct our further approach to this legal system: hybridity, relationality, and dynamics. These concepts indicate that when looking at the legal system we are not investigating a body of elegant simplicity, but rather something we can call a complexity. Therefore we should have a look at the questions of how the concepts of hybridity, relationality, and dynamics are related to the one of complexity and of how the concept of complexity may affect our approach to law in two ways: with regard to both, the material side of law and the methodological one.

2.2.6.1 The Concept of Complexity in the Context of Law

In the sense just introduced, the concept of complexity is opposed to the one of simplicity. It is important to note, though, that it should not be confused with the one of 'complicatedness'.[74] Any arrangement of more than only a few elements can be 'complicated' to understand or to describe or to imagine. But "complexity arises

[72] As for example the Kantian concept of system can be qualified—only *see* the definition of a system given in the Critique of Pure Reason: „Ich verstehe aber unter einem Systeme die Einheit der mannigfaltigen Erkenntnisse unter einer Idee. Diese ist der Vernunftbegriff von der Form eines Ganzen, so fern durch denselben der Umfang des Mannigfaltigen so wohl, als die Stelle der Teile untereinander, a priori bestimmt wird." (Kant, Immanuel. *Kritik der reinen Vernunft*, B 860/A 832).

[73] *See* Ruhl, J. B. (2007–2008). Law's Complexity: A Primer. *Georgia State University Law Review 24*/4, 885–911 (885).

[74] *See* Webb, Julian (2005). Law, Ethics, and Complexity: Complexity Theory & the Normative Reconstruction of Law. Cleveland State Law Review 52, 227–242 (237); Ladeur, Karl-Heinz (1997). Post-modern Constitutional Theory: A Prospect for the Self-Organizing Society. *The Modern Law Review 60*/5, 617–629 (620); Ruhl, J. B. (2008). Law's Complexity: A Primer. *Georgia State University Law Review 24*/4, 885–911 (890). In contrast, explicitly understanding 'complexity' in a much broader sense, including 'complicatedness', Wright, R. George (2000). The Illusion of Simplicity: An Explanation of why the Law can't just be less complex. *Florida State University Law Review 27*, 716–744 (720).

when the dependencies among the elements become important."[75] And complexity involves quite a number of qualities depending on these interdependencies of the elements. Even if it is neither possible nor necessary here to give a precise definition of the traditionally vague concept of complexity,[76] we can state at a very general level of the concept that we call systems complex only if the transformation of at least one element might have a serious impact on the whole system.[77] For example, this is not necessarily the case in a legal system that can be understood as a norm pyramid, where each norm is deduced from a higher norm. In such a pyramid system of norms it would certainly be of great impact on the whole system to remove the basic norm, whereas removing just a simple norm somewhere at the end of a deduction chain could not change the whole system in a significant way. In a hybrid and relational law system, the same operation might have a very different impact on the whole arrangement: since every relationship is constitutive for the whole, any configuration has to be a configuration of the whole. In addition, the here-described law is dynamic, which means that the law is not a stable arrangement but instead is transformed in time. Since these transformations are performed by normative perceptions of earlier perceptions as described above,[78] they are path dependent in the sense that any transformation of the law by the normative perception of one or more norms, decisions, theories, etc. has an impact on the entities that are perceived in such an operation. Therefore, we shall not only refer to the concept of path dependence (which is a typical element of complexity as well as of law),[79] but also to the one of recursivity of law[80]—another often-stated

[75] *See* Miller, John, H. & Page, Scott E. (2007). Complex Adaptive Systems. An Introduction to Computational Models of Social Life. Princeton: Princeton University Press, p. 9.

[76] *See* e.g. already Bain, Read (1929). The Concept of Complexity in Sociology I. *Social Forces 8*, 222–231 (224): "[Complexity] is one of those indefinite blanket-terms that serve to conceal our scientific inadequacy".

[77] This concept of complexity, this is important to state, differs from the one applied by Luhmann and the theory of autopoietic law: Luhmann calls a group of elements 'complex' in the case where not every element might possibly be related to any other element, *see* Luhmann, Niklas (1987). Soziale Systeme. Grundriss einer allgemeinen Theorie. Frankfurt am Main: Suhrkamp, p. 46 ("Als komplex wollen wir eine zusammenhängende Menge von Elementen bezeichnen, wenn auf Grund immanenter Beschränkungen der Verknüpfungskapazität der Elemente nicht mehr jedes Element jederzeit mit jedem anderen verknüpft sein kann."); similarly concerning the difference between Luhmann's concept of complexity and other concepts of complexity *see* Ruhl, J. B. (1996). Complexity Theory as a Paradigm for the Dynamical Law-and-Society System: A Wake-Up Call for Legal Reductionism and the Modern Administrative State. *Duke Law Journal 45*/5, 849–928 (858, note 10).

[78] *See above* Sect. 2.2.4.2.

[79] *See* e.g. Hathaway, Oona A. (2001). Path Dependence in the Law: The Course and Pattern of Change in the Legal System. *Iowa Law Review 86*, 101–165; Roe, Mark J. (1996). Chaos and Evolution in Law and Economics. *Harvard Law Review 109*, 641–668; and of course *see* also Holmes, Oliver Wendell (1897). The Path of the Law. *Harvard Law Review 10*, 457–469.

[80] For a more detailed view on the recursive moment of law *see below* Sect. 2.3.1.

characteristic of complexity, sometimes also called 'feedback'.[81] Another aspect of complexity found in our description of the legal system is its *irreversibility*[82]: once hybridized, hybrid law cannot be separated into different legal systems again. This is of course the case due to the interconnectivity between the originally different legal elements—as soon as they are normatively perceived, an interrelation is established that has to be re-produced every time the establishing perception itself is perceived again (in a later normative perception). In the here-described hybrid, relational and dynamic legal system, a reverse act is unthinkable. It is only thinkable that a certain element *is not* perceived any longer, but even in this case the once-established interrelation cannot be destroyed.

Thus, the complexity of law as introduced here is a concept that essentially refers to the interconnectivity of the elements of a legal system. Therefore, in a first step, the complexity of law points to the assumption that it is important to have a closer look at the basic principles of how the interrelations of the elements of a legal system are established and how they function. This is what we are going to examine in Sect. 2.3 of this chapter.[83]

2.2.6.2 Complexity as a Descriptive Concept

However, the question arises whether or not the concept of complexity determines our conceptual and descriptive approach on law. In the context of law described as hybrid, relational, and dynamic, the concept of complexity may describe certain aspects that are caused by the hybridity, relationality, and dynamics of law. But in a so-described law, these aspects cannot be *due to* its complexity. Rather, the conceptual relationship has to be understood in the inverse sense: because law is hybrid, relational, and dynamic, we can term it 'complex'. Thus, in our context the concept of complexity fulfils nothing but an evocative function. As a descriptive concept, it offers many different and productive perspectives on law,[84] among them

---

[81] *See* e.g. Ruhl, J. B. (2008). Law's Complexity: A Primer. *Georgia State University Law Review 24*/4, 885–911 (pp.898).

[82] Concerning the concept of irreversibility as an aspect of complexity, *see* also Ruhl, J. B. (2008). Law's Complexity: A Primer. *Georgia State University Law Review 24*/4, 885–911 (p.903), referring to Kauffman, Stuart (1995). At Home in the Universe. The Search for Laws of Self-Organization and Complexity. Oxford: Oxford University Press, p. 23.

[83] *See below* Sect. 2.3.

[84] *See* e.g. Ruhl, J. B. (2008). Law's Complexity: A Primer. *Georgia State University Law Review 24*/4, 885–911; Ruhl, J. B. (1996). Complexity Theory as a Paradigm for the Dynamical Law-and-Society System: A Wake-Up Call for Legal Reductionism and the Modern Administrative State. *Duke Law Journal 45*/5, 849–928; Geu, Thomas Earl (1994). The Tao of Jurisprudence: Chaos, Brain Science, Synchronicity, and the Law. *Tennessee Law Review 61*, 933–990; Kades, Eric (1997). The Laws of Complexity and the Complexity of Laws: The Implications of Computational Complexity for the Law. *Rutgers Law Review 49*, 403–484; Wright, R. George (2000). The Illusion of Simplicity: An Explanation of why the Law can't just be less complex. *Florida State University Law Review 27*, 715–744; Webb, Julian (2005). Law, Ethics, and Complexity:

those that observe the behaviour of a legal system towards environment[85] effects. But throughout our approach to law, the concept of complexity does not provide any tools beyond those we have been able to derive already from the concepts of hybridity, relationality, or dynamics. Since these three concepts allow us to apply the concept of complexity while this assertion is not necessarily true in the inverse direction, we shall in this context neglect further investigations of the concept of complexity—except for one methodological consideration we can possibly carry out more easily and in a more intelligible way by falling back upon the concept of complexity rather than upon the more special conceptual triangle we are elaborating here.

2.2.6.3 Methodological Consideration

So, how to investigate complex systems? This is the question constituting the methodological exception I just mentioned. Even if we can avoid further investigations of complexity, we have to deal with one question: are there any aspects that have to be considered when we investigate complex systems but not when investigating ordinary (non-complex) ones? The typical characteristic of a non-complex system lies in its capacity of being described entirely by giving a plan or a function that, if operationalized, provides a perfect representation of the system. For example, if we imagine law as a norm pyramid wherein any norm's normativity is deduced from a higher norm—then we can render the whole system by defining the highest norm (in *Kelsen's* theory this would be called the basic norm) and the deduction rule. For a complex system, this kind of description is not possible because it lacks the necessity of linear cause-and-effect relationships. Hence, the description of law as a complex system in the here-developed sense either requires a very detailed examination of every single element of law and of the former's being related to every single other element of the system. Or else, it requires a qualitative conceptual description of the occurrences by which the elements and their interrelations and their setting are influenced. The first method of investigation is what I would call 'numeric' (in a metaphorical sense). Concerning hybrid, relational and dynamic law, this method shows the deficiency of being incomplete at any moment in time because in law there are too many simultaneous movements; and here, the extensive effort needed to map the whole system of law only at one defined moment in time is not even regarded. Thus, it is the second method of conceptualizing the elements of law, their interrelations, and their setting that remains for us to proceed with our enterprise. Fortunately, we have already taken the first step in outlining our conceptual presuppositions of hybridity, relationality, and dynamics.

Complexity Theory & the Normative Reconstruction of Law. *Cleveland State Law Review 52*, 227–242; Schuck, Peter H. (1992). Legal Complexity: Some Causes, Consequences, and Cures. *Duke Law Journal 42*/1, 1–52.

[85] Even if a greater part of complexity inquiries takes place in the context of environmental law, here the term 'environment' refers to the distinction of a system and its environment.

2.3 The Normativity of Law: Performative, Recursive

But before taking the path towards a perspective on law, there is still a need to theorize the presuppositions already exposed: for there is one question which so far we have neither approximated nor answered: the question *what is law?* Even if this study's topic is not the concept of law—while searching for a perspective on law, we have to have a notion of what we are looking at. Although the previous sections exposed the central presuppositions for such a perspective on law, there is still a lack of theoretical background. Where do these presuppositions come from? How can we talk about a normative perception-based approach, for example; is law not just a system of positive norms? What is meant by the qualification of these normative perceptions as 'events'? And what is to be understood by 'the whole of law'?

Following these questions, the program of this section consists in outlining the theoretical idea on which the previously-exposed presuppositions are based. As we will see, I understand law as a *normative* order. The normativity of law becomes comprehensible through the concept of performativity.[86] Thus, the performativity and the complexity of law[87] constitute the basis for a conceptual and descriptive approach to law.

2.3.1 Normativity through Performativity[88]

Without defining the concept of law, I can acknowledge that it is connected to the concept of normativity. Even a pure legal realism that considers law as fact would not deny that we use the concept of law at least in connection with a claim for normativity. Therefore, even if we denied completely the possibility of a distinction between *Sein* and *Sollen*, even in this case we should have to accept that people use law *as if* it had normativity. For the moment, this kind of link to a 'fictional' normativity is sufficient to suppose the broad hypothesis that the concept of law is connected to the concept of normativity. To explain the notion of normativity that forms the background of the here-ventured approach, it is better to ask the question *How does this legal normativity (whatever ontological level it does occupy) come into the world?* instead of the question *What is legal normativity?*. I.e. the way I look at law is a phenomenological one: I look at the question how we can observe law, not at what it should be like nor at what its concepts could be like. Therefore,

[86] *See below* Sect. 2.3.1.

[87] As we have seen above, cf. Sect. 2.2 in this chapter.

[88] Parts of this section have already been published in German language: *see* Müller-Mall, Sabine (2012). Rechtserzeugung als performativer Vorgang in der Sprache, in: Bäcker, Carsten/Ziemann, Sascha (eds.). *Junge Rechtsphilsophie. Archiv für Rechts- und Sozialphilosophie*, Beiheft 135, Stuttgart: Franz Steiner, pp. 117–126.

the background of this study is an understanding of *Law as Practice*.[89] In this practice of law, as we will see, legal norms have the same functional form as do *signs* in other contexts.[90] Connected to this is the hypothesis that we can explain the generation of legal norms employing a concept of performativity that falls back on both law as practice as well as legal norms as signs.[91] And following the conception of a performative generation of law, legal normativity can be seen as a regressive progress that is expressible only in a recursive formula.[92]

These theoretical foundations of this present approach to hybrid, relational and dynamic law (as far as they concern the normativity of law) I am going to expose now, following the question: *how does legal normativity come into the world?*—presupposing that law is positive law. This limitation, the concentration on positive law, is not a contradiction to the before-described pluralism of law. The notion of plural or hybrid law may include state and non-state law, as well as a pluralism of forms of law, but this is not the case for that of natural law: describing law as possibly going back to different origins and different backgrounds presupposes thinking law as put into the world by human beings. Therefore, in a broad understanding of legal positivism as the idea of law generated by human beings, the law to be described is positive law, not natural law. Following this, the question of this section will not be *whether or not* legal norms come into the world, but *how* legal normativity is generated.[93]

2.3.1.1 Starting Point

In contrast to their great practical relevance, the processes in which positive legal normativity is generated are rarely the objects of legal-theoretical examinations. If we try to explain this in a first (superficial) attempt, a reason for this incompleteness may be seen in the fact that positive legal systems contain coherent explanations of the generation of legal norms in their self-description: legal norms come into the world by procedures established through other legal norms and through legal practice. And these legal norms are by definition normative as soon as they come into force. Therefore, looking at legal theory approaches, the reasons for an almost negligent treatment of these processes can be formulated in a more precise way: almost all positive law theories are based on a categorical separation of the concepts of *Sein* and *Sollen*, and they explain the generation of legal norms mostly along only one of these categories (depending on the direction of the perspective taken in each

---

[89] Concerning the concept of practice, *see* also Sects. 2.3.1.4. and 3.3.1. *below*.

[90] *See below* Sects. 2.3.1.3 and 2.3.1.4.

[91] *See below* Sect. 2.3.1.4.

[92] *See below* Sect. 2.3.1.4.

[93] For a more profound examination of this question, *see* my study *Performative Rechtserzeugung*, Mueller-Mall, Sabine (2012). *Performative Rechtserzeugung. Eine theoretische Annäherung*. Velbrueck: Weilerswist.

case). On the one hand, normativistic theories for instance try to describe law as a normative system, placing the deduction of legal norms from legal norms in the centre of attention.[94] On the other hand, for realistic approaches (treating law as a social fact) it is sufficient to understand the generation of legal norms as socially constituted.

Contrary to that, I am convinced that any explanation of the generation of law necessarily has to include both, *Sein* and *Sollen*. In looking at the positive generation of law we capture exactly this moment, wherein legal normativity is generated through an act of *Sein*. In other words: if we distinguish between the categories of *Sein* and *Sollen*, answering the question of how positive legal norms come into the world will presuppose an explanation of how a *Sollen* can be generated out of the *Sein*. This is the case, because any notion of positive law (that is to be defined by the idea of legal norms coming into the world by procedures, not by an idea of natural existence) necessarily presupposes that at any moment of time *Sein* is transformed into *Sollen*.[95]

---

[94] As paradigmatic in this sense has to be named *Kelsen's Pure Theory of Law*: by this theory, *Kelsen* explains the generation of legal norms in an internal, i.e. exclusively normative, way—"Als Rechtsnorm gilt eine Norm stets nur darum, weil sie auf eine ganz bestimmte Weise zustande gekommen, nach einer ganz bestimmten Regel erzeugt, nach einer spezifischen Methode gesetzt wurde. Das Recht gilt nur als positives Recht, das heißt, als gesetztes Recht." (Kelsen, Hans (2008, orig. 1934). Reine Rechtslehre (1st edition). Tuebingen: Mohr Siebeck, pp.74. *See* also Kelsen, Hans (1934*). Introduction to the Problems of Legal Theory. A Translation of the First Edition of the Reine Rechtslehre or Pure Theory of Law*. New York: Oxford University Press, p. 56: "A norm is valid *qua* legal norm only because it was arrived at in a certain way—created according to a certain rule, issued or set according to a specific method. The law is valid only as positive law, that is, only as law that has been issued or set.") Presupposing an 'act of will' („Willensakt") as precondition for the existence of a legal norm, *Kelsen* connects a legal norm to a factual act, to the sphere of *Sein*. But this act of will is not more than a triggering moment; it is not the cause for the legal norm, because "dabei ist zu beachten, dass die Norm als spezifischer Sinngehalt etwas anderes ist als der psychische Akt, in dem sie gewollt oder vorgestellt wird" (Cf. Kelsen, Hans (2008, orig. 1934). *Reine Rechtslehre* (1st edition). Tuebingen: Mohr Siebeck, p. 20. *See* also Kelsen, Hans (1934*). Introduction to the Problems of Legal Theory. A Translation of the First Edition of the Reine Rechtslehre or Pure Theory of Law*. New York: Oxford University Press, p. 11: "One should note here that the norm *qua* specific meaning is something other than the mental act of intending or imagining the norm."). Since cause and condition are to be distinguished in this context, and since, on the contrary, legal realism that treats acts of *Sein* as *causes* of legal normativity, it is only possible to understand *Kelsen's* position as normativistic, and not as (legal) realistic (for a different opinion concerning this distinction, *see* Jestaedt, Matthias (2008). Einführung, in: Kelsen, Hans (2008). *Reine Rechtslehre*. Mohr Siebeck: Tübingen, p. XXVI.).

[95] Of course it is possible to completely reject this hypothesis. But if in this case one maintains the assumption of *Sein* and *Sollen* as categories that need to be distinguished from one another, then one will have no other choice but to explain the circumstance of the generation of positive law as a paradoxical one—which is not impossible of course, but will not be accepted until all other attempts of description are failed.

How this transformation[96] in turn can be described in a theoretical way is the basic question of every science[97] of positive law: because without answering this question, no secured statements could be made at all on how legal norms are to be applied.[98] Thus, in the following I shall examine the question of how legal *Sollen* arises out of the *Sein*; how legal normativity is generated. In doing so, I shall build on a hypothesis that may be concluded from what was described above: it has to be possible to identify, or at least think, a moment in time that resembles a moment of turnabout. In other words, if we think legal normativity as coming into the world at some transfer point, there must be a moment in time at which *Sein* is transferred into *Sollen*, and this process is what we call the generation of law.[99]

2.3.1.2 Perspective: Generation of Legal Normativity as Language Procedure

I am taking on this present attempt of describing the generation of legal normativity from a special perspective. It is based on a quite simple observation on the one hand, and on a somewhat more complicated hypothesis on the other. The *observation* is that positive legal norms (judicial decisions included[100]) are always

[96] *See* also Vismann, Cornelia (1999). Jurisprudence. A Transfer Science. *Law and Critique 10*, 279–286.

[97] The German legal tradition refers to legal as well as e.g. historical or cultural studies as *sciences*. And even if this may sound unfamiliar for different traditions, I would like to keep up this tradition for the following reason: the goal of most kinds of legal studies will be to find explanations for phenomena, invent models or tools based on these explanations, or to build theories that can approximate law. Even law is not a natural phenomenon; it can be observed, conceptualized and understood as can every other object of a science.

[98] In addition, every theory of legal normativity presupposes a theory of the generation of law, *see* Del Mar, Maksymilian (2007). Legal Norms and Normativity. *Oxford Journal of Legal Studies 27/2*, 355–372 (371).

[99] Until now, this moment in time is an aspect not regarded very often—this is not surprising, since legal theories traditionally, as I pointed out above, either take on the normative perspective or the factual (realistic) one. In both cases, the transfer from one to the other lies more or less on the margin of the set of central questions. But, on the other hand, if we do not take one of these (both very demanding) sides of the medal already at the beginning of our approach, then an attempt to describe this moment of legal generation in more detail could provide a rare opportunity: to examine the generation of law without rashly referring to either normative or social preconditions. Starting from the point of view of this momentum could instead yield some conclusions on both dimensions of law, the *Sein* and the *Sollen*.

[100] By the concept of the generation of legal norms I understand processes of legal norm production governed by all state powers, legislation as well as administrative acts and judicial decision-making. The qualification taken here basically follows *Kelsen* who understands "die meisten Rechtsakte (. . .) zugleich Akte der Rechtserzeugung und Akte der Rechtsvollziehung" (Kelsen, Hans (2008, orig. 1934). Reine Rechtslehre (1st edition). Tuebingen: Mohr Siebeck p. 92; *see* also Kelsen, Hans (1934). *Introduction to the Problems of Legal Theory. A Translation of the First Edition of the Reine Rechtslehre or Pure Theory of Law*. New York: Oxford University Press, p. 70: "Most legal acts are acts of both law creation and law application."). I do not, however, share

generated through language, i.e. by written or oral utterances. The *hypothesis* (which in this context must remain an assumption[101]) can be described as follows: the assumption that the generation of law only happens through language does not only describe a special version of law-generating processes, but it also refers to an intrinsic connection between the generation of law and the language-dependent form of this process.[102] And if this connection exists, the general conditions of generation through language have to be conditions of the generation of law as well. I.e. answers to the question of how we can generate something in language at all, how we can do things with words,[103] may point us to answers to the question of how legal normativity may be generated through language as well. Therefore, the perspective I am taking on the process of law generation concentrates on the language form of this process: what are the conditions for generating anything in language at all, and in what way could these conditions be meaningful in relation to the generation of legal normativity?

From this point of view, it might seem to be a good suggestion to look for criteria applying to utterances that—in case of their fulfilment—lead to such a happy[104] generation of, e.g., a legal norm. We can imagine such criteria for instance thinking of a court, where we could speak of the happy generation of a legal judgment if the following conditions are met: someone who is appointed as a judge by a legitimate authority pronounces a verdict in a courtroom at a date set exclusively for the carrying out of this aim, and the audience present accepts the whole procedure as this—the pronouncement of a verdict. In this case, the utterance "The court sentences you to..." does not describe an action of the judge, but the utterance itself *is* the action. This implicitly opened distinction between descriptive and "acting" utterances, or, in other words, the distinction between constative utterances and speech *acts* goes back to *J. L. Austin*.[105] *Austin* derives this

---

his very presupposing identification of 'execution' and 'application'. Instead, I base this idea on a similar, but less demanding assumption: judicial decisions as well as administrative acts execute legal acts by generating normativity 'as law'. For reasons of clarity, I shall further neglect administrative acts and focus my attention on legislation and judicial decision-making.

[101] For further reasons, again *see* Mueller-Mall, Sabine (2012). Performative Rechtserzeugung. Eine theoretische Annäherung. Velbrück: Weilerswist, chapter 1.

[102] The words of a verdict that a judge has already written but not yet pronounced may illustrate this hypothesis. The pure words do not have a legally normative effect until they are pronounced, which has to happen in a certain legal form. Even if in practice many verdicts are no longer even pronounced—this is not because of renunciation of the pronouncing procedure in a conditional way, but only in an elliptical way. Only the pronouncing of the verdict's words by the judge turns it into a legal judgment, a decision, a verdict that is normative.

[103] Cf. the title of *Austin's* famous lectures: Austin, J. L. (1975). *How to do Things with Words*. Cambridge/Mass : Harvard University Press.

[104] Applying the term 'happy' in this context refers to Austin, J. L. (1975). *How to do Things with Words*. Cambridge/Mass :Harvard University Press, (e.g.) pp. 43.

[105] Central works concerning this distinction and the acting (performative) dimension of speech are: Austin, J. L. (1975). *How to do Things with Words*. Cambridge/Mass. : Harvard University Press, and Austin, J. L. (1979). Performative Utterances, in: Austin, J. L. *Philosophical Papers*. Oxford: Oxford University Press, p. 233–253.

distinction from the observation that besides statements of which the "business" is "to 'describe' some state of affairs", there are "also question and exclamations, and sentences expressing commands or wishes or concessions".[106] Since *Austin's* lectures were published for the first time in 1962, this distinction between constative and 'performative' (as *Austin* calls it)[107] utterances has been very effective in language philosophy until today and has led to a great number of attempts (labelled "speech act theory") to look for criteria of utterances that, as I mentioned above, in case of being met would produce an action, a result.[108]

But such a search for criteria itself proves to be quite problematic and most likely is unable to yield results that could be productive concerning the generation of legal norms. We can sum up the reasons for this misfire in one main argument: apparently it is impossible to distinguish analytically between the process of generation in language and that which is thus generated. And hence, it becomes impossible to state criteria for happy generation in language that have to be fulfilled at the moment of uttering in order for that something which follows temporally (that is the generated) to be in the world: if the process of generation and that which is generated by that process are not categorically differentiable; if we cannot describe this as a linear cause-and-effect-relationship, then any conditional description of happy generation through this process has to be impossible. To underpin the central assumption of this argument—that the process of generation and that which is thus generated are analytically inseparable—we can refer to very different authors, but above all to *Austin* himself: throughout his study, not only the distinction between constative and performative utterances fails,[109] but also a second distinction which he introduces in seeking to rescue his approach—the one of *illocution* and *perlocution*.[110] Furthermore, already for *Wilhelm von Humboldt* it is not possible

---

[106] *See* Austin, J. L. (1975). *How to do Things with Words*. Cambridge/Mass. : Harvard University Press, p. 1.

[107] *See* Austin, J. L. (1975). *How to do Things with Words*. Cambridge/Mass. : Harvard University Press, p. 6: "I propose to call it a *performative sentence* or a performative utterance, or, for short, 'a performative'."

[108] The most prominent attempt is probably the one made by *Searle* – Searle, John (1969). *Speech Acts*. Cambridge: Cambridge University Press.

[109] *Austin* neither finds an unambiguous linguistic criterion to distinguish between constative and performative utterances (*see* Austin, J. L. (1975). *How to do Things with Words*. Cambridge/Mass : Harvard University Press, pp. 47–52; *see* also Bremerich-Vos, Albert (1981). *Zur Kritik der Sprechakttheorie – Austin und Searle*. Weinheim, Basel: Beltz, pp. 34–39), nor does he find a grammatical criterion („Now we failed to find a grammatical criterion for performatives", Austin, J. L. (1975). *How to do Things with Words*. Harvard University Press: Cambridge/Mass., p. 91).

[110] Looking for a more general theory of acting by way of language, *Austin* introduces a distinction to serve no longer for differentiating between several types of utterances, but for describing *every* utterance: the one of *locution*, *illocution*, and *perlocution*. For a detailed definition, *see* Austin, J. L. (1975). *How to do Things with Words*. Cambridge/Mass : Harvard University Press, pp. 92, pp. 98, and pp. 101. Concerning the problems and failures of differentiating between illocution and perlocution, *see* Austin, J. L. (1975). *How to do Things with Words*. Cambridge/Mass : Harvard University Press, pp. 116, but also Davis, Steven (1980). Perlocutions, in: Searle, John & Kiefer, Ferenc & Bierwisch, Manfred (eds.). *Speech Act Theory and Pragmatics*. Heidelberg, New York:

to separate between generation in language and the generated. *Humboldt* understands the use of language as a creative, generative act, but this act takes place only in a field of tension that is constituted by *ergon* (work) and *energeia* (doing something).[111] We can infer quite similar insights from lectures of *Wittgenstein* and *Derrida*: formulating rule-following as a practice (*Wittgenstein*)[112] as well as pointing out that any context of an utterance is indeterminable (*Derrida*),[113] both enterprises can be understood as arguments in favour of the assumption that any description of generation in language is not directed by conditions or criteria that precede this generation in a general and determinable way.[114]

In summary, we cannot uphold the idea that utterances have determinable effects under determinable circumstances. Hence, it is not the assumption of a generating dimension of language in general that has to be given up, but the manner of its description.

2.3.1.3 The Concept of Performativity as Description Tool for Procedures of Generation in Language

I am still on the way in looking for a qualitative description of generation in language, then, but without referring to criteria of happiness that could name the circumstances in which an utterance could possibly generate something, e.g. a legal norm. And although all the searches for criteria were doomed to failure there is one concept that appears more than once throughout the relevant debates in the philosophy of language,[115] a concept that seems to be productive for the description of

---

Springer, p. 37–55 (pp. 46); Savigny, Eike von (1974). *Die Philosophie der normalen Sprache*. Frankfurt am Main: Suhrkamp, pp. 134; Kraemer, Sybille (2001). *Sprache, Sprechakt, Kommunikation* Frankfurt am Main: Suhrkamp, p. 139.

[111] *See* e.g. Humboldt, Wilhelm von (1836). *Über die Verschiedenheit des menschlichen Sprachbaues und ihren Einfluss auf die geistige Entwicklung des Menschengeschlechtes*, §§ 12, 13. *See* also Junker, Klaus (1986). Zur Kritik der Humboldt-Adaption der Neuhumboldtianer, in: Welke, Klaus (ed.). *Sprache – Bewusstsein –Tätigkeit. Zur Sprachkonzeption Wilhelm von Humboldts*. Berlin: Akademie-Verlag, p. 68–93 (pp. 74.); Gipper, Helmut & Schmitter, Peter (1979). *Sprachwissenschaft und Sprachphilosophie im Zeitalter der Romantik. Ein Beitrag zur Historiographie der Linguistik*. Tuebingen: Narr, pp. 90, 95.

[112] Explicitly: Wittgenstein, Ludwig (1984). *Philosophische Untersuchungen*. Frankfurt am Main: Suhrkamp, § 202.

[113] *See* especially Derrida, Jacques (1972). Signature Evénement Contexte, in: Derrida, Jacques, *Marges de la philosophie*. Paris: Editions de Minuit, p. 365–393; Derrida, Jaques (1988). Signature Event Context, in: Graff, Gerald (ed.). *Limited Inc*. Evanston: Northwestern University Press, pp. 1–25.

[114] For a detailed argumentation, *see* Mueller-Mall, Sabine (2012). *Performative Rechtserzeugung. Eine theoretische Annaeherung*.Weilerswist: Velbrueck, chapter 2.

[115] Not only *Austin* applies the term; it appears in philosophical debates on the dimension of language generating something as often and regularly as in cultural studies discourses, where it is not necessarily linked to language, but to processes of generation in a broader sense. *See* e.g.

generation in language: it is the one of *performativity*.[116] Hence, in what follows I will propose an understanding of this concept that might possibly describe how law is generated in and through the application of language; and this proposal will exceed the manner in which criteria such as context, conventionality, or dependence of rules are able to explain this phenomenon.

To approach the concept of performativity it is helpful to take another look at the practice of the use of language, which is always an application of either phonetic or written *signs*. It is a characteristic of a sign to be repeatable. We can call this the quality of being recitable; and this characteristic is what makes the sign a sign in the first place[117]: "Every sign, linguistic or nonlinguistic, spoken or written (...) can be cited, put between quotation marks; thereby it can break with every given context, and engender infinitely new contexts in an absolutely nonsaturable fashion. This does not suppose that the mark is valid outside its context, but on the contrary that there are only contexts without any center of absolute anchoring. This citationality, duplication, or duplicity, this iterability of the mark is not an accident or anomaly, but is that (normal/abnormal) without which a mark could no longer even have a so-called "normal" functioning. What would a mark be that one could not cite? And whose origin could not be lost on the way?"[118] Hence, it is a main capacity of a sign to be repeatable, and following *Derrida* we can call this capacity *iterability*. The concept of iterability even points out that a sign is connected to a different, to a new context by being quoted or cited. I.e. every use of a sign is not a repetition, but an

Culler, Jonathan (2000). Philosophy and Literature. The Fortunes of the Performative. *Poetics Today 21/3*, 503–519; Derrida, Jacques (1993). *Spectres de Marx*. Paris : Galilée; Derrida, Jacques (1972). Signature Evénement Contexte, in: Derrida, Jacques, *Marges de la philosophie*. Paris: Editions de Minuit, p. 365–393 (Derrida, Jaques (1988). Signature Event Context, in: Graff, Gerald (ed.). *Limited Inc*. Evanston: Northwestern University Press, pp. 1–25). Kertscher, Jens & Mersch, Dieter (eds.) (2003). *Performativität und Praxis*. München: Fink; Lyotard, Jean-François (1984). The Postmodern Condition. A Report on Knowledge. Minneapolis: Minnesota Univerity Press; Loxley, James (2007). *Performativity*. London: Routledge; Miller, J. Hillis (2007). Performativity as Performance/Performativity as Speech Act: Derrida's Special Theory of Performativity. *South Atlantic Quarterly 106/2*, 219–235; Wirth, Uwe (2002). Der Performanzbegriff im Spannungsfeld von Illokution, Iteration und Indexikalität, in: Wirth, Uwe (ed.). *Performanz. Zwischen Sprachphilosophie und Kulturwissenschaften*. Frankfurt am Main: Suhrkamp, p. 9–62.

[116] It cannot be very helpful, here, to give a definition of the concept of performativity, since its uses are as different as the contexts of these uses. A productive and useful concept of 'performativity' has yet to be developed, and it should consist in more than just the relation to the already-described generating-dimension of language. A proposal will follow (*see below* in this chapter.).

[117] *Wirth* calls this understanding of the sign „infinite recitability" and „indefinite recontextualizability" [my translation], *see* Wirth, Uwe (2002). Der Performanzbegriff im Spannungsfeld von Illokution, Iteration und Indexikalität, in: Wirth, Uwe (ed.). *Performanz. Zwischen Sprachphilosophie und Kulturwissenschaften*. Frankfurt am Main: Suhrkamp, p. 9–62 (19).

[118] Derrida, Jaques (1988). Signature Event Context, in: Graff, Gerald (ed.). *Limited Inc*. Evanston: Northwestern University Press, pp. 1–25 (12).

event that is new and singular every time.[119] And since in being used a sign is quoted, iterated and repeated (the repetition is exclusively part of the sign, not of its use, which is singular every time), we can conceptualize speaking as a tension between being an event and being the repetition of the sign, which can only happen in the form of *iteration*. This tension occurs in between two poles that we can call citation and new setting, or antecedent and self-referential. A thus-designed dimension of speech (or: the use of language) does not refer to the concept of meaning, but is to be described as a specific externality of the use of signs.[120]

This reflection leads to a way of conceptualizing the performative: the performative includes the characteristic and necessity of speech to be executed on the basis of a tension between antecedents and self-referentiality, and by this, the performative contains what we can call a per-formative power. Hence, there are always these two concepts underlying performativity as I capture it here: changing repetition and new setting, or antecedent and self-referentiality. Antecedent in this sense means referring to earlier uses of a sign, which has to be distinguished from the concept of deduction. And self-referentiality means: in speech, there is always a connection of a sign to a new context, and this connection can only connect to itself. By this connection, we give any sign we use a meaning, we 'add' this meaning to the sign—signs in this description do not carry stable meanings that could immediately represent concepts or things. To the contrary, it is the *use* of a sign that allows us to ascribe a meaning—to this use, not to the sign used.

Performativity in this sense describes the structure of the use of signs, which through the event of uttering executes an antecedent and self-referential connection of a sign to a new context. The connection itself is at the same time a procedure (sign and context get connected), as well as the result of performative generation, *a* connection. The connection itself does not yield any meaning, because a sign as external sign cannot carry any meaning—instead, we as speakers and hearers (or even readers) ascribe meaning to the connection of sign and context.

2.3.1.4 Model of Performative Law Generation: Regressive Normativity

Taking up this description, one could ask further how the structure of the use of language understood as performative event now allows us to make conclusions

[119] Such events are immune of being repeated: „there is only one phrase ‚at a time' [à la fois] (. . .), but only von actual or current ‚time' [une seule ‚fois' actuelle]", Lyotard, Jean-François (1988). *The Differend: Phrases in Dispute*. Minneapolis: Minnesota University Press, p. 136. For the concept of ‚event', *see* also Derrida, Jacques (2007). A Certain Impossible Possibility of Saying the Event. *Critical Inquiry 33*/2, 441–461 (446).

[120] This hypothesis of a „specific externality of signs" (which follows Derrida and Foucault) goes back to *Wirth* and *Wellbery*: *see* Wirth, Uwe (2002). Der Performanzbegriff im Spannungsfeld von Illokution, Iteration und Indexikalität, in: Wirth, Uwe (ed.). *Performanz. Zwischen Sprachphilosophie und Kulturwissenschaften*. Frankfurt am Main: Suhrkamp, p. 9–62 (43), referring to Wellbery, David (1993). Die Äußerlichkeit der Schrift, in: Gumbrecht, Hans-Ulrich & Pfeiffer, K. Ludwig (eds.). *Schrift*. München: Fink, p. 337–348 (343).

concerning the generation of legal norms. With the help of the ascertainments already made, the way to the generation of legal normativity is quite short: if generating in language is a performative process, and if it is not only the case that the generation of law happens in language but that this fact is even constitutive for the generation of law, then we have to assume that the generation of legal normativity is a performative process, as well. Now, how we might recognize this performative structure of the use of language in the process of law production is what I shall try to make explicit in what follows. I will use a model of performative law generation, which again I shall not go beyond outlining here.[121]

Such a model necessarily has to be centred on the sign. Events of law generation,[122] then, can basically be understood as performative speech events, connecting (language) sign chains to contexts.[123] If these events, these generating procedures must explain themselves by way of a performative structure, as we said before for the general use of language, then we have to imagine legal norms working in a manner similar to signs: they might be connected to a context, build a connection to which we can refer afterwards. But we must not imagine legal norms as "normative forces" that have an effect on legal events taking place in the future.

In a concrete event of law generation, e.g. at the pronouncement of a verdict by a judge, the judge connects a (language) sign chain ("The court sentences you to...") to a specific context (here: the courtroom, the public, the date of pronouncement, etc.). And to this connection the people present (but also absent people who receive knowledge of the event afterwards) can ascribe a linguistic meaning. On the other hand and in addition, we can ascribe to this connection something that I call a "normative meaning", e.g. the idea that by way of the pronunciation of the sign chain indicating the verdict, the latter becomes valid.[124] But if legal norms function like linguistic signs, then it is impossible to create a legal norm in a singular event—because a sign cannot come to existence by being 'invented' but once.[125] The entity

---

[121] For a detailed description, *see* again Mueller-Mall, Sabine (2012). *Performative Rechtserzeugung. Eine theoretische Annaeherung*. Velbrueck: Weilerswist, chapter 5.

[122] To understand procedures of law generation as 'events', happening at a certain moment in time, was exactly the starting point of the perspective taken here; the reason for doing so lies in the attempt to describe law generation without any normativistic or social-practical superstructure, in order to uphold the possibility of conclusions concerning both levels, *Sein* and *Sollen*. The advantage of doing so would be not to privilege either of the dimensions of law too early.

[123] This is true for jurisdiction as well as for legislation or giving of a constitution.

[124] I do not presume that every event of this kind necessarily creates these two kinds of meaning ascription. Instead, I am just applying a distinction which originally was introduced by *Austin*: the one between locutionary and other contents of an utterance (*see see* Austin, J. L. (1975). *How to do Things with Words*. Cambridge/Mass : Harvard University Press, pp. 91. Irrespective of the empirical inseparability of each utterance, *Austin* separates analytically into a 'purely linguistic' content of an utterance and a content that is created by performative effects of an utterance. It can be quite important to underline this distinction to allow a perspective on the performative effects of an utterance (here: the generated legal normativity). In contrast to the distinction between illocution and perlocution, the present one does not cause us any problems (neither for *Austin*).

[125] For reasons, *see above* Sect. 2.3.1.3.

arising from the connection of the utterance "The court sentences you to..." to the described context I am going to call a *pre-sign* or a *pre-norm*. It is only by way of an iterative application of this first connection (the re-iteration by perceiving the pre-norm in a subsequent event of legal generation) that a pre-norm can be transformed into a norm. This happens for instance when a second judicial decision builds up on a first one by citing it.[126] A thus-produced norm may be understood as generated only if one or more subsequent performative employments of the original connection have taken place, because the norm's coming into existence is dependent on future events of law generation. Therefore we can say that to understand the generation of legal norms as a performative procedure means to understand normativity as a phenomenon we can only describe in a *recursive* way. In this model, norms do not instantly become effective as prescriptive entities, but they are merely possible subjects of future re-iteration which makes them come into existence in the first place. Thus, normativity proves to be a *passive* concept and a *recursive* concept. And if a norm is only generated by its future application, *then 'application' and 'generation' of a norm have to be different expressions for the same practice.*[127] And this means at the same time that neither the norm itself nor the speaker uttering the original chain of signs may determine whether or not the pre-norm is re-iterated, whether or not the pre-norm becomes a norm. Thus, whether or not the generation of law works out—according to this model, this question depends on facts left to the future, and not on facts that would be either existing or even describable at the moment of the original event of performative generation. Therefore, normativity is not the sequel to a certain event of law generation, but the *result of a practice* which is not completed in the moment of its generation.

In this model, the concept of authority[128] (or: competence understood as the ability to generate legal norms) and the concept of a norm's legitimacy do not appear at all. According to the model, this is not a deficiency, but a necessity. If the

---

[126] It is important to consider at this point what we have said before: that the ascription of a meaning is always a subjective act. This means that succeeding references to earlier events of legal generation do not refer to something like a general meaning, which, once brought into the world, would persist.

[127] Further, it is impossible to describe in a mono-dimensional way *what* exactly it is that is being generated as a norm: what remains in the world after any event of performative law generation is nothing but the norm text which is an embodiment of all ascriptions of meaning that are made referring to the connection between the performative utterance and the context of the event. And, at the same time, the norm text represents the connecting piece that subsequent events of generation might refer to. As soon as it is re-iterated (from an external perspective: a citation), the norm text becomes a sign. New linguistic and normative ascriptions (of meaning) refer to the original ascriptions only implicitly. And here, the original connection of a performative utterance to a context does not even appear any more—it is a necessary condition for the generation of a norm, but not part of the norm.

[128] Concerning the theoretical determination of the concept of authority, *see* e.g. Raz, Joseph (1979). *The Authority of Law*. Oxford: Clarendon Press; Raz, Joseph (2005–2006). The Problem of Authority: Revisiting the Service Conception. *Minnesota Law Review 90*, 1003–1044; Bix, Brian (2005). Authority, and Conceptual Analysis. *The American Journal of Jurisprudence 50*, 311–316.

successful generation of a norm only depends on its later re-iteration, then the authority generating normativity can only be found in this iterative structure itself—not in qualities or competencies that belong to certain subjects, neither in a factual way nor through normative assignments of competencies. Moreover, the legitimacy of such norms might only be generated *ex post*—the category of correctness is not constitutive because the meaning of a norm cannot be determined.[129]

According to this model, *Sein* and *Sollen* constitute interconnected levels that are not separable in a categorical sense: normativity and its factual application merge and are mutually dependent. Only a subsequent use gives rise to the normativity 'used'. As a result, the normativity of legal norms is a 'passive' concept. Therefore I would like to call the originally-named 'transfer point'[130] of *Sein* and *Sollen* at the moment of law generation the "*modulation of* Sein *into* Sollen". This name refers to the musical expression "modulation" which describes the transition from one key to another within the same piece of music. An important characteristic of this musical transition called modulation is that we can only perceive it retrospectively, because it is constituted but through the sound following such a transition.[131]

2.3.1.5 Legal Normativity

This description of the relationship between *Sein* and *Sollen* is not subject to a logical fallacy because it does not *deduce* the *Sollen* from the *Sein*. Rather, both levels prove to be in a persistent reflexive tension which cannot be conceptualized as linearity but can be described by the conception of performativity. The possibility of this description results from the perspective we took on the generation of law: not taking the starting point of either *Sollen* or *Sein* in the search for a reconstruction of the generation procedure, but, to the contrary, making the process of generation the starting point for the examination. The results of this examination do not deny the possibility of legal normativity; instead, they argue for a radical change of perspective on normativity. To explain legal normativity, it does not suffice to rely on the assumption that norms are like formulated rules, but rather we have to look at performative events which can subsequently be understood as law-generating events. Thus, not a scheme that operates with the conceptions of rules and their

[129] Here it should be helpful to mention again that this model does not pursue any normative aims, but is an attempt of a deductive-descriptive explanation.

[130] *See above*, Sect. 2.3.1.1.

[131] An interesting aspect of the musical modulation lies in the fact that a harmonic chord (which has already appeared before the modulation) is often functionally re-interpreted: i.e. the same chord used until then as a subdominant chord, for instance, is now used as the tonic chord of a new key. At the moment of this transition by way of functional re-interpretation, the chord is still perceivable as part of the original key. Only in connection with the subsequent sounds can it be classified as the tonic chord of the new key.

applications should be in the centre of the perspective that further studies in legal theory take, but the configuration of norm generating itself.

With this approach to the question of how legal normativity comes into the world in the background, we have sailed round the problematic distinction of law and non-law. Hopefully, the hidden path we used is quite obvious now: there is no abstract definition that we could formulate of such a distinction. But if we understand legal normativity as generated by the re-iteration of the generative event (*as* a law-generative event), then we can talk about legal normativity. Thus, by explaining legal normativity through the conception of recursivity, we have a test for possible legal norms: if there is an example of re-iteration of the possible norm *as* a legal norm, we can assume it as a legal norm.

2.3.2 Normative Perception/Transformation

Having outlined the recursive conception of normativity, we can now bridge (back) to the two concepts we have already mentioned: the one of normative perception and the one of transformation. Both connect the performative model of law generation to the presuppositions of the approach to law taken here. Above, I described the relationality of law as dynamic, and its dynamics were caused by the event character of normative perceptions, while normative perceptions were exposed as constituting the interrelations of law. Now we can identify these normative perceptions with the performative events of law generation just exposed. In doing so, we see that the object to be described as hybrid, relational, and dynamic law is a set of interconnected events. If we understand legal normativity not as a stable effect, but as exclusively appearing through generative events working recursively, then what we have to look at are these events, not texts of legal norms or decisions. As they iterate former performative events by citing them, and as we call these iterations 'normative perceptions' because they are both, self-referential as well as antecedent acts, every single normative perception transforms the earlier web of interrelations. Thus, concentrating on the single event, we have to understand it as a normative perception, but concentrating on the whole of law, we have to understand each normative perception as a transformative act.

What we understand by law, then, is a system of dynamic interrelations. The application of law in this sense is necessarily the making of law—adding a new normative perception that transforms the topology of the former (which means: made until then) interrelations. In the following, describing law has to be identified with describing the interrelations and their transformability as well as their transformations—it means trying to explain what these transformations are like. And searching for a perspective on law means to find a way to look at this dynamic system that will allow placing us as observers somewhere in this system. In other words, a perspective on law might give us a method of walking through this set in order to let us answer concrete questions that arise in law. For this, we have to admit that concrete questions in law cannot be anything else than questions for determining exactly a certain position in the system.

For the moment, these considerations seem to be quite abstract, but I hope that along the further investigations we will get an insight of what this version of 'taking a perspective' on law could mean in a more concrete sense. At the end of this second chapter, it is important and sufficient to state that the perspective on law for which we are looking has to be able to deal with law as a perceptional system that is constantly in transformation.

References

Abbott, Kenneth W. & Snidal, Duncan (2009). Strengthening International Regulation Transnational New Governance: Overcoming the Orchestration Deficit. *Vanderbilt Journal of Transnational Law 42*, 501–578.

Alexander, Lisa T. (2010). Wisconsin Law Review Symposium Afterword. Part III. *Wisconsin Law Review*, 737–748.

Austin, J. L. (1975). *How to do Things with Words*. Cambridge/Mass.: Harvard University. Press.

Austin, J. L. (1979). Performative Utterances, in: Austin, J. L. *Philosophical Papers*. Oxford: Oxford University Press, pp. 233–253.

Austin, J. L. (1979) *Philosophical Papers*. Oxford: Oxford University Press.

F. v. Benda-Beckmann, K. v. Benda-Beckmann & A. Griffiths (eds.) (2005). *Mobile People, Mobile Law. Expanding Legal Relations in a Contracting World*. Aldershot: Ashgate.

Bäcker, Carsten/Ziemann, Sascha (eds.)(2012). *Junge Rechtsphilsophie. Archiv für Rechts- und Sozialphilosophie*, Beiheft 135, Stuttgart: Franz Steiner.

Bain, Read (1929). The Concept of Complexity in Sociology I. *Social Forces 8*, 222–231.

Barabási, Albert László (2005). Taming Complexity. *Nature physics 1*, 68–70.

Berman, Paul Schiff (2009). The New Legal Pluralism. *Annual Review of Law and Social Science*, 5, 225–242.

Berman, Paul Schiff (2007). Global Legal Pluralism. *Southern California Law Review 80*, 1155–1237.

Berman, Paul Schiff (2010). Towards A Jurisprudence of Hybridity. *Utah Law Review*, 11–29.

Bix, Brian (2005). Authoriy, and Conceptual Analysis. *The American Journal of Jurisprudence 50*, 311–316.

Bremerich-Vos, Albert (1981). *Zur Kritik der Sprechakttheorie – Austin und Searle*. Weinheim, Basel: Beltz.

Bruch, Elisabeth M. (2010). Hybrid Courts: Examining Hybridity through a Post-Colonial Lens. *Boston University International Law Journal 28*/1, 1–38.

Bruch, Elizabeth M. (2011). Is International Law Really Law? Theorizing the Multi-Dimensionality of Law. *Akron Law Review 44*, 333–373.

Burca, Graìnne, de & Scott, Joanne (Eds.) (2006). *Law and New Governance in the EU and the U. S.* Oxford: Hart.

Caldeira, Gregory (1985). The Transmission of Legal Precedent: A Study of State Supreme Courts. *American Political Science Review 79*, 178–194.

Caldeira, Gregory (1988). Legal Precedent: Structures of Communication Between State Supreme Courts. *Social networks 10*, 29–55.

Chandler, Seth S. (2005). The Network Structure of Supreme Court Jurisprudence. *University of Houston Public Law and Legal Theory Series* 2005-W-01.

Cohen, David (2007). "Hybrid" Justice in East Timor, Sierra Leone, and Cambodia: "Lessons Learned" and Prospects for the Future. *Stanford Journal of International Law 43*, 1–38.

Cover, Robert M. (1983). The Supreme Court 1982 Term. Foreword: Nomos and Narrative. *Harvard Law Review 97*, 4–68.
Craig, Paul (2006). *EU Administrative Law*. Oxford: Oxford University Press.
Culler, Jonathan (2000). Philosophy and Literature. The Fortunes of the Performative. *Poetics Today 21*/3, 503–519.
Davis, Steven (1980). Perlocutions, in: Searle, John & Kiefer, Ferenc & Bierwisch, Manfred (eds.). *Speech Act Theory and Pragmatics*. Heidelberg, New York: Springer, pp. 37–55.
Delacroix, Sylvie (2004). Hart's and Kelsen's Concepts of Normativity Contrasted. *Ratio Juris 17*, 501–520.
Del Mar, Maksymilian (2007). Legal Norms and Normativity. *Oxford Journal of Legal Studies 27*/2, 355–372.
Derrida, Jacques (1972). Signature Evénement Contexte, in: Derrida, Jacques, *Marges de la philosophie*. Paris: Editions de Minuit, pp. 365–393.
Derrida, Jacques (1972). *Marges de la philosophie*. Paris: Editions de Minuit.
Derrida, Jaques (1988). Signature Event Context, in: Graff, Gerald (ed.). *Limited Inc*. Evanston: Northwestern University Press, pp. 1–25.
Derrida, Jacques (1993). *Spectres de Marx*. Paris: Galilée.
Derrida, Jacques (2003*). Eine gewisse unmögliche Möglichkeit, vom Ereignis zu sprechen*. Berlin: Merve.
Dickinson, Laura A (2003). The Promise of Hybrid Courts. *American Journal of International Law 97*, 295–310.
Dinwoodie, Graeme B. (2001). International Intellectual Property Litigation: A Vehicle For Resurgent Comparativist Thought. *American Journal of Comparative Law 49*, 429–453.
Elkins, James (1994). The *poetics of perspective*. Ithaca: Cornell University Press.
Erdös, Paul & Rényi, Alfréd (1959). On Random Graphs. *Publicationes Mathematicae 6*, 290–291.
Estermann, Josef (ed.)(2013). *Der Kampf ums Recht*. Beckendried: Orlux.
Figgis, John Neville (1913). *Churches in the Modern State*. London: Longmans, Green.
Fischer-Lescano, Andreas & Teubner, Gunther (2006). *Regime-Kollisionen. Zur Fragmentierung des globalen Rechts*. Frankfurt am Main: Suhrkamp.
Fischer-Lescano, Andreas & Teubner, Gunther (2004). Regime-Collisions: The Vain Search for Legal Unitiy in the Fragmentation of Global Law. *Michigan Journal of International Law* 25, 999–1046.
Fischman, Joshua B. & Law, David S. (2009).What Is Judicial Ideology, and How Should We Measure It? *Journal of Law & Policy 29*, 1–82.
Friedman, Lawrence M. & Kagan, Robert A. & Cartwright, Bliss & Wheeler, Stanton (1981). State Supreme Courts: A Century of Style and Citation. *Stanford Law Review 33*, 773–818.
Fowler, James H. & Jeon Sangick (2008). The Authority of Supreme Court Precedent. *Social networks 30*, 16–30.
Fowler, James H. & Johnson, Timothy R. & Spriggs II, James F. & Jeon, Sangick & Wahlbeck, Paul J. (2007). *Political Analysis 15*, 324–346.
Geu, Thomas Earl (1994). The Tao of Jurisprudence: Chaos, Brain Science, Synchronicity, and the Law. *Tennessee Law Review 61*, 933–990.
Gipper, Helmut & Schmitter, Peter (1979). *Sprachwissenschaft und Sprachphilosophie im Zeitalter der Romantik. Ein Beitrag zur Historiographie der Linguistik*. Tübingen: Narr.
Graff, Gerald (ed.) (1988). *Limited Inc*. Evanston: Northwestern University Press.
Gray, John Chipman (1909). *The Nature and Sources of the Law*. New York: Columbia University Press.
Griffiths, John (1986). What is Legal Pluralism? *Journal of Legal Pluralism 24*, 1–55.
Gumbrecht, Hans-Ulrich & Pfeiffer, K. Ludwig (eds.)(1993). *Schrift*. München: Fink.
Hart, H. L. A. (1958). Positivism and the Separation of Law and Morals. Harvard *Law Review 71*/4, 593–629.
Hart, H. L. A. (^{2}1994). *The Concept of Law*. Oxford: Oxford University Press.

Hart, H. L. A. (1994). Postscript, in: Hart, H. L. A. *The Concept of Law*. Oxford: Oxford University Press, pp. 238–276.
Hassemer, Winfried (2008). Juristische Methodenlehre und richterliche Pragmatik. *Rechtstheorie* 39, 1–22.
Hathaway, Oona A. (2001). Path Dependence in the Law: The Course and Pattern of Change in the Legal System. *Iowa Law Review 86*, 101–165.
Hofmann, Herwig C.H. (2009). Decisionmaking in EU Administrative Law – the Problem of Composite Procedures. *Administrative Law Review 61*, 199–222.
Hofmann, Herwig & Rowe, Gerard C. & Türk, Alexander (2011). *Administrative Law and Policy of the European Union*. Oxford: Oxford University Press.
Holmes, Oliver Wendell (1897). The Path of the Law. *Harvard Law Review 10*, 457–469.
Johnson, Charles A. (1986). Follow-Up Citations in the U. S. Supreme Court. *Western Political Quarterly 39*, 538–547.
Humboldt, Wilhelm von (1836). Über die Verschiedenheit des menschlichen Sprachbaues und ihren Einfluss auf die geistige Entwicklung des Menschengeschlechtes.
Jestaedt, Matthias (2008). Einführung, in: Kelsen, Hans (2008). *Reine Rechtslehre*. Mohr Siebeck: Tübingen, p. XXVI.
Junker, Klaus (1986). Zur Kritik der Humboldt-Adaption der Neuhumboldtianer, in: Welke, Klaus (ed.). *Sprache – Bewusstsein –Tätigkeit. Zur Sprachkonzeption Wilhelm von Humboldts*. Berlin: Akademie-Verlag, pp. 68–93.
Kades, Eric (1997). The Laws of Complexity and the Complexity of Laws: The Implications of Computational Complexity for the Law. *Rutgers Law Review 49*, 403–484.
Kant, Immanuel (1781). Kritik der reinen Vernunft.
Katz, Daniel M. & Stafford, Derek K. & Provins, Eric (2008). Social Architecture, Judicial Peer Effects and the "Evolution" of the Law: Toward a Positive Theory of Judicial Social Structure. *Georgia State University Law Review 24*/4, 975–999.
Katz, Daniel M. & Gubler, Joshua R. & Zelner, Jon & Bommarito II, Michael J. & Provins, Eric & Ingall, Eitan (2011). Reproduction of Hierarchy? A Social Network Analysis of the American Law Professoriate. *Journal of Legal Education 61*, 1–28.
Kauffman, Stuart (1995). At Home in the Universe. The Search for Laws of Self-Organization and Complexity. Oxford: Oxford University Press.
Kelsen, Hans (2008, orig. 1934). Reine Rechtslehre (1st edition). Tuebingen: Mohr Siebeck.
Kelsen, Hans (1934). *Introduction to the Problems of Legal Theory. A Translation of the First Edition of the Reine Rechtslehre or Pure Theory of Law*. New York: Oxford University Press.
Kelsen, Hans (1960). *Reine Rechtslehre*. 2nd Edition. Wien: Deuticke.
Kelsen, Hans (1967). *Pure Theory of Law*. Berkeley and Los Angeles: University of California Press (Translation from the 2nd German Edition).
Kertscher, Jens & Mersch, Dieter (eds.) (2003). *Performativität und Praxis*. München: Fink.
Koskenniemi, Martti (2005). Global Legal Pluralism: Multiple Regimes and Multiple Modes of Thought. http://www.helsinki.fi/eci/Publications/Koskenniemi/MKPluralism-Harvard-05d[1].pdf. Accessed 2 February 2012.
Kosma, Montgomery N. (1998). Measuring the Influence of Supreme Court Justices. *Journal of Legal Studies 27*, 333–372.
Kraemer, Sybille (2001). *Sprache, Sprechakt, Kommunikation*. Frankfurt am Main: Suhrkamp.
Ladeur, Karl-Heinz (1997). Post-modern Constitutional Theory: A Prospect for the Self-Organizing Society. *The Modern Law Review 60*/5, 617–629.
Landes, William M. & Lessig, Lawrence & Solimine, Michael E. (1998). Judicial influence: A Citation Analysis of Federal Courts and Appeals Judges. *Journal of Legal Studies* 27, 271–332.
Landes, William M. & Posner, Richard A. (1976). Legal Precedent: A Theoretical and Empirical Analysis. *Journal of Law & Economics 19*, 249–307.
Leiter, Brian (1997), Rethinking Legal Realism: Toward a Naturalized Jurisprudence. *Texas Law Review 76*, 267–315.
Lewin, Kurt (1951). *Field Theory in Social Science*. New York: Harper & Row.

Loxley, James (2007). *Performativity*. London: Routledge.
Luhmann, Niklas (1987). Soziale Systeme. Grundriss einer allgemeinen Theorie. Frankfurt am Main: Suhrkamp.
Luhmann, Niklas (1995). *Das Recht der Gesellschaft*. Frankfurt am Main: Suhrkamp.
Luhmann, Niklas (1995). Social Systems. Stanford: Stanford University Press.
Luhmann, Niklas (2004). Law as a Social System. Oxford: Oxford University Press.
Lyotard, Jean-François (1988). *The Differend: Phrases in Dispute*. Minneapolis: Minnesota University Press.
Lyotard, Jean-François (1984). The Postmodern Condition. A Report on Knowledge. Minneapolis: Minnesota University Press.
MacCormick, Neil (1993). Beyond the Sovereign State. *The Modern Law Review 56*/1, 1–18.
MacCormick, Neil (1999*). Questioning Sovereignty. Oxford: Oxford University Press.*
Macdonald, Roderick & Kleinhans, Martha-Marie (1997). What is Critical Legal Pluralism? *Canadian Journal of Law and Society (12)*, 25–46.
Merkl, Adolf (1923). *Die Lehre von der Rechtskraft. Entwickelt aus dem Rechtsbegriff*. Leipzig: Deuticke.
Merry, Sally Engle (1988). Legal Pluralism. *Law and Society Review 22*, 869–896.
Merry, Sally Engle (2005), Human Rights and Global Legal Pluralism: Reciprocity and Disjuncture, in: F. v. Benda-Beckmann, K. v. Benda-Beckmann & A. Griffiths, *Mobile People, Mobile Law. Expanding Legal Relations in a Contracting World*. Aldershot: Ashgate, pp. 215–232.
Merryman, John H. (1954). The authority of authority: What the California Supreme Court cited in 1950. *Stanford Law Review* 6, 613–673.
Merryman, John H. (1977). Toward a Theory of Citations: An Empirical Study of the Citation Practice of the California Supreme Court in 1950, 1960, and *1970. Southern California Law Review 50*, 381–428.
Michaels, Ralf (2009). Global Legal Pluralism. *Duke Law School Faculty Scholarship Series*. Paper 185. (http://lsr.nellco.org/duke_fs/185; accessed 12 december 2012).
Michaels, Ralf (2005). The re-*State*-ment of non-state law: the state, choice of law, and the challenge from global legal pluralism. *Wayne Law Review 51*, 1209–1259.
Miller, John, H. & Page, Scott E. (2007). Complex Adaptive Systems. An Introduction to Computational Models of Social Life. Princeton: Princeton University Press.
Miller, J. Hillis (2007). Performativity as Performance/Performativity as Speech Act: Derrida's Special Theory of Performativity. *South Atlantic Quarterly 106*/2, 219–235.
Moore, Michael (1987). Metaphysics, Epistemology and Legal Theory. *Southern California Law Review 60*, 453–506.
Moreno, Jacob (1934). *Who Shall Survive?* Washington, D.C.: Nervous and Mental Desease Publishing.
Müller-Mall, Sabine (2012). *Performative Rechtserzeugung. Eine theoretische Annaeherung*. Weilerswist: Velbrueck.
Müller-Mall, Sabine (2012). Rechtserzeugung als performativer Vorgang in der Sprache, in: Bäcker, Carsten/Ziemann, Sascha (eds.). *Junge Rechtsphilsophie. Archiv für Rechts- und Sozialphilosophie*, Beiheft 135, Stuttgart: Franz Steiner, pp. 117–126.
Örücü, Esin (2001). Public Law in Mixed Legal Systems and Public Law as a „Mixed System". *Electronic Journal of Comparative Law 5*/2.
Osofsky, Hari M. (2011). Multidimensional Governance and the BP Deepwater Horizon Oil Spill. *Florida Law Review 63*, 1077–1137.
Ost, Francois & Van de Kerchove, Michel (2002). *De la pyramide au reseau? Pour une théorie dialéctique du droit*. Brussels: Publications des Facultés universitaires St. Louis Bruxelles.
Paulson, Stanley (1998). Four Phases in Kelsen's Legal Theory? Reflections on a Periodization. *Oxford Journal of Legal Studies 18*, 153–166.
Paulson, Stanley & Lischnewski-Paulson, Bonnie (1998). *Normativity and Norms: Critical Perspectives on Kelsenian Themes*. Oxford: Oxford University Press.

Pospisil, Leopold (1981). Modern and Traditional Administration of Justice in New Guinea. *Journal of Legal Pluralism 19* (93–116).

Post, David G. & Eisen, Michael B. (2000). How Long is the Coastline of the Law? Thoughts on the Fractal Nature of Legal Systems. *Journal of Legal Studies 29*, 545–584.

Raducu, Ioana & Levrat, Nicolas (2007). Le métissage des orders juridiques européens. *Cahiers de Droit Européen*, 111–148.

Rajagopal, Balakrishnan (2005). The Role of Law in Counter-Hegemonic Globalization and Global Legal Pluralism: Lessons from the Narmada Valley Struggle in India. *Leiden Journal of International Law 18*, 345–387.

Raz, Joseph (1979). *The Authority of Law*. Oxford: Clarendon Press.

Raz, Joseph (1998). The Purity of the Pure Theory, in: Paulson, Stanley & Lischnewski-Paulson, Bonnie. *Normativity and Norms: Critical Perspectives on Kelsenian Themes*. Oxford: Oxford University Press, pp. 237–252.

Raz, Joseph (2005–2006). The Problem of Authority: Revisiting the Service Conception. *Minnesota Law Review 90*, 1003–1044.

Riles, Annelise (1994). Representing the In-Between: Law, Anthropology, and the Rhetoric of Interdisciplinarity. *Illinois Law Review*, 597–653.

Roe, Mark J. (1996). Chaos and Evolution in Law and Economics. *Harvard Law Review 109*, 641–668.

Rodriguez Blanco, Veronica (2006). The Methodological Problem in Legal Theory: Normative and Descriptive Jurisprudence Revisited. *Ratio Juris 19* (1), 26–54.

Ruhl, J. B. (1996). Complexity Theory as a Paradigm for the Dynamic Law-and-Society System: A Wake-Up Call for Legal Reductionism and the Modern Administrative State. *Duke Law Journal* 45/5, 849–928.

Ruhl, J. B. (2007–2008). Law's Complexity: A Primer. *Georgia State University Law Review 24*/4, 885–911.

Schuck, Peter H. (1992). Legal Complexity: Some Causes, Consequences, and Cures. *Duke Law Journal* 42/1, 1–52.

Savigny, Eike von (1974). *Die Philosophie der normalen Sprache*. Frankfurt am Main: Suhrkamp.

Schwarze, Jürgen (2005^2), *Europäisches Verwaltungsrecht, Entstehung und Entwicklung im Rahmen der Europäischen Gemeinschaft*. Baden-Baden: Nomos.

Searle, John (1969). *Speech Acts*. Cambridge: Cambridge University Press.

Searle, John & Kiefer, Ferenc & Bierwisch, Manfred (eds.) (1980). *Speech Act Theory and Pragmatics*. Heidelberg, New York: Springer.

Seinecke, Ralf (2013). Rechtspluralismus als Kampf für das Recht – historisch, theoretisch, normativ, in: Estermann, Josef (ed.). *Der Kampf ums Recht*. Beckendried: Orlux, pp. 121–136.

Shapiro, Fred R. (1991). The Most-Cited Articles from The Yale Law Journal. *Yale Law Journal 100*, 1449–1514.

Sirico, Louis J. Jr. (2000). The Citing of Law Reviews by the Supreme Court: 1971–1999. *Indiana Law Journal 75*, 1009–1039.

Slaughter, Anne-Marie (2004). *A New World Order*. Princeton: Princeton University Press.

Slaughter, Anne-Marie (2000/2001). The Accountability of Government Networks. *Indiana Journal of Global Legal Studies 8*, 347–367.

Smith, Thomas A. (2007). The Web of Law. *San Diego Law Review 44*, 309–354.

de Sousa Santos, Boaventura (1987). Law: A Map of Misreading. Toward a Postmodern Conception of Law. *Journal of Law and Society, 14*(3), 279–302.

Spaak, Torben (2008). Relativism in Legal Thinking: Stanley Fish and the Concept of an Interpretative Community. *Ratio Juris 21*/1, 157–171.

Stolleis, Michael (2008). Vormodernes und postmodernes Recht. Quarderni Fiorentini 37, 543–551.

Tamanaha, Brian Z. (2008). Understanding Legal Pluralism. Past to Present, Local to Global, *Sydney Law Review 30*, 375–411.

Tamanaha, Brian Z. (2000). A Non-Essentialist Version of Legal Pluralism. *Journal of Law and Society 27*(2), 296–321.

Teubner, Gunther (1996). Global Bukowina. Legal Pluralism in the World Society, in: G. Teubner (Ed.), *Global Law Without A State*, Aldershot: Dartmouth, pp. 3 – 28.

G. Teubner (Ed.) (1996), *Global Law Without A State*, Aldershot: Dartmouth.

Teubner, Gunther & Korth, Peter (2012). Two Kinds of Legal Pluralism: Collision of Transnational Regimes in the Double Fragmentation of World Society, in: Young, Margaret A. (ed.). Regime Interaction in International Law. Facing Fragmentation. Cambridge: Cambridge University Press, pp. 23–54.

Trubek, David M. & Trubek, Louise G. (2006). New Governance & Legal Regulation: Complementarity, Rivalry, and Transformation. *Columbia Journal of European Law 13*, 539–564.

Vismann, Cornelia (1999). Jurisprudence. A Transfer Science. *Law and Critique 10*, 279–286.

Vesting, Thomas (2007). *Rechtstheorie*. München: C. H. Beck.

Webb, Julian (2005). Law, Ethics, and Complexity: Complexity Theory & the Normative Reconstruction of Law. Cleveland State Law Review 52, 227–242.

Welke, Klaus (ed.)(1986). *Sprache – Bewusstsein –Tätigkeit. Zur Sprachkonzeption Wilhelm von Humboldts*. Berlin: Akademie-Verlag.

Wellbery, David (1993). Die Äußerlichkeit der Schrift, in: Gumbrecht, Hans-Ulrich & Pfeiffer, K. Ludwig (eds.). *Schrift*. München: Fink, pp. 337–348.

Wilkinson, Michael (2007). Between Constitutionalism and Democratic Experimentalism? New Governance in the EU and the U. S. *Modern Law Review 70*/4, 680–700.

Wirth, Uwe (ed.). *Performanz. Zwischen Sprachphilosophie und Kulturwissenschaften*. Frankfurt am Main: Suhrkamp.

Wirth, Uwe (2002). Der Performanzbegriff im Spannungsfeld von Illokution, Iteration und Indexikalität, in: Wirth, Uwe (ed.). *Performanz. Zwischen Sprachphilosophie und Kulturwissenschaften*. Frankfurt am Main: Suhrkamp.

Wittgenstein, Ludwig (1984). *Philosophische Untersuchungen*. Frankfurt am Main: Suhrkamp.

Woodman, Gordon R. (2007). Social and Religious Diversity, Legal Pluralism: Can State Law Survive? *IIUM Law Journal 15*, 154–70 .

Wright, R. George (2000). The Illusion of Simplicity: An Explanation of why the Law can't just be less complex. *Florida State University Law Review 27*, 716–744.

Young, Margaret A. (ed.)(2012). Regime Interaction in International Law. Facing Fragmentation. Cambridge: Cambridge University Press.

Chapter 3
Spatiality

3.1 The Concept of Space as a Tool for Description

Having outlined an understanding of law as a complex system of dynamic interrelations, established by performative events of law generation, we can now take the next step in our investigation. Based on the presuppositions of a hybrid, relational and dynamic law, in this chapter we are on the lookout for a conceptual tool that is suited both for delivering a description of the whole of law and for paving the way for a method: a tool that allows us to position ourselves as observers at specific points within law.

3.1.1 The Problem of Perspective

Of course there are still some obstacles on the way to a plausible approach. One is the problem of perspective which I already indicated in the last chapter. Having recognized the necessity of avoiding one fixed perspective, we have seen that our approach has to *conceptualize the totality of possible perspectives.*[1] The characteristics of law that are the presuppositions of the present investigation—hybridity, relationality, and dynamics—these characteristics reduce the scope of our entire approach by defining the framework we are looking at. There are still two problems: so far, neither have we already conceptualized the totality of possible perspectives, nor developed a method of taking a concrete perspective. We are therefore still in need of a tool, and since we are embarked for a conceptual and descriptive approach; it is quite obvious that this tool has to be a conceptual one. But what concept may serve as such a tool; what could such a concept look like in general?

[1] *See above* Chap. 2, Sect. 2.2.2.

S. Müller-Mall, *Legal Spaces*, DOI 10.1007/978-3-642-36730-4_3,

There is one concept that yields a perspective in many humanities and sciences—the one of time.[2] As do philosophy and physics, the social sciences and law employ the concept of time as a perspective-building tool, albeit assigning it a less central role than does history: if we look at a certain object through the lens of 'time', we can describe developments and evolutions. Investigations based on the scale of time are perfect for describing processes of differentiation. On the other hand, a perspective (purely) based on time cannot allow us to make any statements loaded with qualitative content if we use it to look at simultaneities—because applying a time scale means examining what differences may be observed in an object at different moments of time. As soon as we have to deal with different developments at the same point in time, the concept of time alone is no longer of help, or even forces us to ask the wrong question—the one of change instead of the one of co-operation or relationality of the phenomena appearing simultaneously.

Thus, if we look at law as exposed in the Chap. 2, it will not be sufficient to take a perspective that is based on time: understanding law as a complex set of dynamic interrelations, based on perceptions of other perceptions which are performative events of law generation and which are represented by the terms of norms, judicial decisions, administrative acts, and even legal theory, understanding this law as hybrid, relational, and dynamic, it is intelligible that time is not sufficient for measuring the whole of law. Insights into this law or its theories cannot be extracted by looking at certain norms or certain judicial decisions and their development in time, but such insights necessarily have to go beyond a single, or a discrete point of view.

It is true that all elements of law are subject to permanent renewal and change, and this characteristic is accessible to description through the concept of time. But it is also true that the concept of time will not allow us a *sufficient* description: because linear or evolutionary descriptions inevitably have to stay incomplete, given that the elements of law are not parts of a purely linear development. Even if the elements of law are perceived by later performative events, which themselves are perceived by again succeeding events, due to the hybridity described above[3] every normative perception might break through such a linearity by referring to a very different line of perceptions or to an event of law production occurring simultaneously.

Looking for a conceptual tool for a perspective on law that is able to conceptualize the totality of perspective, we can state here that the concept of time is not the tool for which we are looking. On the other hand, considering the above[4]-described dynamics of law, it has to be a perspective included by the tool for which we are

---

[2] Of course, to this qualification of time as a concept one could object that there is quite a tradition in metaphysical investigations of time (*see* for a very good overview e.g. Callender, Craig (ed.) (2011). *The Oxford Handbook of Philosophy of Time.* Oxford: Oxford University Press.), and I could open the discussion about the ontology of time here. But this would lead too far, since, as we will see in the following lines, the concept of time will not be the one we are looking for.

[3] *See above* Chap. 2, Sects. 2.2.3. and 2.3.2.

[4] *See* Chap. 2, Sect. 2.2.5.

looking. This is the first part of the problem of perspective we have to face here: the conceptual tool to describe the law has to show the capacity of integrating more than one perspective.

Another part of the problem of perspective lies in the distinction between internal and external perspectives. While occurring as a general problem here as well as in other contexts of scientific description, as a problem of placing ourselves as observers, it appears in a specific variation when we consider law: evaluations and decisions, once made by actors and observers within the law, are immediately re-introduced and contributed into the set of all the normative perceptions (that constitute law) and are subjected to the complex system. Therefore, purely internal examinations of law (i.e. those that do not only find their object, but also their scales within the law) might without doubt become valuable for description and are integral components of the law; but they always have to remain selective and thus limited because they change the whole system depending on the point of view taken in each instance.[5] This is the, so-to-speak, 'active side' of internal legal investigations; they cannot escape legal discourse as a system of normative perceptions and therefore remain snapshots. And on the other hand those concepts, decisions, or principles (to which these investigations refer) are themselves subject to the dynamics of law, of which they are components, so that they necessarily lack the capacity of generalization. These aspects are not very dangerous for the construction of theory as long as number and origin of these points of view and of the normative perceptions remain visible at a glance. Or, in other words: they can be ignored if the investigated object is clear and limited, because in this case every single contribution to law is still locatable and the limits of relationality are still comprehensible. Considering hybrid, relational, and dynamic law, in contrast, it is nearly impossible to place every contribution within the whole: the points of reference which connect every judicial decision, every generation of a legal norm, and every construction of a theory explicitly or implicitly with hybrid norm relations, or with hybrid prejudice relationships, or with theoretical traditions—these points of reference are to be qualified as numerous, as incalculable, as vast. In addition, the newer medial and technical possibilities of making such connections on the one hand, and of uncovering them on the other hand, seem to multiply these connections: accessibility produces normative perceptions,[6] and with its increase global mapping seems more and more impossible.

Thus, both internal and external perspectives are full of problems: a purely internal perspective is impossible to take, because it would influence the object of investigation and therefore fail to capture by any means the totality of possible criteria. And a purely external perspective is also impossible to take due to the general observation problem: it is not possible to observe an object without

---

[5] *See* concerning public legal norms e.g. Kelsen, Hans (1960). *Reine Rechtslehre.* 2nd Edition. Wien: Deuticke, pp. 237-242.

[6] *See* for judicial globalization or 'cross-fertilization' Slaughter, Anne-Marie (2004). *A New World Order*. Princeton: Princeton University Press, pp. 65.

influencing it,[7] in other words—as soon as we look at something, we are no longer external to it. And this is even truer for law as a set of elements represented textually: reading any element of law means interpreting it, and interpreting means re-generating it.[8] Hence, internal and external perspectives are not even separable in a categorical way.

The question now, taking the two problems of perspective described in this section together, is how to find a conceptual tool that is able to do both, to integrate several perspectives and conceptualize the totality of possible perspectives we could take on law, and to deal with the problem that neither a purely internal nor a purely external perspective is a possibility. A helpful trick for either escaping such an inevitable problem or for finding a solution to it can often be found in a re-formulation, or a translation of the problem into different terms, and this is what I am going to try in the next section—I shall re-formulate the problem of perspective as a problem of scale.

3.1.2 The Problem of Scale

A summarized formulation of the problem above is: how to find a reference frame from which we can describe the law? And given that any possible reference frame can neither be fully externalized nor purely internalized, how can we grasp it? And, to make the whole job even more complicated, how can we moreover adopt different reference frames, depending on which concrete question we want to examine?

Parallel to the two-fold strategy already mentioned above[9]—of looking for a conceptual description of law as well as a method of zooming in on concrete problems within law—one can recognize this strategy as mirrored in the questions just formulated: we are looking for answers to the question of what characteristics a reference frame must have in general to allow theorizing hybrid, relational, and dynamic law. *And* we are looking for answers to the question of which conceptualization of this law allows adopting more than one and different reference frames suited, respectively, to each of the concrete questions we have to law. In other words: the question is not only, in what relationship concepts, norms, principles, or

[7] The probably less controverse references in this context: Chalmers, Alan (2007). *What is This Thing Called Science?* St. Lucia: University of Queensland Press, pp. 19 and of course Brown, Harold (1979). *Perception, Theory and Commitment. The New Philosophy of Science*. Chicago: University of Chicago Press.

[8] It is not possible to explain this relationship more deeply in this short study, but I may refer to Augsberg, Ino (2009). Die Lesbarkeit des Rechts. Texttheoretische Lektionen für eine postmoderne juristische Methodenlehre. Weilerswist: Velbrück, pp. 95 and Müller-Mall, Sabine (2010). Interpretation *als* Rechtserzeugung, in: Groh, Thomas & Lorenz, Jörn (eds.). Interpretatio Mundi. Wie deuten die Wissenschaften ihre Welt?, pp. 235-251.

[9] *See* Chap. 2, Sect. 2.2.2.

decisions as elements of law are to each other, but also, how such relationships can be described in general, or towards which coordinates descriptions of law must be oriented in order to allow a localization. And this question of locating, or of a reference frame,[10] is not only important for legal theory, but also for legal science as well as for legal practice. This is the case because both the generation of theoretical concepts and the practical delimitations of legal concepts are hardly feasible without a reference frame.

For a consistent and systematic system of law, this question does not pose a problem, because every possible reference frame is generated by the legal system itself: e.g. norms assign other norms a rank in a so-called norm hierarchy to which we can refer, and we also might refer to legal definitions or decisions on basic questions of delimitation.[11] But if the pure number of different hierarchy systems of globalized law is so high that norm and competence conflicts have to be qualified as 'regime-collisions',[12] then no single norm hierarchy and no single precedent family can be understood as the reference frame ready for further deductions for future norm applications or judicial decisions. Thus, considering hybrid, relational, and dynamic law we can no longer proceed from the assumption that we can use norm hierarchies and competence orders as reference frames.

But how can we grasp a reference frame for the description of law, then? Only one solution remains: if we cannot deduce any reference frames from the law we are going to describe (as we have seen in developing the problem of perspective), then we have to create them as we are describing them. *Description has to be identified, then, with setting new good standards.* Every description of law that can be more than the pure representation of different fragments, every description that is open to conceptualization and categorization and thus normatively utilizable, and every such description has to develop its own reference frame, or, to introduce an additional helpful term: every such description has to develop its own *scaling*.

In what follows I will add the concept of scaling to the one of a reference frame because the term 'reference frame' alone is suspicious of suggesting that there is a stable, well-defined basis that can give any observation an objectivity of the kind we have just excluded from the set of theoretical possibilities. The concept of scaling underlines that the development of a reference frame is a possible process of

---

[10] I consider a successful *placing* of an element of law as identical with a relationship established between this element and an intelligible reference frame.

[11] I have to add that even in such a well-arranged configuration the question occurs whether for description one takes a perspective of observer or of participant. In law, this question is often circumvented by qualifying an observer's perspective as one of social science, while only the perspective of a participant would be an originally legal one. Quite clear concerning this differentiation e.g. Koller, Peter (2008). Der Begriff des Rechts und seine Konzeptionen, in: Brugger, Wilfried & Neumann, Ulfrid & Kirste, Stephan (eds). *Rechtsphilosophie im 21. Jahrhundert.* Frankfurt am Main: Suhrkamp, p. 157-180 (pp.176).

[12] Fischer-Lescano, Andreas & Teubner, Gunther (2004). Regime-Collisions: The Vain Search for Legal Unitiy in the Fragmentation of Global Law. *Michigan Journal of International Law* 25, 999-1046; Fischer-Lescano, Andreas & Teubner, Gunther (2006). Regime-Kollisionen. Zur Fragmentierung des globalen Rechts. Frankfurt am Main: Suhrkamp.

proportionalization, but not a necessary one. We can use different scales; we can even use multiple scales at the same time. A scale is by definition relative. And still it will be very helpful for the description of law because scaling includes two important aspects we need for our approach to law: on the one hand, scaling allows measurement. This means that it allows the proportionalization of relationships between elements of law—an indispensable tool for any qualitative description of law.[13] And, second, the concept of scale includes the one of *dimension*, since any scale has to have a (or more than one) direction(s), and since any direction of extension is what we call a dimension. And because we are embarked for the conceptualization of the totality of possible perspectives we can take on law, the concept of dimension will become an important one for the present approach: dimensions are markers for perspectives.

What we are looking for on our conceptual track, then, is a concept that describes not only the hybridity, relationality, and dynamics of law, but that is able to let us apply scales to law while investigating it. That is quite a lot of features to be in search of, but the good thing about this complexity is that all these features are conceptually connected, as we will see. Before proceeding on this route, it could be helpful to illustrate the considerations made thus far by an example drawn from the context of very traditional European Administrative Law.[14]

3.1.3 Example: Subjective-Public Rights

This example is set around questions of subjective-public rights, which seem to allow us to show in a quite intelligible way the difficulties of treating simultaneity and relationality, of hybridities and questions of scale.

Referring to this object, we can initially distinguish three different levels of consideration: the one of theoretical text documents—which is the one of theories and concepts, of doctrine; then the one of legal norms and legal principles, which strictly speaking is the level of legal documents; and last, the level of judicial decisions. On account of simplicity, I will in the following call these three levels theories, norms, and decisions.

On the level of theories, the most general, maybe typical question regarding subjective-public rights would be: what is to be understood by a 'subjective-public right'? Obviously, we have to deal with a conceptual question, here. Trying to answer it, one would probably look for definitions and theories of this concept, and put them into chronological order, and maybe also describe the origin and the

[13] We will come back to this issue in Chap. 4, Sects. 4.1.2.2 and 4.2.3.2.

[14] I consider it important to choose a very classical example in view of the quite abstract reflections made here, just to the purpose of better comprehensibility. As we will see later on, such an example is not well suited for producing new insights or revolutionary discoveries, but it might be helpful to keep track of the way of legal investigation, in order to find new and revolutionary insights in subsequent studies.

development of the concept,[15] in order to—in the best case—develop an understanding of the actual concept of a subjective-public right, seen in the light of its evolution: embedded in the time of German Constitutionalism, the question of subjective-public rights became a controversial and broadly discussed central question in the middle of the nineteenth century—the question of the relationship between a citizen and the executive power.[16] Around the end of constitutionalism, *Jellinek* succeeded in helping the concept receive serious recognition[17] with his reformulation of the subjective-public right as the ability to set legal norms into motion for individual interest.[18] Finally, the concept got its process dimension with *Bühler* who identified the right in this sense with a claim, a subjective law,[19] falling back (as *Jellinek* did) upon the "Interessentheorie" of *Jhring*[20]: for *Bühler*, a subjective-public right is this legal relationship between a citizen and the state, in which the citizen may claim something from the state or do something against the state.[21] During the time of National Socialism in Germany, then, the idea of a

---

[15] *See* of the extensive literature e.g.: Stolleis, Michael (2001). *Public Law in Germany, 1800-1914.* Oxford/New York: Berghahn, pp. 347; Bauer, Hartmut (1986). *Geschichtliche Grundlagen der Lehre vom subjektiven öffentlichen Recht.* Berlin: Duncker & Humblot; Huber, Peter-Michael (1991). *Konkurrenzschutz im Verwaltungsrecht.* Tübingen: Mohr Siebeck; Masing, Johannes (1997). *Die Mobilisierung des Bürgers für die Durchsetzung des Rechts. Europäische Impulse für eine Revision der Lehre vom subjektiv-öffentlichen Recht. Berlin*: Duncker & Humblot, pp. 56; Reiling, Michael (2004). *Zu individuellen Rechten im deutschen und Gemeinschaftsrecht. Ein Vergleich ihrer Gründe, Ermittlung und Durchsetzung.* Berlin: Duncker & Humblot, pp. 65; Caldwell, Peter C. (1997). *Popular Sovereignty and the Crisis of German Constitutional Law. The Theory and Practice of Weimar Constitutionalism.* Durham: Duke University Press, pp. 34.

[16] *See* Gerber, Carl Friedrich von (1852). Über öffentliche Rechte. Tübingen: Laupp & Siebeck. *See* also Gozzi, Gustavo (1997). Rechtsstaat *and Individual Rights in German Constitutional History,* in: Costa, Pietro & Zolo, Danilo (eds.). The Rule of Law. History, Theory and Criticism. Berlin/Heidelberg/New York: Springer, pp. 237-259 (pp. 247).

[17] *See* Masing, Johannes (1997). *Die Mobilisierung des Bürgers für die Durchsetzung des Rechts. Europäische Impulse für eine Revision der Lehre vom subjektiv-öffentlichen Recht. Berlin*: Duncker & Humblot, p. 63.

[18] The original wording is: subjective public right as "Fähigkeit, Rechtsnormen im individuellen Interesse in Bewegung zu setzen", cf. Jellinek, Georg (1892). System der subjektiven öffentlichen Rechte. Freiburg: Mohr, p. 48.

[19] Cf. Reiling, Michael (2004). *Zu individuellen Rechten im deutschen und Gemeinschaftsrecht. Ein Vergleich ihrer Gründe, Ermittlung und Durchsetzung.* Berlin: Duncker & Humblot, p. 71.

[20] *See* Jellinek, Georg (1892). System der subjektiven öffentlichen Rechte. Freiburg: Mohr, pp. 41; Bühler, Ottmar (1914). Die subjektiven öffentlichen Rechte und ihr Schutz in der deutschen Verwaltungsrechtsprechung. Stuttgart: Kohlhammer, pp. 92 and pp. 62: concerning the influence of civil law on the doctrine of subjective public law, *see* especially Masing, Johannes (1997). *Die Mobilisierung des Bürgers für die Durchsetzung des Rechts. Europäische Impulse für eine Revision der Lehre vom subjektiv-öffentlichen Recht.* Berlin: Duncker & Humblot, pp. 64.

[21] The famous formulation in its original wording is: "subjektives öffentliches Recht ist diejenige rechtliche Stellung des Untertanen zum Staate, in der er auf Grund eines Rechtsgeschäfts oder eines zwingenden, zum Schutz seiner Individualinteressen erlassenen Rechtssatzes, auf den er sich der Verwaltung gegenüber soll berufen können, vom Staat etwas verlangen kann oder ihm

subjective-public right was nearly given up in favour of collective interests.[22] *Bühler*'s definition was revived finally in the newly-founded Bundesrepublik, nevertheless extended through concepts such as "Willensmacht"[23] ('power of will') or "Rechtsmacht" ('power of law').[24,25]

Instead of following the concept through its chronological development, we could also examine current definitions of the concept directly, without any historical considerations—even if there are grounds for the assumption that current discussions give priority to questions of actually-installed legal protection instruments rather than to conceptual considerations. However, in what follows we will try to look at present-day occurrences of subjective-public rights, and we shall do so referring to a second level of consideration[26]: the one of norms.

Here, a question with which to begin could be formulated as follows: in which cases is legal protection assured due to a subjective-public law?

There are two,[27] maybe three[28] systems to be distinguished, all of them realized in different legal orders. Most authors distinguish between a subjective legal concept and an objective legal concept for administrative law, ascribing the first concept to the German, the second one to the French tradition of administrative law.[29] With regard to the narrowing to be undertaken here, we can describe the concepts as follows: while the German administrative procedure mainly aims to

---

gegenüber etwas tun darf." Bühler, Ottmar (1914). *Die subjektiven öffentlichen Rechte und ihr Schutz in der deutschen Verwaltungsrechtsprechung*. Stuttgart: Kohlhammer, p. 224.

[22] Cf. Stolleis, Michael (2004). *Public Law in Germany, 1914-1945*. Oxford: Oxford University Press, p. 388; Bauer, Hartmut (1986). *Geschichtliche Grundlagen der Lehre vom subjektiven öffentlichen Recht*. Berlin: Duncker & Humblot, pp. 102, 128; 4; Reiling, Michael (2004). *Zu individuellen Rechten im deutschen und Gemeinschaftsrecht. Ein Vergleich ihrer Gründe, Ermittlung und Durchsetzung*. Berlin: Duncker & Humblot, pp. 72.

[23] *See* Bachof, Otto (1951). *Die verwaltungsgerichtliche Klage auf Vornahme einer Amtshandlung*. Tübingen: Mohr Siebeck, p. 64.

[24] *See* Huber, Ernst Rudolf (1953). *Wirtschaftsverwaltungsrecht*. Vol. 1, 2nd ed. Tübingen: Mohr Siebeck, p. 681.

[25] *See* in general concerning this issue: Reiling, Michael (2004). *Zu individuellen Rechten im deutschen und Gemeinschaftsrecht. Ein Vergleich ihrer Gründe, Ermittlung und Durchsetzung*. Berlin: Duncker & Humblot, pp. 73.

[26] For a distinction and exposition of the different levels of consideration, *see* at the beginning of this section.

[27] Distinguishing *two* systems e.g. Calliess, Christian (2006). Feinstaub im Rechtsschutz deutscher Verwaltungsgerichte. *Neue Zeitschrift für Verwaltungsrecht*, pp. 1-7 (pp.1); Masing, Johannes (1997). *Die Mobilisierung des Bürgers für die Durchsetzung des Rechts. Europäische Impulse für eine Revision der Lehre vom subjektiv-öffentlichen Recht*. Berlin: Duncker & Humblot, pp. 83.

[28] As *Nettesheim* does, who distinguishes basically a German, a French and an English system, cf. Nettesheim, Martin (2007). Subjektive Rechte im Unionsrecht, *Archiv des öffentlichen Rechts 132*, pp. 333-392 (339).

[29] *See* e.g. Nettesheim, Martin (2007). Subjektive Rechte im Unionsrecht, *Archiv des öffentlichen Rechts 132*, pp. 333-392 (pp. 339); Masing, Johannes (1997). *Die Mobilisierung des Bürgers für die Durchsetzung des Rechts. Europäische Impulse für eine Revision der Lehre vom subjektiv-öffentlichen Recht*. Berlin: Duncker & Humblot, pp. 83.

safeguard the defence of subjective rights of the individual citizen,[30] in French administrative procedure legal protection principally aims at an objective control of the executive power.[31] Accordingly, in France an individual citizen might trigger an objective legal control without being himself subject of a substantive right.[32] The most important procedure in practice,[33] the "recours pour excès de pouvoir", is an objective law procedure.[34] In that respect, the citizen is understood as "procureur du droit", as 'advocate of law'[35]; of course this procedure might incidentally defend individual rights, without changing its overall character as an objective law procedure. But for a right to bring proceeding ("intérêt donnant qualité d'agir") in this sense, it is sufficient to have a 'grief moral', a moral claim, which can only be concluded from a collective interest.[36] On the other hand, the subjective law approach in German administrative procedural law is written down explicitly in § 42 (2) and § 113 of the *Verwaltungsgerichtsordnung* (Administrative Procedure Code), on a constitutional level in art. 19 (4) Grundgesetz. The administrative procedural rules lay down that an individual citizen may only take legal action on behalf of a public right if at the same time there is a corresponding substantive law.[37] The question *whether or not* there is such a substantive subjective-public law is regularly determined by the so-called "theory of standard protection".[38]

If we turn our perspective now from these descriptions of national administrative law systems to the European level and its descriptions, we often find a qualification of the European legal protection system as one that is to a large extent objective,

---

[30] *See* Danwitz, Thomas von (2008). *Europäisches Verwaltungsrecht*. Berlin/Heidelberg/New York: Springer, p. 24.

[31] *See* Danwitz, Thomas von (2008). *Europäisches Verwaltungsrecht*. Berlin/Heidelberg/New York: Springer, pp. 24

[32] *See* Nettesheim, Martin (2007). Subjektive Rechte im Unionsrecht, *Archiv des öffentlichen Rechts 132*, pp. 333-392 (p. 340), referring to Galmot, Yves & Bonichot, Jean-Claude (1988). La Cour de Justice des Communautés européennes et la transposition des directives en droit national. *Revue Francaise de Droit Administratif 4*, pp. 1.

[33] *Cf.* Masing, Johannes (1997). *Die Mobilisierung des Bürgers für die Durchsetzung des Rechts. Europäische Impulse für eine Revision der Lehre vom subjektiv-öffentlichen Recht*. Berlin: Duncker & Humblot, p. 197; Danwitz, Thomas von (2004). Aarhus-Konvention: Umweltinformation, Öffentlichkeitsbeteiligung, Zugang zu den Gerichten. *Neue Zeitschrift für Verwaltungsrecht*, pp. 272-282-(279).

[34] Laubadère, André de & Venezia, Jean-Claude & Gaudemet, Yves (1995). Droit administratif, 15th ed. Paris : LGDJ, pp. 105.

[35] Formulation in Chapus (1993), Droit administrative général, 7th ed. Paris , cited after Masing, Johannes (1997). *Die Mobilisierung des Bürgers für die Durchsetzung des Rechts. Europäische Impulse für eine Revision der Lehre vom subjektiv-öffentlichen Recht*. Berlin: Duncker & Humblot, p. 199.

[36] Cf. Danwitz, Thomas von (2008). *Europäisches Verwaltungsrecht*. Berlin/Heidelberg/New York: Springer, pp. 24, p. 65.

[37] Nettesheim, Martin (2007). Subjektive Rechte im Unionsrecht, *Archiv des öffentlichen Rechts 132*, pp. 333-392 (340).

[38] *See* Wahl, Rainer (2010). Vorbemerkungen § 42 Abs. 2, in: Schoch, Friedrich & Schmidt-Aßmann, Eberhard &. Pietzner,Rainer. *Verwaltungsgerichtsordnung. Kommentar*. München: CH. Beck 20th ed. No. 94.

mostly following the French model.[39] This fact might seem covered up by the legal construction—the individual in the European legal protection system has quite far-reaching subjective rights at her disposal, and these subjective rights are legally enforceable. Still, this arrangement is not sufficient for qualifying it as a subjective system because these rights are only and explicitly accorded for the aim of controlling that the member states respect Community Law.[40] Whether claims are actionable does not depend on the question whether any rights are affected; to the contrary, it is sufficient that interests are affected, so that the (objective) control is encompassed. Thus, the citizens of the member states are mobilized to enforce Union law.[41] As mentioned above, this arrangement is often compared to the French system of legal protection in administrative law, by name to the 'recours pour excès de pouvoir',[42] but sometimes, conversely, also to a subjective system, because far-reaching subjective rights are guaranteed.[43] In any case, this conception runs contrary to the relevant conditions for the protection of individual rights against Union legislation,[44] which presuppose individualization and a direct concern.[45]

Maybe this—though very short—presentation of the legal protection system in different normative systems can reveal, at least to some extent, how little descriptive power the applied concepts have with regard to the respective body of standards. The terms 'subjective legal system' or 'objective legal system' do not deliver more than names for the arrangement found respectively. However, the concepts do not help us in describing the European system of legal protection in

[39] Masing, Johannes (1997). *Die Mobilisierung des Bürgers für die Durchsetzung des Rechts. Europäische Impulse für eine Revision der Lehre vom subjektiv-öffentlichen Recht.* Berlin: Duncker & Humblot, pp. 218; Danwitz, Thomas von (1996). *Verwaltungsrechtliches System und europäische Integration.* Tübingen: Mohr Siebeck, p. 225; *see* for a different evaluation: Reiling, Michael (2004). *Zu individuellen Rechten im deutschen und Gemeinschaftsrecht. Ein Vergleich ihrer Gründe, Ermittlung und Durchsetzung.* Berlin: Duncker & Humblot,, pp. 444 Nettesheim, Martin (2007). Subjektive Rechte im Unionsrecht, *Archiv des öffentlichen Rechts 132*, pp. 333-392 (pp. 339).

[40] ECJ (1963). Van Gend en Loos, Case 26/62 *ECR* 1963, p. 1 (26); *see* also Danwitz, Thomas von (2008). *Europäisches Verwaltungsrecht.* Berlin/Heidelberg/New York: Springer, p. 283.

[41] *Cf.* already the title of *Masing*'s study which so far is programmatic for this opinion: Masing, Johannes (1997). *Die Mobilisierung des Bürgers für die Durchsetzung des Rechts. Europäische Impulse für eine Revision der Lehre vom subjektiv-öffentlichen Recht.* Berlin: Duncker & Humblot. (The Mobilization of the Citizen for the Enforcement of Law; translation S.MM.).

[42] *Cf.* Danwitz, Thomas von (2008). *Europäisches Verwaltungsrecht.* Berlin/Heidelberg/New York: Springer, p.282; Schwarze, Jürgen (1999). Die Entwicklung der französischen Verwaltungsgerichtsbarkeit aus deutscher Sicht. *Deutsche Verwaltungsblätter*, pp. 261-269 (265).

[43] E.g. Reiling, Michael (2004). *Zu individuellen Rechten im deutschen und Gemeinschaftsrecht. Ein Vergleich ihrer Gründe, Ermittlung und Durchsetzung.* Berlin: Duncker & Humblot p. 454.

[44] Art. 263 (4) TFEU: Any natural or legal person may, under the conditions laid down in the first and second paragraphs, institute proceedings against an act addressed to that person or which is of direct and individual concern to them, and against a regulatory act which is of direct concern to them and does not entail implementing measures.

[45] *See* also the so-called "Plaumann Formula", ECJ (1963). Plaumann. Case 25/62. ECR 1963, 95.

administrative law; in cases of doubt, we have to fall back upon separate criteria. And if we add the dynamics also of the normative development, we have to state that the German administrative law system recognizes more and more generously the character of norms to protect third parties and with that the character of subjective-public rights,[46] while the French system experiences openings, e.g. with regard to application for interim measures.[47] Of course the influence of European law on the member states' systems of administrative law is obvious, for instance if the Union legislation (or jurisdiction) gives enforceable subjective rights to the citizens. I.e., the description power of a purely subjective or objective legal system cannot be this strong if we apply the concepts to the whole arrangement of European Administrative Law. By these concepts, it is neither possible to answer the question in which cases there is legal protection due to subjective rights, nor is it possible, regarding the first level of consideration, to make any statements as to the concept of the subjective right in Union Law by referring to the historicization of the concept of the subjective right.[48] On the third level of consideration (the one of decisions), in turn, the judicial history of the EU directive on particulate matter in Germany might serve as an excellent example for how difficult it is to answer the question of subjective rights in a concrete case—nevertheless, for the moment we have to do without this case study so as not to exceed the frame of this example.[49]

However, these examples show quite clearly some of the problems that any description of European Administrative Law has to face: *descriptions of the development* have to be based on a certain thesis of linearity. The discussions on the concept of subjective rights in Germany may be put into a chronological order and maybe even categorized in this sense. But thereby they will not allow statements on simultaneous processes in France or on conditions of subjective rights in Europe. On the other hand, snapshots for describing different systems of administrative law in Europe by conceptual categories and comparative analysis may be meaningful for singular, concretely defined points of comparison. But they meet with great difficulties as soon as the points of comparison are no longer stable but fluid, because in this case the points of reference as well as categories deduced from them cannot be identified with each other, which in turn would be necessary for the description.

On the one hand one might argue that descriptions of development or evolution can be taken on from different starting points and perspectives, which gives us the opportunity to approximate a view on the whole; and on the other hand one could

---

[46] E.g. BVerwGE 94, pp. 151; 101, pp. 157 (decisions of the Federal Administrative Court of Germany, in short: BVerwGE).

[47] *See* Marsch, Nikolaus (2011). *Subjektivierung der gerichtlichen Verwaltungskontrolle in Frankreich*. Baden-Baden: Nomos,

[48] Constating a deficit of theoretical investigation concerning the concept of subjective rights in Union law, Nettesheim, Martin (2007). Subjektive Rechte im Unionsrecht, *Archiv des öffentlichen Rechts 132*, pp. 333-392 (339).

[49] For a more detailed examination of the judicial history of this directive in Germany, *see below* Chap. 4, Sect. 4.3.2.2.

argue that it is also possible to create new snapshots that adapt to the dynamics each time, just as it is not impossible to adapt the categories of description. Both alternatives are thinkable. But the exclusivity of such approaches—even if it were possible to take them on again and again with immeasurable scientific capacities—the exclusivity would always signify that we would never get a global perspective on European Administrative Law that could be able to describe the dynamics, hybridity, and relationality of this in any way different than by a dense network of snapshots. This idea, a dense network of snapshots, is in turn very problematic if we want to form scales that provide the option of measuring or qualifying the object to be described along these scales. In this case scales would only refer to these snapshots and would not allow any statements that would include a larger scope of application than the respective snapshot from the respective perspective. Then, for example, one could state from the perspective of a subjective rights approach that the concept of subjective rights is softened or contaminated, if suddenly the rights of legal action were to be enhanced for the individual. This valuation again contains a temporal moment of comparison, which is laid out in a linear way and refers to the difference between two snapshots (before: pure, after: contaminated).

What this kind of examination never contains is a description and explanation of the dynamics, of the simultaneous relationality, and of the hybridity of law as specific peculiarities of this arrangement. If we presuppose that its dynamics in the sense of a perpetual change by way of new generations of norms, by way of new judicial decisions, by way of new theorizing is a characteristic throughout all levels of European Administrative Law, then the description of such evolutionary processes is interesting and even central; but for a global perspective on this constellation of law it is no less important to describe how singular changes behave in relation to other, simultaneous changes. Answering this question is more significant to the description of dynamic complexities in so far as it could allow us to attempt prognosis or build categories as scales which can stay applicable to the arrangement even after new changes.

As we see through this example of European Administrative Law, looking for a specific perspective on those configurations that are characterized by dynamics, relationality, and hybridity gains in interest. But if such a perspective will meet the here-exposed criteria, it has to take up the hybridities and relationships of the law that generate and convey the latter's dynamics. Therefore the aim of this study is not to look for a perspective that would be dedicated to replace other (already existing) perspectives of legal theory and science; instead, it is to look for one that might supplement existing approaches by enabling us to take a look at law's constellation. In the best case, such a perspective would be different from already existing ones. It is even conceivable, though, that such a perspective already exists in the world of theories but has to be re-formulated in line with the objectives developed here.

3.1.4 *Spatiality as Perspective/Space as a Description Tool*

Obviously, for the description of hybrid, relational, and dynamic law, concepts such as network or system could open far-reaching perspectives—and they already do in network and system theories.[50] However, both show two imperfections that do not occur in most of the contexts in which they are used in a very fruitful way, but that perturb the aim we are pursuing *here*: first, on a conceptual level, system and network approaches do not allow us to extract dimensions (understood as directions of extension) of the arrangement, which is a necessary condition for applying scales[51]; and second, the concepts of network and/or system do not deal in a satisfying way with the peculiarity of law, not being conceptually separable into norm and action, but being constituted as law only by performative (perceptional) events that are both at the same time norm-generating and norm-applying[52]—the application and the generation of norms are thus not distinguishable on conceptual grounds.

Even though the concepts of network or system are to a large extent adequate to what I called hybridity, relationality, and dynamics of law, they do not deliver the perspective on law for which we are looking. And still, their imperfections will

[50] *See* as examples only Slaughter, Anne-Marie (2004). *A New World Order*. Princeton: Princeton University Press (network approach) and Luhmann, Niklas (1995). *Das Recht der Gesellschaft*. Frankfurt am Main: Suhrkamp (system approach), for further sources *see above* Chap. 2, Sect. 2.2.4.3.

[51] *See* for this consideration *above* Chap. 2, Sect. 2.2.4.4.

[52] Again, for more detailed considerations *see above* Chap. 2, Sects. 2.3.1.4 and 2.3.1.5. I would not say that systems theory in the luhmannian version in particular exposes this special condition of normativity in law. But this approach falls back upon an *aporia* (as *Derrida* calls it, *see* Derrida, Jacques (1992). Force of Law: The "Mystical Foundation of Authority", in: Cornell, Drucilla & Rosenfeld, Michel & Carlson, David Gray (eds.). *Deconstruction and the Possibility of Justice*, New York: Routledge pp. 3-67 (pp. 24) .) or *paradox* (as *Luhmann* and calls it, cf. Luhmann, Niklas (1995). *Das Recht der Gesellschaft*. Frankfurt am Main: Suhrkamp, p. 308 and Luhmann, Niklas (1993), Die Paradoxie des Entscheidens, *Verwaltungsarchiv 84*, pp. 287-310.): basically, as they describe it, the relationship between norm and decision in law is paradoxical, because only a legal problem that is *not* decidable needs a judicial decision; the characteristic of being undecidable, then, is a condition for a decision. This description further leads to an approach that is centered around the situation of decision. The reason why this is not compatible with our present approach lies in the problematic use of the terms decision and decidability, or in general: normativity—because these approaches solve the problem that arises due to the (in my approach shared) concept of normativity on which the idea of law is based in a hardly convincing way. When they qualify an arrangement as undecidable, they understand by decision a conclusion mechanism: such a situation cannot be solved simply by applying a norm. But in saying that the paradoxical moment lies in the situation's need of still being and becoming decided (which is only a result of being undecidable), they are applying the term 'decidable' in a different sense: a sense that transgresses the notion of the application of norms as simple subsuming towards a notion of 'decision as creation'. In Derrida's version, this observation is a deconstructive lecture of the legal decision moment, which only allows approaches as the one we are taking here. But in systems theory, this observation is formalized, and thus the different use of the same concepts contains a mistake that creates a far-reaching paradoxology which I am trying not to follow here.

disappear if their scope is to be extended—and along this line we are now approaching a possible perspective that might lead to the conceptual and descriptive approach at which this study aims.

However, the perspective for which we are looking is indicated by the concept of a network, included in our description of law's relationality, and it will prove to be able to include law's hybridity, and it will also turn out to be connected to law's dynamics: the perspective will be built on the *concept of space*. Every kind of relationality is necessarily imagined in the geometrical idea of space: "relationality renders the spatial perspective unavoidable".[53] Thus, the proposal is: to try to *think law as space*. This is hardly as farfetched as it might at first appear—we shall see this throughout the next sections. Spaces will prove to include conceptually relational constellations, but they also necessarily have dimensions, are even multidimensional.[54] Therefore, they have the capacity of being described in dependence of reference frames. Temporality, too, can be part of spatial dimensions—which turns out to be quite comfortable for a description of dynamic law. The perspective of space allows us to develop tools and instruments for gathering processes, structures, and relations that constitute law and for whose description with regard to their simultaneity and interactions traditional conceptual tools are not well suited. The concept of a legal space could thus be meaningful for legal science beyond a simple reference to a political-geographical point of departure.

Anyway, we shall pass through these aspects slowly and more systematically in the next sections. For now, we might satisfy ourselves with reflecting on the status a concept like space can have in a theory of law. Law is not a material object that we might perceive as we perceive a tree or a sheet of paper, by optic or acoustic or haptic radar. It is true that we can read written laws and hear judges speaking, but we would not find any helpful descriptions of law if we were to measure the acoustic or optic signals we perceive in listening to a judge or looking at a written legal norm in a book. And still I am constantly writing about a perspective on law, about being on the lookout for such a perspective, about a point of view: these terms only indicate the metaphorical level that is necessary for talking about conceptual objects at all. We *can* observe law, but not like we can see a bird flying above our heads; rather, we observe things like law in a mode of conceptual perception. Before, I called this specific mode of perception *normative perception*: a manner of perception that includes all, presupposing, recognizing, and applying concepts at the same time. A short thought experiment might show what is meant by this 'presupposing, recognizing and applying concepts at the same time': if we imagine ourselves to have never heard of such a thing as law, and we then see a courtroom with a judge, a prosecutor, some lawyers, an defendant, the public, etc. We listen to the questions of the judge, the answers of the defendant, the whispering of the public. We see everyone leaving the room and coming back the next day, we see

[53] Bachmann-Medick, Doris (2006). *Cultural Turns. Neuorientierungen in den Kulturwissenschaften*. Hamburg: Rowohlt, p. 287 (translation S. MM.)

[54] *See below* Sect. 3.2.

and hear the judge reading a text, the journalists in the room hurrying to hack lines into their notebooks, the defendant starting to cry or turning pale, a policeman putting handcuffs on the defendant's wrists. What could we tell or think of what we have seen? That someone tells others what he has or has not done; the next day one of the latter tells the former what will happen to him in the future. We could possibly think of it as theatre, because the constellation is similar to what we know as theatre.[55] We could think of it as a meeting of friends, giving themselves an artistic form of telling each other stories of what has happened to them. Without any concept of law we could never classify what we have seen as court proceedings, as a hearing of evidence, as pleading, and as applying law to a specific case leading to a court decision followed by sanctions—just because we had no concepts of what the judge is reading as sentence. To the contrary, if we have a concept of law that includes court proceedings, then we can qualify the entire happening as a process and the sentencing as the application of legal norms to a specific case. And in so qualifying it, we apply the concept of law to the situation we see. Above, I called this version of perception 'perception', and I referred to what we have seen before, even if we have not made any statement on the general use of concepts. We called performative events of law generation 'perception'—falling back upon antecedent and self-reference understood as the characteristics of these perceptional events. What I have done now is to identify the use of a concept such as law with the performative event of law generation by calling both of them 'perception'. This is not a logical identification, of course[56]; it is an application of a concept to itself; and this application is driven by the aim of understanding the one through the understanding we have of the other. This is the case because drawing this kind of analogy[57] permits us to make comparisons, and thus, to scale—a scale is nothing but a tool for proportionality considerations.[58] Furthermore, both comparisons and scales give rise to the possibility of forming new concepts to describe and differentiate already existing concepts. Of course, as observers we remain in the regressive situation of constructing concepts based on concepts by way of concepts.[59] And yet, we shall now try to apply the concept of space to the concept of law in order to receive a new conceptual perspective.

---

[55] To the similarities of court and theatre, only *see* e. g. Vismann, Cornelia (1999). "Rejouer les Crimes." – Theater vs. Video. *Cardozo Studies in Law and Literature 11*/2, 161-177 and Vismann, Cornelia (2011). *Medien der Rechtsprechung*. Frankfurt am Main: S. Fischer, pp. 19.

[56] Even though I am convinced that it must be analytically possible to analogize the application of concepts and the application of law—along the line of argument that legal concepts are also concepts. But probably the argument cannot be run as simply as the formulation sounds right now. This question has to be left for different investigations.

[57] Concerning the interesting and varied concept of analogy and its role in science, *see* e.g. Hallyn, Fernand (ed.) (2000). *Metaphor and Analogy in the Sciences*. Dordrecht: Kluwer.

[58] We will have a deeper look at the concepts of scale and proportionality below, *see* Chap. 4, Sect. 4.2.

[59] *See* already *above* Chap. 2, Sect. 2.2.2.

3.2 A Concept of Space

In a first step, I have to point out that until now the most common use of the concept of space referring to law is quite inconspicuous. Terms like 'legal space', 'space of law',[60] 'European legal space'[61] are ubiquitous in legal literature—even in norm texts. The Treaty on European Union, for example, even contains a section heading called: "Area of Freedom, Security, and Justice".[62] The term used in the treaty is 'area', though, not 'space'—but because other languages and official translations use the terms 'espace' and 'Raum' which are very close—and probably closest to the English word 'space', we can neglect the terminological difference here.

The concept of space in these contexts has an inconspicuous appearance because it does not contain any reference that would transcend the concept of a political-geographical space: a legal space in this sense is equivalent to the political-geographical space in which a specific normative order is valid.[63] Such a concept of space therefore has no further value as scientific knowledge. Despite these reservations, the concept of space thus used can be understood as a category of the application of law. It either specifies the geographical area in which the facts of a case have to be situated for a certain norm to be applicable to the case; or it indicates the geographical area in which certain norms are applicable by the executive or the judicial power. In addition, legal domains such as zoning law or emission control law treat the space as an object that is a natural unit to be governed by law. As different as these applications of the concept of space may appear, they still are to be assigned to two very similar categories[64]: "The concept of space appears in law either as a constructed area that is tailor-made in three dimensions (. . .) or as a clearly delimited part of the earth's surface that is typically perceived from a two-dimensional perspective of a (topographical) map."[65] The concept of

---

[60] Especially in German legal literature the terms 'Verwaltungsrechtsraum' (Space of Administrative Law) or 'Verwaltungsraum' (Space of Administration) are very common—*see* for example Debus, Alfred G. et. al. (eds.)(2011). *Verwaltungsrechtsraum Europa*. Baden-Baden: Nomos; Schmidt-Aßmann, Eberhard (1999). Strukturen des Europäischen Verwaltungsrechts: Einleitende Problemskizze, in: Schmidt-Aßmann, Eberhard & Hoffmann-Riem, Wolfgang (eds.). *Strukturen des Europäischen Verwaltungsrechts*. Baden-Baden: Nomos, p. 9-43 (12).

[61] See e. g. Weiler, Joseph (1999). Fundamental Rights and Fundamental Boundaries: on the Conflict of Standards and Values in the Protection of Human Rights in the European Legal Space, in: Weiler, Joseph. *The Constitution of Europe*. Cambridge: Cambridge University Press, pp. 102-129; De Bellis, Maurizia (2011). Public Law and Private Regulators in the Global Legal Space. *International Journal of Constitutional Law 9*, pp. 425-448.

[62] *See* title V, art. 67 TEU.

[63] Referring to the European "Area of Freedom, Security, and Justice" e.g. Monar, Jörg (2009). Der Raum der Freiheit, der Sicherheit und des Rechts in: von Bogdandy, Armin & Bast, Jürgen (eds). *Europäisches Verfassungsrecht*. Berlin/Heidelberg: Springer. P. 749-798 (757).

[64] This qualification is borrowed from *Dreier* and *Wittreck*, cf. Dreier, Horst & Wittreck, Fabian (2009). Rechtswissenschaft, in: Günzel, Stephan (ed.). *Raumwissenschaften*. Frankfurt am Main: Suhrkamp, p. 338-353.

[65] Dreier, Horst & Wittreck, Fabian (2009). Rechtswissenschaft, in: Günzel, Stephan (ed.). *Raumwissenschaften*. Frankfurt am Main: Suhrkamp, p. 338-353 (338) (translation S. MM.).

space thus appears to be associated with the description of objects of law, of natural, three-dimensional spaces. We could also say: of container spaces, but we will get to that concept later.[66] Legal spaces, then, are natural spaces that are of a certain legal relevance; they do not provide any description of law, instead they are for their part described by law.

So far, this inconspicuous use of the term 'space' in law does not seem all that suitable for the conceptual and descriptive approach to law for which we are looking. But in being made so often in legal contexts, the reference to the concept of space might still serve as an indication: it should be understood as an allusion to the assumption that the apparently self-suggesting connection between law and space promises further insights. And it is quite a simple consideration that leads to this assumption: the striking frequency of the concept's appearance in legal contexts is very probably not due to lawyers needing to place emphasis on the territorial scope of application all the time. This might sometimes be the reason for a reference to the space of law, but most likely only in cases that concern collisions of different normative orders. Instead, we better hypothesize that the use of the term legal space indicates a metaphorical approach to law: in using the concept of space, one can easily refer to a certain normative order or a part of such an order without being obliged to give a precise definition of all ambiguities. The term 'space' then names a structure or a formation, but seems not to indicate any further exact details about this structure. The aim of this chapter, now, is first to show that the term 'space', contrary to this assumption, contains quite a lot of details; and second we are going to see in what sense these details could provide a plausible description of law and thus allow us further insights. To obtain these insights, we now have to investigate and maybe speculate on possible formulations of the connection between law and space.

3.2.1 Space as a Non-Territorial Concept

As we have seen, one of the most common formulations of this connection is the one referring to space as a political-geographical concept; the inconspicuous use of the concept of space in many pieces of legal literature is mirrored in more advanced conceptualizations treating the connection between law and space: the latter often confront law with space as its geocentrical material.[67] Other considerations of this

[66] *See below* Sect. 3.2.2.

[67] *See* e.g. Erbsen, Allan (2011). Constitutional Spaces. *Minnesota Law Review* 95, 1168-1267; Blomley, Nicholas D. (1994). *Law, Space, and the Geographies of Power*. London: Guilford; Blomely, Nicholas D. & Delaney, David & Ford, Richard (eds.) (2001). *The Legal Geographies Reader*. Oxford: Wiley-Blackwell; Holder, Jane & Harrison, Carolyn (eds.)(2003). *Law and Geography*. Oxford: Oxford University Press; Pottage, Alain (1994). The Measure of Land. *Modern Law Review* 57/3, 361-384; Cooper, Davina (1998). *Governing out of Order: Space, Law and the Politics of Belonging*. London: Rivers Oram; Massey, Doreen. (1994). *Space, Place*

connection can be found concerning the issues of the law of cyberspace[68] or of cartographical techniques[69] as a method to gain a view of a scientific field. All of them presuppose space as a territorial concept—even concepts of cyberspace do so in confronting cyberspace as virtual space with real space, understood as natural space. Maybe it is only the last version of the connection that shows a different understanding of space, or at least, indicates it: in applying cartographical techniques to law, in *mapping* law, these approaches employ topographical methods for developing law. In more exact terms: they use methods of measuring and mapping natural space in order to do the same with law. Such approaches thus analogize law and natural space. They do not necessarily give up an understanding of space as territorial-based or natural, but they open the way towards a different understanding of space by applying methods of spatial measurement to a different object—the law. If this is possible, then it must at least be thinkable for space to be a concept that is only contingently linked to a three-dimensional natural sphere.[70] In other words: a use of the concept of space where it refers to different objects is not impossible. This is an important insight for our present approach, because such a natural sphere, or the territory, has not yet been a striking element of the law described here. The question of how law and its validity are related to a certain territory or natural space has not arisen to this point: it was not the delimitations of different legal orders but their overlap that was our starting point. In hybrid, relational, and dynamic law the reference to a certain territorial area does not differ from any other connection that a performative event of law generation creates: a connection of a legal norm to a context may include a location, a place. But the abstract concept of space is not part of the concept of normativity exposed above. A concept of territorial space, therefore, is neither what we are looking for nor what we need to presuppose in our understanding of law. Instead, we shall focus on non-territorial concepts of space in what follows.

and Gender. Oxford: Blackwell; Butler, Chris (2003). *Law and the Social Production of Space*. Thesis, Griffith University Queensland (Australia).

[68] *See* e.g. Cohen, Julie E. (2007). Cyberspace as/ and Space. *Columbia Law Review 107*, 210-256.

[69] *See* e.g. McGhee, Derek & Moran, Leslie (1998). Perverting London: the cartographic practices of law. *Law and Critique 9*/2, 207-224; Twining, William (1999). Mapping Law. *Northern Ireland Legal Quarterly* 50/1, 12-49; Philippopoulos-Mihalopoulos, Andreas (2001). Mapping Utopias: A Voyage to Placenessless. *Law and Critique* 12, 135-157; Patterson, Dennis & Teubner, Gunther (1998). Changing Maps: Empirical Legal Autopoiesis. *Social and Legal Studies* 7/4, 451-486; Grabham, Emily. (2006). Taxonomies of Inequality: Lawyers, Maps and the Challenge of Hybridity. *Social and Legal Studies 15*/1, 5-23; Economides, Kim & Blacksell, Mark & Watkins, Charles (1986). The spatial analysis of legal systems: towards a geography of law? *Journal of Law and Society 13*/2, 161-181; Chatterjee, Bela (2006). Text and terrain: Mapping Sexuality and Law. *Law and Critique 17*, 293-323.

[70] The notion of contingency in the sense applied here means: possible, but not necessary.

3.2.2 *Towards a Concept of Relative Space*

On the way to a concept of space that might provide a conceptual and descriptive perspective on law, it will be helpful to delve a little deeper into cultural and social studies; because these areas of research have grappled with the concept of space already for a while. The spatial perspective has gained a lot of interest there since around the 1980s, and this interest is even growing.[71] The reason for this development is similar to the one leading us to look for a new perspective on law that is not only based on time: researchers have come to propose that the simultaneous and globalized overlap of diverse social, cultural, political and not least legal developments should be understood spatially; because this perspective allows making visible and readable overlaps, duplications, and alternating currents.

But while the cultural and social studies are already concerned with a *spatial turn*,[72] it is still to be examined whether and in what way it could be meaningful to describe the spatiality of law. In this context, the reception of cultural and social studies is necessary for at least two reasons: first, law can be understood as a cultural technique among others, and its study by such methods is thus indicated. And second, the development of an originally spatial perspective on law without references to already-developed conceptualizations in other disciplines does not seem suitable.

3.2.2.1 From Time to Space

For a long time, "the word 'space' had a strictly geometrical meaning: the idea it evoked was simply that of an empty area".[73] Space is thus understood as a physical entity, stable and not exposed to time or dynamics; this space is a material object. Time, in contrast, has been understood as a socially-constituted concept, a social product. And on a first, not yet theoretical level this opposition bears some plausibility: "Let everyone look at the space around them. What do they see? Do they see *time*? They live time, after all; they are *in* time. Yet all anyone sees is movements."[74] Space appears as a natural area, physically perceivable, that we can measure while its size is stable—but we cannot perceive time with our senses as we can see, smell, or hear.

---

[71] *See* Bachmann-Medick, Doris (2006). *Cultural Turns. Neuorientierungen in den Kulturwissenschaften.* Hamburg: Rowohlt, pp. 286.

[72] Some exemplary literature about the spatial turn (out of real floods of studies on the topic): Hubbard, Phil & Kitchin, Rob (eds.) (2011). *Key Thinkers on Space and Place.* 2nd edition. London: Sage; Crang, Mike & Thrift, Nigel (eds.) (2000). *Thinking Space.* London, New York: Routledge; Ward, Barney & Arias, Santa (eds.) (2008). *The Spatial Turn: Interdisciplinary Perspectives.* New York: Routledge; Döring, Jörg & Thielmann, Tristan (2008). *Spatial Turn. Das Raumparadigma in den Kultur- und Sozialwissenschaften.* Bielefeld: Transcript.

[73] Lefebvre, Henri (1991 (orig. 1974)). *The Production of Space.* Blackwell: Oxford, p. 1.

[74] Lefebvre, Henri (1991 (orig. 1974)). *The Production of Space.* Blackwell: Oxford, p. 95.

The opposition between time as something that is socially produced and space as a physically stable area changed most radically[75] with the upcoming of a 'spatial turn' in the social and cultural studies. The second half of the twentieth century saw a changing perspective on space: from the described opposition—still maintained in distinctions between physical space and social space[76]—towards a postulation of a social construction of space in general.[77] Finally, most certainly by the 1980s,[78] but probably going back to the late 1960s,[79] we can speak of a manifest 'spatial turn': "Contemporary critical studies have experienced a significant spatial turn. In what may be seen as one of the most important intellectual and political developments in the late twentieth century, scholars have begun to interpret space and spatiality of human life with the same critical insight and emphasis that has traditionally been given to time and history on the one hand, and to social relations and society on the other."[80]

I would locate the turning point or the birth of a new attention towards the spatial dimension in societal life with the famous lecture by *Michel Foucault* titled "Of Other Spaces".[81] In this lecture *Foucault* proclaims the age of space as well as indicating the reason for this change of perspective: "The great obsession of the

---

[75] Of course in philosophy and even physics, but also in sociology and cultural studies there had been turns towards the concept of a relative and/or socially constructed space before (*see* e.g. *Leibniz* in Clarke, Samuel (1717). *A collection of papers which passed between the late learned Mr. Leibniz and Dr. Clarke in the years 1715/1716 relating to the principles of natural philosophy and religion.* London: Knapton; Kant, Immanuel (1770). Von dem Raume, in: *Schriften zur Metaphysik und Logik I.* (Werkausgabe, Bd. 5. Frankfurt am Main: Suhrkamp), p. 56-69; Nietzsche, Friedrich (1967, ed. and tr. by Kaufmann, Walter). *The Will to Power.* Random House: New York, p. 293, cited after Lefebvre, Henri (1991 (orig. 1974)). *The Production of Space.* Blackwell: Oxford, p. 22; Einstein, Albert (1930). Raum, Äther und Feld in der Physik. *Forum Philosophicum* I, pp. 173-180; Durkheim, Émile (1969 (orig. 1897)). Note sur la morphologie sociale, in: Durkheim, Èmile (ed.). *Journal sociologique.* Paris: Presses Universitaires de France, pp. 181-182; Simmel, Georg (1903). Über räumliche Projektionen sozialer Formen, in: *Aufsätze und Abhandlungen 1901-1908.* Gesamtausgabe, vol. 7. Frankfurt am Main: Suhrkamp, p. 201-220.).

[76] E.g. in *Durkheim*'s study, who already distinguished physical space from social space and concentrated on the latter, *see* Durkheim, Émile (1969 (orig. 1897)). Note sur la morphologie sociale, in: *Journal sociologique.* Presses Universitaires de France: Paris, pp. 181-182.

[77] *See* Dünne, Jörg (2006). Einleitung, in: Dünne, Jörg & Günzel, Stephan (eds.). *Raumtheorie. Grundlagentexte aus Philosophie und Kulturwissenschaften.* Frankfurt am Main: Suhrkamp, pp. 289-302 (289).

[78] Mostly referring to Soja, Edward (1989). *Postmodern Geographies. The Reassertion of Space in Critical Social Theory.* London/New York: Verso.

[79] As *Soja* himself dates the turning point, alluding to early works of "postmodern critical human geography", *see* Soja, Edward (1989). *Postmodern Geographies. The Reassertion of Space in Critical Social Theory.* London/New York: Verso, pp. 12.

[80] Soja, Edward (1996). *Thirdspace. Journeys to Los Angeles and other Real-and-Imagined Places.* London/New York: Verso, *cover text.*

[81] *Foucault* originally gave this lecture in 1967, but it was only published in 1984 (translated to English in 1986): Foucault, Michel (1984). Des espaces autres. *Architecture, mouvement, continuité 5*, p. 46-49 and Foucault, Michel (1986). Of Other Spaces. *Diacritics 16*, p. 22-27.

nineteenth century was, as we know, history: with its themes of development and of suspension, of crisis, and cycle, themes of the ever-accumulating past, with its great preponderance of dead men and the menacing glaciation of the world. The nineteenth century found its essential mythological resources in the second principle of thermodynamics. The present epoch will perhaps be above all the epoch of space. We are in the epoch of simultaneity: we are in the epoch of juxtaposition, the epoch of the near and far, of the side-by-side, of the dispersed. We are at a moment. I believe, when our experience of the world is less that of a long life developing through time than that of a network that connects points and intersects with its own skein [. . .] In any case I believe that the anxiety of our era has to do fundamentally with space, no doubt a great deal more than with time. Time probably appears to us only as one of the various distributive operations that are possible for the elements that are spread out in space."[82] Even if *Soja* states that „the contributions of Foucault to the development of critical human geography must be drawn out archeologically, for he buried his percursory spatial turn in brilliant whirls of historical insight",[83] we can extract some observations from these words. If *Foucault* calls already the 1960s an age of simultaneity, of juxtaposition, and of fragmentation, and if he concludes from these observations an age of space instead of time, then it is probably hardly surprising that the 'spatial turn' has not lost its relevance until today and even spread out into almost all fields of social studies and humanities.[84] Because "fast technologies of transport, transmission of information almost simultaneously around the world, and finally the new opportunities of moving in virtual spaces"[85]—all this produces simultaneity, juxtaposition, and fragmentation of the processes of living up to a degree never known. It is thus the 'at the same time', the 'juxta', the fragmented that makes the perspective of time less and the one of space more important. The use of terms like 'juxta' indicates a spatial setting already conceptually: we cannot think even just two things in juxtaposition to each other without having at least a pre-conceptual notion of space. Moreover, these relations in social life are no longer stable: with growing possibilities of moving physically and virtually, the configurations change all the

---

[82] Foucault, Michel (1986). Of Other Spaces. *Diacritics 16*, pp. 22-27 (pp.22)

[83] Soja, Edward (1989). *Postmodern Geographies. The Reassertion of Space in Critical Social Theory*. London/New York: Verso, p. 16.

[84] *See* for the present-day significance e.g. Bachmann-Medick, Doris (2006). *Cultural Turns. Neuorientierungen in den Kulturwissenschaften*. Hamburg: Rowohlt; Crang, Mike & Thrift, Nigel (eds.) (2000). *Thinking Space*. London, New York: Routledge; Döring, Jörg & Thielmann, Tristan (2008). *Spatial Turn. Das Raumparadigma in den Kultur- und Sozialwissenschaften*. Bielefeld: Transcript; Elden, Stuart (2001). Politics, Philosophy, Geography: Henri Lefebvre in Recent Anglo-American Scholarship. *Antipode 33*/5, p. 809 - 825; Günzel, Stephan (ed., 2007). *Topologie. Zur Raumbeschreibung in den Kultur- und Medienwissenschaften*. Bielefeld: Transcript; Günzel, Stephan (ed., 2009). Raumwissenschaften. Frankfurt am Main: Suhrkamp; Law, John (2002). Objects and Spaces. *Theory Culture Society 19*, p. 91 - 105; Löw, Martina (2001). *Raumsoziologie*, Frankfurt am Main: Suhrkamp; Warf, Barney & Arias, Santa (eds.) (2008). The Spatial Turn: Interdisciplinary Perspectives. New York: Routledge.

[85] Löw, Martina (2001). *Raumsoziologie*, Frankfurt am Main: Suhrkamp, p. 10 (tr. S. MM.)

time. The turn of the perspective is thus neither surprising nor revolutionary; it is quite an obvious change of concentration resulting from a change of circumstances: if I stay at the same place for a long time, seeing the same surroundings, meeting the same people, taking the same walk every day, then I concentrate on questions of temporality. But if I never stay at the same place, take a plane to a different region every day, see different people every day, and walk different promenades, then, of course, my thoughts concentrate on questions of spatiality.

But in this example as well as in the beginnings or preliminaries of the 'spatial turn', the concept of space may refer to a purely physical space without any self-contradictions. It is not yet entirely clear why a non-physical space should be a necessary concept, or even thinkable. In the example of staying in one place versus moving around all the time, we will find an indication for a certain connection that presupposes a non-physical, or at least a not-only-physical concept of space: the space I perceive if I stay in the same place and the space I perceive when I am moving, both depend on my movement. In walking north for 100 meters, I see a different space than in walking south. If a new house has been built in my street and I look down the street for the first time after its construction, I see a different space than before. *My perception of space changes with what I do. There must therefore be a certain connection between perception, action, and space.* What this very simplified example indicates is a connection that we will pursue in the next two sections along the line of far more elaborated approaches.

3.2.2.2 A Non-physical—But Still Material—Space

Most of cultural studies' approaches to space that form part of the spatial turn do not only aim at abandoning classical (geographical) concepts of physical space, but they postulate the 'social production of space'. And probably most prominent among these approaches is that of *Henri Lefebvre*, elaborated in a book bearing this programme as its title: "La production de l'espace" (The Production of Space).[86] A French neo-Marxist philosopher, Lefebvre influenced an entire generation of neo-Marxist human geographers, among them *Edward Soja*[87] and *David Harvey*.[88,89] His core thesis, "that (social) space is a (social) product",[90] that

---

[86] Lefebvre, Henri (1974). *La production de l'espace*. Anthropos: Paris. In English: Lefebvre, Henri (1991, 2011). *The Production of Space*. Blackwell: Oxford.

[87] Soja, Edward (1989). *Postmodern Geographies. The Reassertion of Space in Critical Social Theory*. London/New York: Verso; Soja, Edward (1996). *Thirdspace. Journeys to Los Angeles and other Real-and-Imagined Places*. London/New York: Verso.

[88] Harvey, David (1989). The Condition of Postmodernity. Basil Blackwell: Oxford.

[89] Cf. Dünne, Jörg (2006). Einleitung, in: Dünne, Jörg & Günzel, Stephan (eds.). *Raumtheorie. Grundlagentexte aus Philosophie und Kulturwissenschaften*. Frankfurt am Main: Suhrkamp, pp. 289-302 (297).

[90] Lefebvre, Henri (1991, 2011). *The Production of Space*. Blackwell: Oxford, p. 30.

"(physical) nature space is disappearing",[91] leads at the same time to a different understanding of space from that of Marxist tradition *and* to a structurally Marxist argument: on the one hand, Lefebvre contradicts Marx in conceiving of space as something that is not a purely physical entity, nor an entity that would only serve as 'means of production' and which is "an unnecessary complication"—as Marx' theory holds.[92] For Lefebvre, time and space are both important and even connected: "The fact is that space 'in itself' is ungraspable, unthinkable, unknowable. Time 'in itself', absolute time, is no less unknowable. But that is the whole point: time is known and actualized in space, becoming a social reality by virtue of a spatial practice. Similarly, space is known only in and through time. Unity in difference, the same in the other (and vice versa), are thus made concrete".[93] And on the other hand, as for the structurally Marxist argument—Lefebvre does not investigate space as a physical object, but as something that is produced socially: "Like Marx, who examines the products of industry not in their material form but as the outcome of a societal production process, Lefebvre develops a critical approach permitting the investigation of space as a product of society."[94]

That the concept of space refers to a socially-produced space, and no longer to a physical or natural space—this is the core of the paradigm of the spatial turn from the 1970s onwards, and Lefebvre's work is among the most influential for the development of this paradigm. And at the core of his work, again, we can find a triangular model of spatiality—this will be a far-reaching conceptualization[95] also for our approach, even if it will be on a different side of spatiality, as we will see later.[96] The conceptual triad introduced by *Lefebvre* contains the 'Spatial practice' ('espace perçu'),[97] the 'Representations of space' ('espace conçu'),[98] and

---

[91] Lefebvre, Henri (1991, 2011). *The Production of Space*. Blackwell: Oxford, p. 30.

[92] *See* Soja, Edward (2008). New Twists on the *Spatial Turn*, in: Döring, Jörg & Thielmann, Tristan. *Spatial Turn. Das Raumparadigma in den Kultur- und Sozialwissenschaften*. Bielefeld: Transcript, pp. 241-262 (245).

[93] Lefebvre, Henri (1991, 2011). *The Production of Space*. Blackwell: Oxford, pp. 218.

[94] Löw, Martina (2008). The Constitution of Space. The Structuration of Spaces Through the Simultaneity of Effect and Perception. *European Journal of Social Theory* 11/1, 25-49 (27).

[95] It was especially *Edward Soja* who took up the triadic conception, *see* Soja, Edward (1996). *Thirdspace. Journeys to Los Angeles and other Real-and-Imagined Places*. London/New York: Verso.

[96] *See below*, Sect. 3.3.

[97] Lefebvre, Henri (1991, 2011). *The Production of Space*. Blackwell: Oxford, p. 38: "The spatial practice of a society secretes that society's space; it propounds and presupposes it, in a dialectical interaction; it produces it slowly and surely as it masters and appropriates it. From the analytic standpoint, the spatial practice of a society is revealed through the deciphering of its space." *See* also Soja, Edward (1996). *Thirdspace. Journeys to Los Angeles and other Real-and-Imagined Places*. London/New York: Verso, p. 74-78, calling this space 'Firstspace'.

[98] Lefebvre, Henri (1991, 2011). *The Production of Space*. Blackwell: Oxford, pp. 38: "conceptualized space, the space of scientists, planners, urbanists, technocratic subdividers and social engineers, as of a certain type of artist with a scientific bent—all of whom identify what is lived and what is perceived with what is conceived. (. . .) This is the dominant space in any society (or mode of production)." *See* also Soja, Edward (1996). *Thirdspace. Journeys to Los Angeles and*

'Representational spaces' ('espace vecu').[99] 'Spatial practice' refers to space as a material form,[100] to objects in space, to behaviour in space, to the use, while 'representations of space' are concerned with a mental dimension: how we conceptualize space, how we think space—"it is the ideological, cognitive aspect of space, its representation, mathematical and physical models and plans".[101] We could grasp the first as objective space and the second as subjective space.[102] The third 'representational spaces' finally add the symbolic dimension to space; they complement practice and cognition[103] with imagination they are 'lived' spaces due to their symbols and thus transcend the first and second spaces. "It is this aspect of space that can undermine prevailing orders and discourses and envision other spaces."[104] By adding this third dimension, *Lefebvre* seeks to escape all problems borne by dual oppositions, or, in other words, the antagonism of subjectivity and objectivity.[105] But this triad is far from being an "abstract 'model'"[106]; it is to capture the concrete, and its elements are interconnected with each other through a dialectical relationship.[107] A space thus understood is socially produced by way of perception, use, and appropriation, and linked to symbolic representation.[108] It is therefore to be distinguished from natural and physical spaces, but it is still a

other Real-and-Imagined Places. London/New York: Verso, p. 78-81, calling this space 'Secondspace'.

[99] Lefebvre, Henri (1991, 2011). *The Production of Space*. Blackwell: Oxford, p. 39: "space as directly *lived* through its associated images and symbols, and hence the space of 'inhabitants' and 'users', but also of some artists and perhaps of those, such as a few writers and philosophers, who *describe* and aspire to do no more than describe. This is the dominated—and hence passively experienced—space which the imagination seeks to change and appropriate. It overlays physical space, making symbolic use of its objects. Thus representational spaces may be said, though again with certain exceptions, to tend towards more or less coherent systems of non-verbal symbols and signs." *See* also Soja, Edward (1996). *Thirdspace. Journeys to Los Angeles and other Real-and-Imagined Places*. London/New York: Verso, p. 53-82.

[100] *See* Soja, Edward (2008). New Twists on the *Spatial Turn*, in: Döring, Jörg & Thielmann, Tristan. *Spatial Turn. Das Raumparadigma in den Kultur- und Sozialwissenschaften*. Bielefeld: Transcript, p. 241-262 (250).

[101] Löw, Martina (2008). The Constitution of Space. The Structuration of Spaces Through the Simultaneity of Effect and Perception. *European Journal of Social Theory* 11/1, 25-49 (28).

[102] Similarly Soja, Edward (2008). New Twists on the *Spatial Turn*, in: Döring, Jörg & Thielmann, Tristan. *Spatial Turn. Das Raumparadigma in den Kultur- und Sozialwissenschaften*. Bielefeld: Transcript, p. 241-262 (251).

[103] Löw, Martina (2008). The Constitution of Space. The Structuration of Spaces Through the Simultaneity of Effect and Perception. *European Journal of Social Theory* 11/1, 25-49 (28).

[104] Löw, Martina (2008). The Constitution of Space. The Structuration of Spaces Through the Simultaneity of Effect and Perception. *European Journal of Social Theory* 11/1, 25-49 (28).

[105] *See* Lefebvre, Henri (1991, 2011). *The Production of Space*. Blackwell: Oxford, p. 39.

[106] *See* Lefebvre, Henri (1991, 2011). *The Production of Space*. Blackwell: Oxford, p. 40.

[107] *See* Lefebvre, Henri (1991, 2011). *The Production of Space*. Blackwell: Oxford, p. 39.

[108] *See* Bachmann-Medick, Doris (2006). *Cultural Turns. Neuorientierungen in den Kulturwissenschaften*. Hamburg: Rowohlt, p. 292.

materialized space: one that structures and anchors social relationships[109]—it is never a purely (e.g. medially) constituted spatiality, but always a lived spatiality[110] that characterizes *Lefebvre's* space as space. The 'objective' dimension of space, the 'percu' that we can find in spatial practices constitutes space just as the two other axes do; with *Lefebvre*, any description of space that concentrates on only one of the three aspects will not be sufficient. But even if "(physical) nature space is disappearing"[111] in this conception, its ontological existence is not denied—*Lefebvre* proposes a turn of perspective on social life; he provides a perspective on how we can understand space as something we produce by way of our social lives, and not social life as something we do *in* space.

Because of the material dimension at the heart of this conceptualization, it does not fit all that well into our project of finding a perspective on hybrid, relational, and dynamic law: in this study we are rather focussing on a non-material description of law. Law is understood here as a normative complexity, a perceptional, relational system constituted by performative events of generation that are clearly non-material. But, and this is why we are undertaking this short look at *Lefebvre's* ideas, we can find here a concept of space that is basically constituted by a triangular relationship between action, perception, and a symbolic level. And this approach shows a strong similarity to the one we are taking on law here: there, too, we have seen the law constituted by performative *acts* that are characterized and fulfilled by the normative *perception* of a symbolic level—the texts of law representing (other) performative acts of generation. Finally, we can read *Lefebvre* on this basic and maybe reductive level as an example of how triangular relationships between action, perception, and a representational side might be placed in relation to the concept of space.

One aspect on which neo-Marxist human geographers in the following of *Lefebvre* as well as he himself do not concentrate so explicitly, but which has played a central role in the description of law we have already exposed throughout this study, is relationality. The establishing of relations is not only a side-effect of performative law generation, but this is what we can understand as law's (complex) order—its relationality, which is itself dynamic. Therefore, a concept of space that is to offer a perspective on law must be able to encompass law's relationality. And even if we have already seen that space does not necessarily have to be understood as physical space, as a three-dimensional container on the surface of a territory, it is yet to be shown that space does not necessarily have to be an absolute entity, neither changeable nor dynamic nor relative in its structure. The concept of space needs to

---

[109] *See* Schmid, Christian (2003). Raum und Regulation. Henri Lefebvre und der Regulationsansatz, in: Brand, Ulrich & Raza, Werner (eds.). *Fit für den Postfordismus*. Münster: Dampfboot, pp. 217-242 (233).

[110] Similarly, Siegert, Bernhard (2005). Repräsentationen diskursiver Räume – Einleitung, in: Böhme, Hartmut (ed.). *Topographien der Literatur. DFG-Symposion 2004*. Stuttgart/Weimar: Metzler, pp. 3-11.

[111] Lefebvre, Henri (1991, 2011). *The Production of Space*. Blackwell: Oxford, p. 30.

include the concept of relativity if it is to be suitable for a hybrid, relational, and dynamic law—which cannot possibly be understood as an absolute structure, existing independently of everything we do to it and with it—as we have already seen.[112]

3.2.2.3 Absolute vs. Relative Space

Our next step on the way to a concept of space that will let us grasp law as hybrid, relational and dynamic will therefore prepare us for developing a concept of a relative legal space. The opposition between absolute and relative space (parallel to absolutistic versus relativistic concepts of space) also unfolds in *Lefebvre's* work discussing "qualities *of space*" rather than "qualities embedded *in space*",[113] but we can develop it on a more general level: while absolutistic concepts of space conceive of both (mostly physical) objects and space as creating a dualistic relationship, relativistic concepts, in contrast, understand space as a result of the relative locations of objects.[114] The relativistic concept of space as constituted by relations is—this seems to be quite obvious—not the intuitively grasped notion we have of space: because the most common use of the term space in ordinary language is when we refer to the space in which we live, not to a space constituted in whatever way. Relativistic concepts of space therefore have to provide arguments for their legitimacy.[115] At this point of our study, we are not going to undertake historical examinations of the development of absolutistic and relativistic concepts of space; this is a very complex history with many turning points, it is even a history of interdisciplinary interchange at its best, one that probably will not find many debates comparable in this respect. But not to lose sight of the main idea of this present study we cannot delve deeper into such an investigation.[116] Nor shall we have a deeper look at conceptualizations of an absolute space: since there is no doubt that we are looking for a relativistic concept of space that can help us develop our approach to law, we shall concentrate on the conceptualization of relative space. As to the scope of this study, we shall not look for a *general* approach to conceptualizations of relative space, but for a special one. Since we have already

[112] *See above* Chap. 2.

[113] Lefebvre, Henri (1991, 2011). *The Production of Space*. Blackwell: Oxford, p. 230.

[114] Löw, Martina (2001). *Raumsoziologie*. Frankfurt am Main: Suhrkamp, p. 17. Concerning the distinction between absolute and relative spaces in geography, *see* Smith, Neil (2008). *Uneven Development: Nature, Capital and the Production of Space*. University of Georgia Press: Athens.

[115] Löw, Martina (2001). *Raumsoziologie*. Frankfurt am Main: Suhrkamp, p. 19.

[116] Among the numerous interesting examinations are e.g. the one by *Whittaker* (Whittaker, Sir Edmund (1949). From Euclid to Eddington. A Study if Conceptions of the External World. Cambridge: Cambridge University Press)or the one by *Jammer* (Jammer, Max (1969). Concepts of Space: The History of Theories of Space in Physics. Cambridge/Mass.: Harvard University Press.).

noticed that different concepts of relative space are thinkable,[117] our next step will consist in the development and the proposal of a concept of relative space that might be helpful for a conceptual and descriptive approach to law.

3.2.3 *Performative Production of Relative Space*

But what are the characteristics of the concept of relative space for which we are looking? At least we do not have to look for a concept in the whole set of possible formulations of relative space, because we have some indications of what essential ideas a concept of space has to include if it is to be a productive tool for our approach to law. Narrowing the scope to our presuppositions does not mean to conclude a concept from itself or apply a concept to itself. We are searching here for similarities between a concept of space and the description we have of law until now. In the case that such similarities allow us to apply a concept of space to our description of law, we might at best find some aspects of the concept of space that would allow us to take a new perspective on law. But we will not be able to make any conclusions that could be valid as proof for the one or the other concept of law.

Earlier, we presupposed law to be hybrid, relational, and dynamic, and as generated by performative acts of generation that consist in normative perceptions. Its relationality is constituted by normative perceptions of other performative acts of generation—we can thus imagine law as a web of interrelations constituted by normative perceptions of other normative perceptions through performative events. And if the whole constellation takes on a different appearance with each new performative event, we can speak of law as related to both, a certain structure, and to acts or events. The two levels are connected through the concept of performativity. In literature we can find both—a sociological concept of space that is built upon the dualism of structure/order and act/action, as well as a concept of space that is based on a theory of performativity: on the one hand the 'spatial

[117] *See* e.g. *Leibniz* in Clarke, Samuel (1717). *A collection of papers which passed between the late learned Mr. Leibniz and Dr. Clarke in the years 1715/1716 relating to the principles of natural philosophy and religion.* London: Knapton (referring to this debate, *see* Ballard, Kaith (1960). Leibniz's Theory of Space and Time. *Journal of the History of Idea 21*, p. 49-65; Erlichson, Herman (1967). The Leibniz-Clarke Controversy: Absolute Versus Relative Space and Time. *American Journal of Physics 35*, p. 89-98.); Kant, Immanuel (1770). Von dem Raume, in: *Schriften zur Metaphysik und Logik I.* (Werkausgabe, Bd. 5. Frankfurt am Main: Suhrkamp), p. 56-69; Nietzsche, Friedrich (1967, ed. and tr. by Kaufmann, Walter). *The Will to Power.* Random House: New York, p. 293, cited after Lefebvre, Henri (1991 (orig. 1974)). *The Production of Space.* Blackwell: Oxford, p. 22; Einstein, Albert (1930). Raum, Äther und Feld in der Physik. *Forum Philosophicum* I, p. 173-180; Durkheim, Émile (1969 (orig. 1897)). Note sur la morphologie sociale, in: Durkheim, Èmile (ed.). *Journal sociologique.* Paris: Presses Universitaires de France, pp. 181-182; Simmel, Georg (1903). Über räumliche Projektionen sozialer Formen, in: *Aufsätze und Abhandlungen 1901-1908.* Gesamtausgabe, vol. 7. Frankfurt am Main: Suhrkamp, p. 201-220.

sociology' by the German sociologist *Martina Löw*[118] and on the other hand a concept that is part of a study in 'The Practice of Everyday Life' by the French philosopher *Michel de Certeau.*[119] We shall not analyse these two approaches in depth; because this would transcend the scope of our investigation here. Through the consideration of *de Certeau's* approach, we will get an idea of how we could think of space in a relative and relational sense that is very much connected to a dualism of action on the one hand and order on the other. With this idea in mind we can finally go a step further and try to outline an idea of how to think law as space.[120]

Michel de Certeau, originally a Jesuit priest working on medieval mysticism,[121] after 1968 turned to what today we would probably call 'urban studies'.[122] He wrote studies in this area, but also in philosophy, all centred on his main project, to investigate 'everyday life'.[123] In his main book concerned with spatial issues, *The Practice of Everyday Life* ,[124] *de Certeau* exposes spatial thinking that is deeply connected to a theory of performativity that in turn is built upon ordinary language philosophy.[125] In looking for a point of access to language strictly through ordinary language, *de Certeau* takes up *Wittgenstein's* late philosophy, which is driven by the intention of bringing "words back from their metaphysical to their everyday use".[126] *Wittgenstein*'s understanding of the use of language as a practice that is accessible to everyone and part of any human being even serves *de Certeau* as a 'model'. He considers it as a radical critique of the expert, and also: a critique of the philosopher as expert[127]: "it is also possible to turn to a philosophy which furnishes a "model" and which undertakes to carry out a rigorous examination of ordinary

[118] Löw, Martina (2001). *Raumsoziologie*. Frankfurt am Main: Suhrkamp.

[119] De Certeau, Michel (1984). *The Practice of Everyday Life*. Berkeley/Los Angeles: University of California Press

[120] *See below*, Sect. 3.3.

[121] E.g. De Certeau, Michel (1987). *La fable mystique*. Gallimard: Paris.

[122] *See* for biographical information Crang, Mike (2011). Michel de Certeau, in: Hubbard, Phil & Kitchin, Rob (eds.). *Key Thinkers on Space and Place*. 2nd edition. London: Sage, pp. 106-112 (106).

[123] Central works include de Certeau, Michel (1980). On the oppositional practices of everyday life. *Social Text 1*, pp. 3-43; de Certeau, Michel (1984). *The Practice of Everyday Life*. Berkeley/Los Angeles: University of California Press; de Certeau, Michel (1986). *Heterologies: Discourses on the Other*. Manchester University Press: Manchester.

[124] *See* originally de Certeau, Michel (1980). L'Invention du Quotidien. 1. Arts de faire. Paris: Gallimard.

[125] *See* Dünne, Jörg (2006). Einleitung, in: Dünne, Jörg & Günzel, Stephan (eds.). *Raumtheorie. Grundlagentexte aus Philosophie und Kulturwissenschaften*. Frankfurt am Main: Suhrkamp, pp. 289-302 (299).

[126] Wittgenstein, Ludwig (1976). *Philosophical Investigations*. Blackwell: Oxford, §§ 116, 48. *See* also de Certeau, Michel (1984). *The Practice of Everyday Life*. Berkeley/Los Angeles: University of California Press, p. 9.

[127] De Certeau, Michel (1984). *The Practice of Everyday Life*. Berkeley/Los Angeles: University of California Press p. 9.

language: that of Wittgenstein."[128] There are (among others) two core aspects that *de Certeau* borrows from *Wittgenstein* and that are of specific interest for our approach to law: first, a rejection of "the purifying process that, by eliminating the ordinary use of language (everyday language), makes it possible for science to produce and master an artificial language". Along with a very similar consideration, also building on *Wittgenstein's* late philosophy, we have come to describe law neither as a system of 'purified' artificial set of rules that are formulated in norm texts, nor as the exteriority of language, a "metaphysical overflow beyond what speech *can* say",[129] but rather as a 'practice'.[130] The second aspect refers to the possibilities we have concerning the description of any phenomenon that is connected to language: "We are subject to, but not identified with, ordinary language. As in the ship of fools, we are embarked, without the possibility of an aerial view or any sort of totalization."[131] Of course in urban theory this question of taking a total perspective is more vivid.[132] But did we not arrive at this point in our study on the search for a perspective on law that will allow us to have an idea of the whole as well as to take singular viewpoints, just because of the impossibility of a total perspective, the impossibility of being an objective observer when taking a global point of view?

Another similarity—and now we are approximating *de Certeau's* conceptualization of space—can be seen in the turn to performativity. Our conclusion in Chap. 2 was to understand law by way of performative events of its generation: this followed from the hypothesis that it is impossible to understand legal norms as general meanings of concrete texts. We thus introduced both, the necessity to concentrate on law as a practice rather than law as a system of norms and a conceptualization of the generating moment as a performative one. *De Certeau*,

[128] De Certeau, Michel (1984). *The Practice of Everyday Life*. Berkeley/Los Angeles: University of California Press, p. 9.

[129] Citation in: De Certeau, Michel (1984). *The Practice of Everyday Life*. Berkeley/Los Angeles: University of California Press, p. 9.

[130] *See above*, Chap. 2, Sect. 2.3.1.

[131] De Certeau, Michel (1984). *The Practice of Everyday Life*. Berkeley/Los Angeles: University of California Press, p. 9.

[132] *See* only the famous passage of the chapter "Walking in the City": "Seeing Manhattan from the 110th floor of the World Trade Center. Beneath the haze stirred up by the winds, the urban island, a sea in the middle of the sea, lifts up the skyscrapers over Wall Street, sinks down at Greenwich, then rises again to the crests of Midtown, quietly passes over Central Park and finally undulates off into the distance beyond Harlem. A wave of verticals. Its agitation is momentarily arrested by vision. The gigantic mass is immobilized before eyes. It is transformed into a texturology in which extremes coinicide (….). Unlike Rome, New York has never learned the art of growing old by playing on all its pasts. Its present invents itself, from hour to hour, in the act of throwing away its previous accomplishments and challenging the future. (. . .) The spectator can read in it a universe that is constantly exploding.(. . .) To what erotics of knowledge does the ecstasy of reading such a cosmos belong? Having taken a voluptuous pleasure in it, I wonder what is the source of this pleasure of "seeing the whole", of looking down on, totalizing the most immoderate of human texts.(. . .)"; de Certeau, Michel (1984). *The Practice of Everyday Life*. Berkeley/Los Angeles: University of California Press, pp. 91.

now, investigating the 'practice of everyday life', distinguishes *space* as constituted by relational connections in practice (and through experience or perception) and *place* (lieu) as a certain point within a conventional, artificial (and structured) system. *Space* hence has a performative component: "A place (*lieu*) is the order (of whatever kind) in accord with which elements are distributed in relationships of coexistence. It thus excludes the possibility of two things being in the same location (*place*). The law of the 'proper' rules in the place: the elements taken into consideration are *beside* one another, each situated in its own 'proper' and distinct location, a location it defines. A place is thus an instantaneous configuration of positions. It implies an indication of stability. // A *space* exists when one takes into consideration vectors of direction, velocities, and time variables. Thus space is composed of intersections of mobile elements. It is in a sense actuated by the ensemble of movements deployed within it. Space occurs as the effect produced by the operations that orient it, situate it, temporalize it, and make it function in a polyvalent unity of conflictual programs or contractual proximities."[133] It was necessary for me to cite this entire passage because it seems to be the exposition of the program of our approach that is to conceptually capture a totality of perspectives on law as well as allow us to adopt various concrete perspectives, methodically adopt a certain point of view on the exploration of law—or should I say adopt a "place", a "location"? But to show the plausibility of applying this notion of space to our approach to law, we will have to analogize slowly.

If *place* is not independent of artificial systems, for example of a reference frame—then it is a certain point within a system of points, and there are no two points in the same location; all of them are 'beside one another', coexisting. If we think of law as a hierarchical norm pyramid, we imagine it as a system of locations where every norm is precisely locatable, each of them 'proper' to the system and its specific location—'the location it defines'. *Place* thus becomes a secondary result of a fixation in a geometrical space[134]; we should add: in a well-defined space. A place therefore presupposes a reference frame, for instance a definition of dimensions, or, as is the case with the legal norm pyramid, a definition through deduction. A *space*, to the contrary, is constituted by practices, by movements, and it presupposes 'vectors of direction, velocities, and time variables'. *Space*, then, cannot be described as a stable system, like a reference system that *place* in turn presupposes. *Space* is relational and dynamic, and, in distinction to *place*, it does not preclude simultaneity or hybridity.

If we now look at the whole of contemporary law in its hybridity, relationality, and dynamics, then we cannot draw a map of this law—and the reason is not the large number of elements of this law, the reasons are its dynamics, its relationality,

[133] De Certeau, Michel (1984). *The Practice of Everyday Life*. Berkeley/Los Angeles: University of California Press, p. 117.

[134] Dünne, Jörg (2006). Einleitung, in: Dünne, Jörg & Günzel, Stephan (eds.). *Raumtheorie. Grundlagentexte aus Philosophie und Kulturwissenschaften*. Frankfurt am Main: Suhrkamp, pp. 289-302 (300).

which does not necessarily remain two-dimensional, and its hybridity, which precludes the possibility of every element having only one defined location in this map. Law is not *place*, it is not a systematic order that makes it possible to define distinctly any place contained in it. Instead, law is space, it is constituted through practices, and these practices might be simultaneous and overlapping. We can think law as space in *de Certeau*'s sense. This in turn includes the possibility of taking a place, but again, restricted by the conditions above—among the most important being: we need a reference frame, a secondary set of definitions to locate ourselves in law. *To take a place in law means to enter law at a specific moment in time and to look at a specific, well-defined location.*

De Certeau extracts a further important aspect of *place* and *space* from their relationship: place can be transformed into space by being used, by being practiced. "In short, *space is a practiced place*. Thus the street geometrically defined by urban planning is transformed into a space by walkers."[135] Again, if we think of law, the relationship becomes quite plausible, too: if we think of a specific legal norm, we can define it within a system of norms, so that it is located. But as soon as we apply it or interpret it, we are in the space of law, we are for instance adding a meaning to the norm, or we are giving the norm a direction, we are orienting it, situating, temporalizing it.[136]

This transfer of *de Certeau*'s considerations of space and place to law might seem somewhat reductive or speedy, but it is not completely illegitimate, and the reason for this is furnished by the author himself: "In the same way, an act of reading is the space produced by the practice of a particular place: a written text, i.e., a place constituted by a system of signs."[137] *De Certeau* shows explicitly in this passage that he thinks space and place as concepts that are applicable to texts and to doing things with texts, e.g. reading. We could also replace the term 'reading' by 'interpreting' or, more general, 'doing something with a text'. The proximity to law and to 'doing things with law' as in 'doing things with texts' thus becomes obvious. At the same time, we must recognize that the concept of space offered by this author has already overcome the conventional complicity between space and (physical) objects. Space in this conception is no longer bound to matter or surrounding matter; rather it is disentangled from the necessity of being thought in relation to matter.

What we find in the study of *de Certeau* is a specific formulation of the relationship between structural order and procedural action, which is the dichotomy underlying almost every social study.[138] The special feature of *de Certeau*'s

[135] De Certeau, Michel (1984). *The Practice of Everyday Life*. Berkeley/Los Angeles: University of California Press, p. 117.

[136] De Certeau, Michel (1984). *The Practice of Everyday Life*. Berkeley/Los Angeles: University of California Press, p. 117.

[137] De Certeau, Michel (1984). *The Practice of Everyday Life*. Berkeley/Los Angeles: University of California Press, p. 117.

[138] *See* for a spatial (sociological) study that is explicitly based on this dichotomy Löw, Martina (2001). *Raumsoziologie*. Frankfurt am Main: Suhrkamp, and Löw, Martina (2008). The

conceptualization of space lies in the inversion he adds to this relationship by privileging space over place: whereas a conventional understanding of order and practice subordinates practice to order by interpreting practice as the application of an order, as something that we can *do to* an order without changing the order, *de Certeau* develops the secondary level of any order, the 'artificial'—and hence distinguishes it from the whole, the space. A practiced place, then, can never be part of the order anymore; as soon as a place becomes the object of a practice, it is space. The basic idea is that we can never have place and space at the same time. A street can be seen as a place in an order that is defined by an urban plan—but as soon as someone walks on this street, we are in the sphere of space; the map has no significant meaning anymore because it cannot grasp the practice.

Everything we have said in Chap. 2 about hybrid, relational, and dynamic law argues for a similar inversion of the relationship between order and practice in law: the characteristics of law are not to be identified with, they are even contrary to the concept of order—we therefore described law's order as complex in using the term 'complex' as a term for hybridity, relationality, and dynamics. The idea of a normative order that we can define and describe and from the definition of which we can conclude locations of specific elements—this idea is not compatible with hybrid, relational, and dynamic law. On a purely theoretical level, we therefore went on to concentrate on the performative event of generating legal normativity in order to learn about the concept of legal normativity.[139] But on the way towards a conceptual description of and methods of exploring hybrid, relational, and dynamic law, we have to delve deeper into the idea of thinking law as space, and, after reading *de Certeau*, place. This means, then, to examine different ways and methods of exploring spaces and of taking locations in order to scrutinize them for their adaptability to the investigation of law.

3.3 Spatiality of Law

How can we imagine a productive way, in the following, to think law as space? In this section we shall try to become familiar with the idea of thinking law as space and as place (Sect. 3.3.1). In particular, we have to develop further the possibilities of exploring law as space (Sect. 3.3.2). And finally we shall be prepared to describe a first topology of law (Sect. 3.3.3). How we can employ such an approach to law towards a conceptual description and methods of investigating law—offering possible answers to this question will be the purpose of the succeeding chapter.[140]

Constitution of Space. The Structuration of Spaces Through the Simultaneity of Effect and Perception. *European Journal of Social Theory* 11/1, 25-49.

[139] *See* Chap. 2, Sect. 2.3.1.

[140] *See below* Chap. 4.

3.3.1 Law as Space/Places in Law

As a consequence of *de Certeau*'s conception of space that qualifies space as 'the practiced' in distinction to any (artificial) systematic order, it is important for the present approach to transfer this distinction to the sphere of law. This may not exactly correspond to many among the theories of law. But, as we will see in the next chapter, it is exactly this proposal that prepares the conceptual ground for both: investigating the conceptual description of law as distinct from the method of exploring law on the one hand, and on the other hand formulating the relationship between these distinct tasks.

Seen from the description of law we have extracted from our presuppositions,[141] it is not a great step anymore to transfer the notion of space as 'the practiced' to law. The essential understanding of law we have developed is based on the idea that law is to be understood as a practice.[142] Law as a system of performative events of law generation (rather than a system of norms) not only indicates but already involves the notion of 'practice': we cannot grasp thus-described law without action, without doing something, because it is constituted by *acts*. We have even seen the impossibility of distinguishing between generating and 'something that is generated' as the result of this process, or in other words, of understanding 'Sein' and 'Sollen' as independent spheres.[143] At this point, we can enrich our approach with the considerations of *de Certeau* concerning space and place by interpreting them as follows:

Space is always and already relational, and space is dynamic; movement is necessarily inscribed in the concept of space. *Place*, on the other hand, is a dead concept, since 'place' means a stable, a fixed and specified location. But, and this appears crucial for the whole conception, from the perspective of space we cannot conceive of any place as this dead, fixed location. The reason for this impossibility lies in the distinction between an artificial order (or a reference frame that allows the location of a place) and space—the two are not identifiable. Space is not even compatible with any reference frame that would allow locating places, because the concept of space excludes the notion of a stable frame, while the concept of a reference frame excludes the multidimensional relationality, the hybridity, and the dynamics of space. From the perspective of space we hence do not have the conceptual tools for grasping a place understood as location within a reference frame. The only possibility of integrating places into spaces lies in a different modus of place: looking at it as a *practiced place*. Here, now, we find an obvious similarity between our approaches to law and to space: we have seen that looking at law does not mean looking at legal norms (that are fixed within a normative order) on the one hand and the application of legal norms on the other, but it means looking at performative events of the generation of legal norms. From such a

[141] *See above* Chap. 2.

[142] *See above*, Chap. 2, Sect. 2.3.1.

[143] *See above* Chap. 2, Sect. 2.3.1.

perspective it is simply not possible to refer to a norm as a discrete (locatable) entity, because it is always and already inscribed in a dynamic, relational, and hybrid—space of law. As a consequence, talking about the 'spatiality of law' means referring to this hybrid, relational, and dynamic constellation we described above.[144] Since this constellation cannot be understood as a motionless system, we cannot describe it as such. Ways of description have to begin with the conceptual grounds we have termed hybridity, relationality, and dynamics. So far we have not gotten further than we were in Chap. 2. And still, as we will indicate in the next sections and work out more deeply in the following chapter,[145] the concept of space will help us find conceptual ways of investigating these grounds; it allows us to do so, and here we shall surpass *de Certeau*'s approach, because this concept is a relatively well-studied one in different disciplines. So we will avail ourselves of this opportunity and test some of these discoveries as to their applicability in the present context.

Moreover, what may it look like to explore law under these conditions of spatiality? With respect to this question, again, we find some indications in *de Certeau*'s conception of space *and place*. If the location of places in law presupposes what *de Certeau* calls an artificial system and what we have before called a reference frame, but if at the same time this reference frame is not to be identified with law in its spatiality, then it should be important to learn what such a reference frame could be like, and how it would be related to law in its spatiality. In other words: what could it mean to take a place in law, or, as we have called it before, how can we take a concrete perspective on a concrete location in law? In any case, we must answer this question in a first step as follows: to take any concrete perspective on law, to answer any concrete legal question, we need a location in law. And this presupposes that we have a well-defined reference frame, which allows us to locate a place. Such a reference frame could for instance be a hierarchical norm pyramid or territorial limitation, such as: European law, or a time scale together with an institutional indication (e.g. all court decisions of the year of 2005)—in short: any imaginable order to which a certain set of elements of law might be imagined to be subject. The most important aspect of any of these conceivable reference frames is their *contingency*: we can lay them onto any extract of law at a specific moment in time, but this extract is only thinkable as extract due to the respective reference frame. And as soon as we look at such an extract, we are no longer in the sphere of law's spatiality; because we are referring to the reference frame that was not compatible with law's spatiality. In the sphere of taking places, taking concrete perspectives on law by locating ourselves in frames of references, every conceivable reference frame can be chosen, but none necessarily has to be chosen.

The concepts of space and place allow (and dictate) an important distinction: the one of law as a phenomenon of practice (that can be described by spatial concepts in

[144] *See above* Chap. 2.

[145] *See below* Sect. 3.3.2. and Chap. 4.

a general perspective) *and* law as a multitude of conceivable concrete perspectives (that are defined by specific reference frames, respectively). Both sides of the story presuppose the respective other side, while it is impossible to take both perspectives at the same time because they are not compatible. It is no accident that this description is very similar to the one of the relationship of *Sein* and *Sollen* we gave earlier.[146] I even believe that this version of thinking law as space and place is just a different re-formulation of that relationship: while we can easily concentrate on either the *Sein* of law or the *Sollen* of law, it is not possible to take both sides into account at the same time or in one perspective. And still, referring to the concept of recursivity, we described their relationship as respectively presupposing each other.[147] I would not dare to identify *Sein* and *Sollen* with *space* and *place*, of course. Rather, what we negotiate in law as well as in this conception of space is the question of how to describe a practice, and even more complex: how to describe a multiplicity of practices that exist at the same time, given that as observers we are unable to take a safe and stable starting point.

The concept of space offers two epistemological strategies to this problem, and in the following we are going to try to transfer them onto the description of law.

3.3.2 Differentiating the Perspective: Topography vs. Topology

On our way of investigating the spatiality of law and the perspectives on law that we are gaining by adopting the spatial point of view, we shall now extract these epistemological strategies of spatial exploration. In another step, then, we have to scrutinize them with regard to their applicability to the description of law. In general, there are two kinds of approaches that allow building theories on space and into which most spatial theories may be subsumed: topography and topology.

Topo*graphy* in general negotiates different forms of spatial representation, the most common being cartography, the study of creating maps.[148] Approaches from this field do not concentrate so much on a substantial description of space in the sense of a discrete entity.[149] They rather scrutinize space as a constellation that is

---

[146] *See above* Chap. 2, Sect. 2.1.5.

[147] *See* again *above* Chap. 2, Sect. 2.1.5.

[148] For studies in cartography *see* e.g. Jacob, Christian (1996). Toward a Cultural History of Cartography: *Imago Mundi 48*, pp. 191-198; Cosgrove, Denis (2001). *Appolo's Eye: A Cartographic Genealogy of the Earth in the Western Imagination*. Baltimore: John Hopkins University Press; Harley, J. B. (2001). *The New Nature of Maps: Essays in the History of Cartography*. Baltimore: John Hopkins University Press.

[149] Günzel, Stephan (2007). Raum – Topographie – Topologie, in: Günzel, Stephan (ed.). *Topologie. Zur Raumbeschreibung in den Kultur- und Medienwissenschaften*. Bielefeld: Transcript, pp. 14-29 (14).

constituted by a functional relationship between nature and culture[150] and therefore as an entity that cannot be described independently. Corresponding to this, many topographical approaches are connected to the idea of physical space, even if they do not refer to notions of given, unchangeable spaces. We have already decided that—in the scope of the description of law for which we are looking—the connection to physical space and geographies at best might be a special object of our investigation, but not in the centre. This is the case because the concept of space we are negotiating is derived from the idea of a relative space. Further, any topographical approach to hybrid, relational, and dynamic law has to be limited to a chosen extract, one that is contingent and only one of numerous possible extracts.[151] A topographical analysis covering the whole of law is therefore impossible, and any approximation of it using a multitude of different representations of extracts, e.g. an *atlas of law*, would go beyond the scope as well as the possibilities of the present study, though it could be very fruitful for law.

We shall therefore focus on a rather topo*logical* approach to law's spatiality, and the advantages of this way of proceeding will hopefully become intelligible in the next few lines. In our context of a search for a conceptual description of law, it seems to be most promising to look for a spatial approach to law that is oriented towards those structures or relational coherences that remain stable. Of course, if we ask the question this way, we do not neglect what we have stated before—the conceptual necessity of space being in motion at any given time. Asking the question this way round presupposes the dynamics of the space of law: provided that the legal space is in a process of changing at any given time, are there any constellations, any structures, any characteristics that appear as continuities, at least for a while? Seen like that, the question is a fundamentally topological one. We can say that, because topology, looking to a lesser extent at the conditions of space, but rather at the conditions of spatiality, negotiates exactly these kinds of questions.[152] Its aim is to describe correspondences and similarities *in difference*.[153] The recourse to *topology*, which has become quite familiar in cultural and social studies[154] and even occurs in legal studies,[155] is always a recourse to

[150] Günzel, Stephan (2007). Raum – Topographie – Topologie, in: Günzel, Stephan (ed.). *Topologie. Zur Raumbeschreibung in den Kultur- und Medienwissenschaften*. Bielefeld: Transcript, pp. 14-29 (14).

[151] *See* also *above* Sect. 3.2.1.

[152] Günzel, Stephan (2007). Raum – Topographie – Topologie, in: Günzel, Stephan (ed.). *Topologie. Zur Raumbeschreibung in den Kultur- und Medienwissenschaften*. Bielefeld: Transcript, pp. 14-29 (21).

[153] Günzel, Stephan (2007). Raum – Topographie – Topologie, in: Günzel, Stephan (ed.). *Topologie. Zur Raumbeschreibung in den Kultur- und Medienwissenschaften*. Bielefeld: Transcript, pp. 14-29 (21).

[154] As an almost classical example, see only Lewin, Kurt (1951). *Field Theory in Social Science*. New York: Harper & Row,

[155] *See* e.g.; Katz, Daniel M. & Stafford, Derek K. & Provins, Eric (2008). Social Architecture, Judicial Peer Effects and the "Evolution" of the Law: Toward a Positive Theory of Judicial Social

mathematics.[156] The term 'topology', also in mathematics, developed relatively late (in the late nineteenth or finally in the beginning twentieth century)[157]—even if the first problems of this discipline occurred already in the eighteenth century.[158] As topology's precedent, the 'analysis situs' was considerably shaped by *Gottfried W. Leibniz* who was seeking a new mathematical method to negotiate spatial relations.[159] But in 1932 *David Hilbert* could reasonably state that of all fields of mathematics, topological research was one of the most fruitful and successful at that time.[160] One of the most influential texts in the development of topology was written by *Felix Klein*: the 'Erlangen program'.[161] In this book, *Klein* developed an

---

Structure. *Georgia State University Law Review 24/4*, 975-999 (985); Meyerson, Michael I. (2002). Political Numeracy: Mathematical Perspectives on Our Chaotic Constitution. New York:Norton; Meyerson, Michael I. (2002). Mathematics and the Legal Imagination. A Response to Paul Edelman. *Constitutional Commentary 19*, 477-481; Tribe, Laurence H. (1989). The Curvature of Constitutional Space: What Lawyers Can Learn from Modern Physics. *Harvard Law Review 103*, 1-39.

[156] *See* e.g. *Serres*: „Une paresse relative aux mathématiques induit à penser que l'espace, en géometrie, se lie à une métrique ou même à la mesure en général. Bergson et Heidegger répètent à loisir la même bévue et y entraînent leurs obligés, sans observer qu'autour d'eux les topologues, et, comme d'habitude, avant les savants, des artistes comme Maupassant, surent peindre le voisinage et ses proximités sans nul besoin de la distance ni de quantité pur la mesurer. [...] La topologie épouse l'espace, autrement, et mieux. Pour ce faire, elle use du fermé (*dans*), de l'ouvert (*hors*), des intervalles (*entre*), de l'orientation et de la direction (*vers, devant, derrière*), du voisinage et de l'adhérence (*près, sur, ceontre, suivant, touchant*), du plongement (*parmi*), de la dimension... et ainsi de suite, toutes le réalités sans mesure et avec relations.", Serres, Michel (1994). *Atlas*. Paris: Éditions Julliard, p. 71. I owe *Benjamin Wihstutz* for the hint to this beautiful passage to, *see* Wihstutz, Benjamin (2012). Der andere Raum. Politiken sozialer Grenzverhandlung im Gegenwartstheater. Zürich/Berlin: Diaphanes, p.63. *Der andere Raum* is a great example of a recourse to the mathematical concept of topology in the humanities (concerning this topic, *see* especially pp. 61).

[157] *See* Crilly, Tony (1999). The Emergence of Topological Dimension Theory, in: James, I. M. (ed.). *History of Topology*. Amsterdam: Elsevier, pp. 1-24 (10ff.); Heuser, Marie-Luise (2007). Die Anfänge der Topologie in Mathematik und Naturphilosophie, in: Günzel, Stephan (ed.). *Topologie. Zur Raumbeschreibung in den Kultur- und Medienwissenschaften*. Bielefeld: Transcript, pp. 183-200 (183).

[158] Hilbert, David & Cohn-Vossen, Stephan (2011, orig. 1932). Anschauliche Geometrie. Springer: Heidelberg/Berlin, p. 254.

[159] *See* Leibniz, Gottfried W. (1693). De analysi situs, in: Leibniz, Gottfried W. (1858, ed. By Gerhardt, Carl Immanuel). *Mathematische Schriften*. Hildesheim: Olms, pp. 178-183 and *Leibniz* in Clarke, Samuel (1717). *A collection of papers which passed between the late learned Mr. Leibniz and Dr. Clarke in the years 1715/1716 relating to the principles of natural philosophy and religion*. London: Knapton. *See* also Heuser, Marie-Luise (2007). Die Anfänge der Topologie in Mathematik und Naturphilosophie, in: Günzel, Stephan (ed.). *Topologie. Zur Raumbeschreibung in den Kultur- und Medienwissenschaften*. Bielefeld: Transcript, pp. 183-200 (pp. 185) and Freudenthal, Hans (1972). Leibniz und die Analysis situs. *Studia Leibnitiana 4*, 61-69.

[160] "In der Gegenwart gehören unter allen Zweigen der Mathematik die topologischen Forschungen zu den fruchtbarsten und erfolgreichsten." Hilbert, David & Cohn-Vossen, Stephan (2011, orig. 1932). Anschauliche Geometrie. Springer: Heidelberg/Berlin, p. 254.

[161] Klein, Felix (1872). *Vergleichende Betrachtungen über neuere geometrische Forschungen*. Deichert: Erlangen.

approach to geometry based on groups "that made it possible to qualify different geometries not according to their objects but according to their basic behaviour or transformations".[162] The central idea is that spatial constellations have geometrical characteristics. These geometrical characteristics show stability even if certain spatial transformations take place—they are even produced by these transformations.[163] There are several aspects we have to emphasize here: first, we can recognize spatial constellations that can be found in a space. Of course this idea is only conceivable on the basis of a relational understanding of space—for a geometrical thinker like *Klein* at the end of nineteenth century this is already quite common, simply because geometry at the time provides the option of thinking space as a set of points. Then of course you can also look at parts of this set of points—spatial constellations inside a space. Further, these constellations only become visible through spatial transformations: if some or even all relations change, e.g. if distances are increased or reduced, there are some characteristics of the relations that remain unchanged. This creates a certain spatial constellation. Another remarkable aspect is that spatial transformations are only conceivable as transformations that affect the totality of spatial constellations and thus, the space.[164]

But where does such theorizing lead—except to mathematical knowledge? Basically, it allows two approaches to the concept of space: on the one hand an imagination of relational space, independent of any natural space, and on the other hand tools for describing certain spatial constellations on the basis of transformations. This last aspect could become very important for our present approach to law, because until now we had no means of differentiating between relationality and dynamics of law in a conceptual way. This means that we can of course follow a mapping strategy and create maps of law for a series of moments in time, as a result of which we would probably receive a description of concrete developments in time. But on a general, a conceptual level, we do not yet have any means to say more than: law is dynamic. Since we are on the way towards a conceptual description of law, a more advanced set of conceptual tools referring

[162] Heuser, Marie-Luise (2007). Die Anfänge der Topologie in Mathematik und Naturphilosophie, in: Günzel, Stephan (ed.). *Topologie. Zur Raumbeschreibung in den Kultur- und Medienwissenschaften.* Bielefeld: Transcript, pp. 183-200 (pp. 197, tr. S.MM.).

[163] "Es gibt nun räumliche Transformationen, welche die geometrischen Eigenschaften räumlicher Gebilde überhaupt ungeändert lassen. Geometrische Eigenschaften sind nämlich ihrem Begriffe nach unabhängig von der Lage, die das zu untersuchende Gebilde im Raume einnimmt, von seiner absoluten Größe, endlich auch von dem Sinne, in welchem seine Theile geordnet sind. Die Eigenschaften eines räumlichen Gebildes bleiben also ungeändert durch alle Bewegungen des Raumes, durch seine Aehnlichkeitstransformationen, durch den Process der Spiegelung, sowie durch alle Transformationen, die sich aus diesen zusammensetzen." Klein, Felix (1872). *Vergleichende Betrachtungen über neuere geometrische Forschungen.* Deichert: Erlangen, p. 6.

[164] "Wir denken von den Transformationen immer die Gesammtheit der räumlichen Gebilde gleichzeitig betroffen und reden deshalb schlechthin von Transformationen des Raumes." Klein, Felix (1872). *Vergleichende Betrachtungen über neuere geometrische Forschungen.* Deichert: Erlangen, p. 5, note 2.

to law's relationality, hybridity, and dynamics would be helpful. Similarly to *de Certeau*, who inversed our understanding of space by explicating it as 'practiced place', these (of course quite non-mathematically formulated) mathematical ideas may help us find a specification of how a spatial perspective on law could be developed further: the idea that there are topological structures, constellations within a topological space that are defined by a certain stability on the basis of transformations, just inverses the point of view. If we try to find constellations in law that show these characteristics, we do not first have to observe and describe certain constellations in order to recognize their differences in different moments. But we have to try to define what transformation of the space of law means in order to distinguish relational (sub-)spaces that can be understood as stable in a specific sense, even if their constellation (including all their constituting elements) is subject to a transformation. In the next chapter we will see that concepts such as dimension, distance, scale play a role in such an attempt. But let us look at one easily-imaginable example from the sphere of mathematical topology, before we undertake a first sketch of what the term 'law's topology' could signify. The example is as simple as it is famous: we can imagine a topological structure that displays a spherical shape. Maybe it is made of dough. We can play with it in our fingers, and we can change its shape a little, for example into a more elliptical shape. Maybe at the end it looks more like an egg than like a doughnut. We can even form a cylinder without undertaking any fundamental operations. What is important is what fundamental could mean in this context: e.g. it could mean to tear a hole, or it could mean to cut the entire piece of dough into two. On a figurative level this stands for instance for making a doughnut out of the (spherical) ball. These kinds of transformation are what topology investigates—the question to be formulated in this case would be: how can we explain that making an egg out of the ball can be qualified as 'not changing the (topological) structure' of the piece of dough even if every atom in it changes its relational situation; and how is this related to the case of turning the ball into a doughnut, which we could qualify as 'changing the structure'? In other words, the topological question concerning the egg would be: what is it in this structure that stays the same, even if every single point therein changes its relational position? The crux of topological studies lies in the idea that the concept of transformation is a presupposition for recognizing structure. Thinking of a ball and an egg without the idea of transforming one into another would never let us think of similarities (at first), but seduce us to look for differences. It is even the case that we can recognize the continuities *only* if we think of the transformation. In the following, we shall consider this idea in addition to the conceptualizations of space and place, in order to outline a first picture of where such thinking of law's spatiality might bring us.

3.3.3 Law's Topology: Norms, Judgment, Theory

Before,[165] we have said that the concepts of space and place allowed the distinction of law as a phenomenon of practice (to be described by the concept of space) and law as a multitude of thinkable concrete perspectives (defined by respectively chosen frames of reference) or taken places. On conceptual grounds, these two sides of the story are linked to the concept of *practice* which in the case of law is to be re-formulated as normative perception, executed by a performative event of the generation of law.[166] But it does not yet seem entirely clear how the two are connected in ways and methods of description of law—this is what we are going to concretize throughout the next chapter. The connection between describing law either as space or from the perspective of concrete places that are to be defined through reference frames is not obvious at first sight, but the previous topological considerations will help us find the way there.

So far, we have seen three different kinds of approach to spatial law: first, a global notion of law as space, characterized by hybridity, relationality, and dynamics. This space has been re-formulated then as the product of places—practiced places constitute space. And, third, by places we have understood locations in law that are defined by external reference frames. We can imagine this as follows: the space of law is constituted by acts of normative perception. These do not only form the dynamics of law, but also its relationality: relations are acts of normative perception that necessarily show points of action as well as references to other acts of normative perception. In exploring concrete constellations of law, we might pick out one single act of normative perception, for example one legal decision. If we want to locate this decision, it is impossible to apply the whole complex space of law, because the latter is a fluid relationality with many events occurring at the same time, overlapping each other. But we can pick it out in a literal sense, which means to extract it from the space of law, and locate it within another system, a reference frame we create and adjust to our needs, e.g. to the questions we have regarding this decision. Of course, this procedure is not identical to the pure invention of a reference frame—it is rather a process of selection: out of all conceivable dimensions the space of law might have, we choose those that allow a meaningful location of the decision. Meaningful here is to be determined according to the questions or reasons for analyzing this specific decision. But even if this procedure of choosing a reference frame and hence the location of the decision is not completely invented (in a fictional sense), it is still arbitrary: it could just as well be chosen differently, depending only on the aim one is pursuing with the act of locating. If we decided to attempt general conclusions about constellations in the space of law, any such localization would not help, though—not only because of its arbitrariness, but also because of the incompatibility with the perspective of space that we have attributed to the one of place. The latter was the sphere of the dead, the

---

[165] *See above* Sect. 3.3.2.

[166] *See above* Chap. 2, Sect. 2.3.

singular perspective, while the former was the general one; under the restriction that no extrapolation from the location sphere could ever reach the space, which is the sphere of dynamic relationality. It is exactly at the threshold of this gap that the topological considerations come into play.

In order to achieve the possibility of extrapolation, of making general statements about specific constellations, we have to concentrate on several acts of normative perception at the same time. We can specify their relational constellation by choosing one reference frame for all of them, but we still have to negotiate one complication: we can only avoid the dynamics of the space if we concentrate on a single element of the space of law. As soon as we look at more than one, we are lost in the relativity of dynamic relationality, so that we cannot find a precise location of any configuration. But, and this is the great advantage of topology—we can examine constellations in the space of law by means of topological approaches: this means integrating the constant transformation by constructing the whole perspective on it. The vehicle for doing so is to ask for continuities within these constellations, presupposing that they are constantly subject to transformations. How this could be done, and how all these three aspects of approaching legal spaces could be specified and developed further—we will approach these questions in the next chapter.

References

Augsberg, Ino (2009). Die Lesbarkeit des Rechts. Texttheoretische Lektionen für eine postmoderne juristische Methodenlehre. Weilerswist: Velbrück.

Bachmann-Medick, Doris (2006). Cultural Turns. Neuorientierungen in den Kulturwissenschaften. Hamburg: Rowohlt.

Bachof, Otto (1951). Die verwaltungsgerichtliche Klage auf Vornahme einer Amtshandlung. Tübingen: Mohr Siebeck.

Ballard, Kaith (1960). Leibniz's Theory of Space and Time. Journal of the History of Idea 21, p. 49-65.

Bauer, Hartmut (1986). Geschichtliche Grundlagen der Lehre vom subjektiven öffentlichen Recht. Berlin: Duncker & Humblot.

Blomley, Nicholas D. (1994). Law, Space, and the Geographies of Power. London: Guilford.

Blomely, Nicholas D. & Delaney, David & Ford, Richard (eds.) (2001). The Legal Geographies Reader. Oxford: Wiley-Blackwell.

Bogdandy, Armin von & Bast, Jürgen (eds)(2009). Europäisches Verfassungsrecht. Berlin/ Heidelberg: Springer.

Böhme, Hartmut (ed.)(2005). Topographien der Literatur. DFG-Symposion 2004. Stuttgart/ Weimar: Metzler.

Brand, Ulrich & Raza, Werner (eds.)(2003). Fit für den Postfordismus. Münster: Dampfboot.

Brown, Harold (1979). Perception, Theory and Commitment. The New Philosophy of Science. Chicago: University of Chicago Press.

Brugger, Wilfried & Neumann, Ulfrid & Kirste, Stephan (eds)(2008). Rechtsphilosophie im 21. Jahrhundert. Frankfurt am Main: Suhrkamp.

Bühler, Ottmar (1914). Die subjektiven öffentlichen Rechte und ihr Schutz in der deutschen Verwaltungsrechtsprechung. Stuttgart: Kohlhammer.

Butler, Chris (2003). Law and the Social Production of Space. Thesis, Griffith University Queensland (Australia).

Caldwell, Peter C. (1997). Popular Sovereignty and the Crisis of German Constitutional Law. The Theory and Practice of Weimar Constitutionalism. Durham: Duke University Press.

Calliess, Christian (2006). Feinstaub im Rechtsschutz deutscher Verwaltungsgerichte. Neue Zeitschrift für Verwaltungsrecht, pp. 1-7.

Chalmers, Alan (2007). What is This Thing Called Science? St. Lucia: University of Queensland Press.

Chatterjee, Bela (2006). Text and terrain: Mapping Sexuality and Law. Law and Critique 17, 293-323.

Clarke, Samuel (1717). A collection of papers which passed between the late learned Mr. Leibniz and Dr. Clarke in the years 1715/1716 relating to the principles of natural philosophy and religion. London: Knapton.

Cohen, Julie E. (2007). Cyberspace as/ and Space. Columbia Law Review 107, 210-256.

Cooper, Davina (1998). Governing out of Order: Space, Law and the Politics of Belonging. London: Rivers Oram.

Cosgrove, Denis (2001). Appolo's Eye: A Cartographic Genealogy of the Earth in the Western Imagination. Baltimore: John Hopkins University Press.

Costa, Pietro & Zolo, Danilo (eds.)(1997). The Rule of Law. History, Theory and Criticism. Berlin/Heidelberg/New York: Springer.

Crang, Mike & Thrift, Nigel (eds.) (2000). Thinking Space. London, New York: Routledge.

Crang, Mike (2011). Michel de Certeau, in: Hubbard, Phil & Kitchin, Rob (eds.). Key Thinkers on Space and Place. 2nd edition. London: Sage, p. 106-112.

Cornell, Drucilla & Rosenfeld, Michel & Carlson, David Gray (eds.)(1992). Deconstruction and the Possibility of Justice, New York: Routledge.

Crilly, Tony (1999). The Emergence of Topological Dimension Theory, in: James, I. M. (ed.). History of Topology. Amsterdam: Elsevier, pp. 1-24.

Danwitz, Thomas von (2008). Europäisches Verwaltungsrecht. Berlin/Heidelberg/New York: Springer.

Danwitz, Thomas von (2004). Aarhus-Konvention: Umweltinformation, Öffentlichkeitsbeteiligung, Zugang zu den Gerichten. Neue Zeitschrift für Verwaltungsrecht, pp. 272-282.

Danwitz, Thomas von (1996). Verwaltungsrechtliches System und europäische Integration. Tübingen: Mohr Siebeck.

De Bellis, Maurizia (2011). Public Law and Private Regulators in the Global Legal Space. International Journal of Constitutional Law 9, pp. 425-448.

De Certeau, Michel (1980). On the oppositional practices of everyday life. Social Text 1, 3-43.

De Certeau, Michel (1980). L'Invention du Quotidien. 1. Arts de faire. Paris: Gallimard.

De Certeau, Michel (1984). The Practice of Everyday Life. Berkeley/Los Angeles: University of California Press.

De Certeau, Michel (1986). Heterologies: Discourses on the Other. Manchester University Press: Manchester.

De Certeau, Michel (1987). La fable mystique. Gallimard: Paris.

Debus, Alfred et. al. (eds.)(2011). Verwaltungsrechtsraum Europa. Baden-Baden: Nomos.

Derrida, Jacques (1992). Force of Law: The "Mystical Foundation of Authority", in: Cornell, Drucilla & Rosenfeld, Michel & Carlson, David Gray (eds.). Deconstruction and the Possibility of Justice, New York: Routledge, pp. 3-67.

Döring, Jörg & Thielmann, Tristan (2008). Spatial Turn. Das Raumparadigma in den Kultur- und Sozialwissenschaften. Bielefeld: Transcript.

Dreier, Horst & Wittreck, Fabian (2009). Rechtswissenschaft, in: Günzel, Stephan (ed.). Raumwissenschaften. Frankfurt am Main: Suhrkamp, pp. 338-353.

Dünne, Jörg (2006). Einleitung, in: Dünne, Jörg & Günzel, Stephan (eds.). Raumtheorie. Grundlagentexte aus Philosophie und Kulturwissenschaften. Frankfurt am Main: Suhrkamp, p. 289-302.

Dünne, Jörg & Günzel, Stephan (eds.)(2006). Raumtheorie. Grundlagentexte aus Philosophie und Kulturwissenschaften. Frankfurt am Main: Suhrkamp.
Durkheim, Émile (1969 , orig. 1897). Note sur la morphologie sociale, in: Durkheim, Èmile (ed.). Journal sociologique. Paris: Presses Universitaires de France, pp. 181-182.
Durkheim, Èmile (ed.) (1969, orig. 1897). Journal sociologique. Paris: Presses Universitaires de France.
Economides, Kim & Blacksell, Mark & Watkins, Charles (1986). The spatial analysis of legal systems: towards a geography of law? Journal of Law and Society 13/2, pp. 161-181.
Einstein, Albert (1930). Raum, Äther und Feld in der Physik. Forum Philosophicum I, pp. 173-180.
Elden, Stuart (2001). Politics, Philosophy, Geography: Henri Lefebvre in Recent Anglo-American Scholarship. Antipode 33/5, pp. 809 – 825.
Erbsen, Allan (2011). Constitutional Spaces. Minnesota Law Review 95, pp. 1168-1267.
Erlichson, Herman (1967). The Leibniz-Clarke Controversy: Absolute Versus Relative Space and Time. American Journal of Physics 35, pp. 89-98.
Fischer-Lescano, Andreas & Teubner, Gunther (2004). Regime-Collisions: The Vain Search for Legal Unitiy in the Fragmentation of Global Law. Michigan Journal of International Law 25, pp. 999-1046.
Fischer-Lescano, Andreas & Teubner, Gunther (2006). Regime-Kollisionen. Zur Fragmentierung des globalen Rechts. Frankfurt am Main: Suhrkamp.
Foucault, Michel (1984). Des espaces autres. Architecture, mouvement, continuité 5, pp. 46-49.
Foucault, Michel (1986). Of Other Spaces. Diacritics 16, pp. 22-27.
Freudenthal, Hans (1972). Leibniz und die Analysis situs. Studia Leibnitiana 4, pp. 61-69.
Galmot, Yves & Bonichot, Jean-Claude (1988). La Cour de Justice des Communautés européennes et la transposition des directives en droit national. Revue Francaise de Droit Administratif 4, pp. 1.
Gerber, Carl Friedrich von (1852). Über öffentliche Rechte. Tübingen: Laupp & Siebeck.
Gozzi, Gustavo (1997). Rechtsstaat and Individual Rights in German Constitutional History, in: Costa, Pietro & Zolo, Danilo (eds.). The Rule of Law. History, Theory and Criticism. Berlin/ Heidelberg/New York: Springer, pp. 237-259.
Grabham, Emily (2006). Taxonomies of Inequality: Lawyers, Maps and the Challenge of Hybridity. Social and Legal Studies 15/1, pp. 5-23.
Groh, Thomas & Lorenz, Jörn (eds.)(2010). Interpretatio Mundi. Wie deuten die Wissenschaften ihre Welt? Dresden: Thelem.
Günzel, Stephan (2006). Einleitung, in: Dünne, Jörg & Günzel, Stephan (eds.). Raumtheorie. Grundlagentexte aus Philosophie und Kulturwissenschaften. Frankfurt am Main: Suhrkamp, pp. 19 – 43.
Günzel, Stephan (2007). Raum – Topographie – Topologie, in: Günzel, Stephan (ed.). Topologie. Zur Raumbeschreibung in den Kultur- und Medienwissenschaften. Bielefeld: Transcript, pp. 14-29.
Günzel, Stephan (ed.)(2007). Topologie. Zur Raumbeschreibung in den Kultur- und Medienwissenschaften. Bielefeld: Transcript.
Günzel, Stephan (ed.) (2009). Raumwissenschaften. Frankfurt am Main: Suhrkamp.
Harley, J. B. (2001). The New Nature of Maps: Essays in the History of Cartography. Baltimore: John Hopkins University Press.
Harvey, David (1989). The Condition of Postmodernity. Basil Blackwell: Oxford.
Heuser, Marie-Luise (2007). Die Anfänge der Topologie in Mathematik und Naturphilosophie, in: Günzel, Stephan (ed.). Topologie. Zur Raumbeschreibung in den Kultur- und Medienwissenschaften. Bielefeld: Transcript, pp. 183-200.
Hilbert, David & Cohn-Vossen, Stephan (2011, orig. 1932). Anschauliche Geometrie. Springer: Heidelberg/Berlin.
Holder, Jane & Harrison, Carolyn (eds.)(2003). Law and Geography. Oxford: Oxford University Press.

Hubbard, Phil & Kitchin, Rob (eds.) (2011). Key Thinkers on Space and Place. 2nd edition. London: Sage.
Huber, Ernst Rudolf (1953). Wirtschaftsverwaltungsrecht. Vol. 1, 2nd ed. Tübingen: Mohr Siebeck.
Huber, Peter-Michael (1991). Konkurrenzschutz im Verwaltungsrecht. Tübingen: Mohr Siebeck.
Jacob, Christian (1996). Toward a Cultural History of Cartography: Imago Mundi 48, pp. 191-198.
Jammer, Max (1969). Concepts of Space: The History of Theories of Space in Physics. Cambridge/Mass.: Harvard University Press.
Jellinek, Georg (1892). System der subjektiven öffentlichen Rechte. Freiburg: Mohr.
Kant, Immanuel (1770). Von dem Raume, in: Schriften zur Metaphysik und Logik I. (Werkausgabe, Bd. 5. Frankfurt am Main: Suhrkamp), pp. 56-69.
Katz, Daniel M. & Stafford, Derek K. & Provins, Eric (2008). Social Architecture, Judicial Peer Effects and the "Evolution" of the Law: Toward a Positive Theory of Judicial Social Structure. Georgia State University Law Review 24/4, pp. 975-999.
Kelsen, Hans (1960). Reine Rechtslehre. 2nd Edition. Wien: Deuticke.
Klein, Felix (1872). Vergleichende Betrachtungen über neuere geometrische Forschungen. Deichert: Erlangen.
Koller, Peter (2008). Der Begriff des Rechts und seine Konzeptionen, in: Brugger, Wilfried & Neumann, Ulfrid & Kirste, Stephan (eds). Rechtsphilosophie im 21. Jahrhundert. Frankfurt am Main: Suhrkamp, pp. 157-180.
Law, John (2002). Objects and Spaces. Theory Culture Society 19, pp. 91 – 105.
Laubadère, André de & Venezia, Jean-Claude & Gaudemet, Yves (1995). Droit administratif, 15th ed. Paris: LGDJ.
Lefebvre, Henri (1991 (orig. 1974)). The Production of Space. Blackwell: Oxford.
Leibniz, Gottfried W. (1693). De analysi situs, in: Leibniz, Gottfried W. (1858, ed. By Gerhardt, Carl Immanuel). Mathematische Schriften. Hildesheim: Olms, pp. 178-183.
Lewin, Kurt (1951). Field Theory in Social Science. New York: Harper & Row.
Löw, Martina (2001). Raumsoziologie, Frankfurt am Main: Suhrkamp.
Löw, Martina (2008). The Constitution of Space. The Structuration of Spaces Through the Simultaneity of Effect and Perception. European Journal of Social Theory 11/1, pp. 25-49.
Luhmann, Niklas (1993), Die Paradoxie des Entscheidens, Verwaltungsarchiv 84, pp. 287-310.
Luhmann, Niklas (1995). Das Recht der Gesellschaft. Frankfurt am Main: Suhrkamp.
Marsch, Nikolaus (2011). Subjektivierung der gerichtlichen Verwaltungskontrolle in Frankreich. Baden-Baden: Nomos.
Masing, Johannes (1997). Die Mobilisierung des Bürgers für die Durchsetzung des Rechts. Europäische Impulse für eine Revision der Lehre vom subjektiv-öffentlichen Recht. Berlin: Duncker & Humblot.
Massey, Doreen. (1994). Space, Place and Gender. Oxford: Blackwell.
McGhee, Derek & Moran, Leslie (1998). Perverting London: the cartographic practices of law. Law and Critique 9/2, pp. 207-224.
Medick, Doris (2006). Cultural Turns. Neuorientierungen in den Kulturwissenschaften. Hamburg: Rowohlt.
Meyerson, Michael I. (2002). Mathematics and the Legal Imagination. A Response to Paul Edelman. Constitutional Commentary 19, pp. 477-481.
Meyerson, Michael I. (2002). Political Numeracy: Mathematical Perspectives on Our Chaotic Constitution. New York: Norton.
Monar, Jörg (2009). Der Raum der Freiheit, der Sicherheit und des Rechts in: von Bogdandy, Armin & Bast, Jürgen (eds). Europäisches Verfassungsrecht. Berlin/Heidelberg: Springer, p. 749 - 798.
Müller-Mall, Sabine (2010). Interpretation als Rechtserzeugung, in: Groh, Thomas & Lorenz, Jörn (eds.). Interpretatio Mundi. Wie deuten die Wissenschaften ihre Welt? Dresden: Thelem, pp.235-251.

Nettesheim, Martin (2007). Subjektive Rechte im Unionsrecht, Archiv des öffentlichen Rechts 132, pp. 333-392.

Nietzsche, Friedrich (1967, ed. and tr. by Kaufmann, Walter). The Will to Power. Random House: New York, cited after Lefebvre, Henri (1991 (orig. 1974)). The Production of Space. Blackwell: Oxford, p. 22.

Patterson, Dennis & Teubner, Gunther (1998). Changing Maps: Empirical Legal Autopoiesis. Social and Legal Studies 7/4, pp. 451-486.

Philippopoulos-Mihalopoulos, Andreas (2001). Mapping Utopias: A Voyage to Placenessless. Law and Critique 12, pp. 135-157.

Pottage, Alain. (1994). The Measure of Land. Modern Law Review 57/3, pp. 361-384.

Reiling, Michael (2004). Zu individuellen Rechten im deutschen und Gemeinschaftsrecht. Ein Vergleich ihrer Gründe, Ermittlung und Durchsetzung. Berlin: Duncker & Humblot.

Schmid, Christian (2003). Raum und Regulation. Henri Lefebvre und der Regulationsansatz, in: Brand, Ulrich & Raza, Werner (eds.). Fit für den Postfordismus. Münster: Dampfboot, pp. 217-242.

Schmidt-Aßmann, Eberhard (1999). Strukturen des Europäischen Verwaltungsrechts: Einleitende Problemskizze, in: Schmidt-Aßmann, Eberhard & Hoffmann-Riem, Wolfgang (eds.). Strukturen des Europäischen Verwaltungsrechts. Baden-Baden: Nomos, pp. 9-43.

Schmidt-Aßmann, Eberhard & Hoffmann-Riem, Wolfgang (eds.)(1999). Strukturen des Europäischen Verwaltungsrechts. Baden-Baden: Nomos.

Schoch, Friedrich & Schmidt-Aßmann, Eberhard &. Pietzner, Rainer (2010). Verwaltungsgerichtsordnung. Kommentar. München: CH. Beck.

Schwarze, Jürgen (1999). Die Entwicklung der französischen Verwaltungsgerichtsbarkeit aus deutscher Sicht. Deutsche Verwaltungsblätter, pp. 261-269.

Serres, Michel (1994). Atlas. Paris: Éditions Julliard.

Siegert, Bernhard (2005). Repräsentationen diskursiver Räume – Einleitung, in: Böhme, Hartmut (ed.). Topographien der Literatur. DFG-Symposion 2004. Stuttgart/Weimar: Metzler, pp. 3-11.

Simmel, Georg (1903). Über räumliche Projektionen sozialer Formen, in: Aufsätze und Abhandlungen 1901-1908. Gesamtausgabe, vol. 7. Frankfurt am Main: Suhrkamp, pp. 201-220.

Slaughter, Anne-Marie (2004). A New World Order. Princeton University Press: Princeton.

Smith, Neil (2008). Uneven Development: Nature, Capital and the Production of Space. University of Georgia Press: Athens.

Soja, Edward (1989). Postmodern Geographies. The Reassertion of Space in Critical Social Theory. London/New York: Verso.

Soja, Edward (1996). Thirdspace. Journeys to Los Angeles and other Real-and-Imagined Places. London/New York: Verso.

Soja, Edward (2008). New Twists on the Spatial Turn, in: Döring, Jörg & Thielmann, Tristan. Spatial Turn. Das Raumparadigma in den Kultur- und Sozialwissenschaften. Bielefeld: Transcript, pp. 241-262.

Stolleis, Michael (2001). Public Law in Germany, 1800-1914. Oxford/New York: Berghahn.

Stolleis, Michael (2004). Public Law in Germany, 1914-1945. Oxford: Oxford University Press.

Tribe, Laurence H. (1989). The Curvature of Constitutional Space: What Lawyers Can Learn from Modern Physics. Harvard Law Review 103, pp. 1-39.

Twining, William (1999). Mapping Law. Northern Ireland Legal Quarterly 50/1, pp. 12-49.

Vismann, Cornelia (1999). "Rejouer les Crimes." – Theater vs. Video. Cardozo Studies in Law and Literature 11/2, pp. 161-177.

Vismann, Cornelia (2011). Medien der Rechtsprechung. Frankfurt am Main: S. Fischer.

Wahl, Rainer (2010). Vorbemerkungen § 42 Abs. 2, in: Schoch, Friedrich & Schmidt-Aßmann, Eberhard &. Pietzner, Rainer. Verwaltungsgerichtsordnung. Kommentar. München: CH. Beck. 20th ed.

Ward, Barney & Arias, Santa (eds.) (2008). *The Spatial Turn: Interdisciplinary Perspectives.* New York: Routledge.

Weiler, Joseph (1999). The Constitution of Europe. Cambridge: Cambridge University Press.
Weiler, Joseph (1999). Fundamental Rights and Fundamental Boundaries: on the Conflict of Standards and Values in the Protection of Human Rights in the European Legal Space, in: Weiler, Joseph. The Constitution of Europe. Cambridge: Cambridge University Press, pp. 102-129.
Weiler, Joseph (1999). The Constitution of Europe. Cambridge: Cambridge University Press.
Whittaker, Sir Edmund (1949). From Euclid to Eddington. A Study of Conceptions of the External World. Cambridge: Cambridge University Press.
Wihstutz, Benjamin (2012). Der andere Raum. Politiken sozialer Grenzverhandlung im Gegenwartstheater. Zürich/Berlin: Diaphanes.
Wittgenstein, Ludwig (1976). Philosophical Investigations. Blackwell: Oxford.

Chapter 4
Legal Spaces

The question this chapter negotiates is how to develop a conceptual and descriptive approach to law—proceeding from the assumptions we have made in the previous chapters. More precisely formulated, the question would then be: how to make the spatial perspective fruitful for exploring hybrid, relational, and dynamic law? Our aim was to find a perspective on law that would make possible a conceptual description of law as well as methods of its exploration. In the following, we therefore have to illustrate how the concept of space, the space-place dichotomy as well as a topological view on law could serve us in reaching this goal. The following illustrations provide some clues as to what a spatial theory of law could look like. In this sense, we will first see how thinking law as space might yield a conceptual perspective (Sect. 4.1). Furthermore, we shall try to explain how taking concrete perspectives on law might be described in terms of a spatial perspective. In doing so, we shall see that a spatial approach indicates how a method of exploring concrete legal questions—we could also say: a legal method—could be developed if we start from the assumption that law can be thought as space (Sect. 4.2). And, finally, we shall discover a connection from a conceptual description in this sense to the outlined legal method. This connection is mediated by the conceptual tool, the concept of space, that is presupposed on both sides of the coin; but it is also based on the topological considerations that we have undertaken in the last part of Chap. 3 (Sect. 3.3).

4.1 Thinking Law Spatially

What does it mean, now, to think law spatially? Although we have already found some indications, we still have to outline a general picture of law's spatiality. In trying to do so, we build upon the concept of space that we have developed in the previous chapter: space is understood as a relational, dynamic structure composed of different elements—the relations that are established through and in between these elements constitute the space. These moments of establishment, the relations

S. Müller-Mall, *Legal Spaces*, DOI 10.1007/978-3-642-36730-4_4,

themselves, are not stable entities; instead, they are dynamic movements, performative acts that do not only re-create a new space in every act but also presuppose dynamics. Space is thus not thinkable without the notion of practice. Without someone doing something, there is no space.

4.1.1 Legal Spaces: Norms, Judgment, Theory

Seen from the perspective of our presuppositions concerning law that we described in chapter II, a transfer of the concept of space to the description of law no longer seems so far-fetched: we understood law as a hybrid, relational and dynamic constellation, whose relationality was constituted by performative acts of normative perception. These acts have two main features: they create the connections between the different elements of law (which are constituted by the different events) *and* they build up the relations in between these elements. This two-fold character of the elements that constitute law is grounded in the structure of the performative acts, which is a structure of normative perception and thus necessarily refers to the outside of the act itself, refers to a different entity, a different element of law. We were therefore able to expose that "hybrid, relational, and dynamic law is a set of interconnected events".[1]

According to our conception, now, space does not necessarily have to be understood in a Euclidean sense as a three-dimensional entity, but might take different forms; because it is defined only by its elements and their relational connections.[2] In this formulation, the proximity to our description of law becomes obvious: it includes exactly this relationship between elements and their relational connections, which constitute law. In addition, the understanding of this relationship through a performative concept of practice, which is borrowed from *de Certeau*,[3] finds a parallel in our description of the elements of law as performative acts of generation.[4] Considering this analogy we might grasp the ways along which the normative perception connects the perceiving and the perceived, the law-generating act to other acts of law generation as relations. In the following, we shall understand these relations as ones that produce space.

The concept of space, hence, is part of a cover-up tactic: we try to grasp the hardly definable (or only recursively describable) normativity of law in this web of interconnected events by applying to law a concept of space. This concept has very similar implications, then, to the ones we worked out for the description of law employing our presuppositions, so that it seems legitimate, or at least not forbidden, to carry out this analogy. In the second step, now, we have to learn from the concept

---

[1] *See* Chap. 2, Sect. 2.3.2.

[2] Similarly, Law, John (2002). Objects and Spaces. *Theory Culture Society* 19, pp. 91-105 (94).

[3] *See above* Chap. 3, Sect. 3.2.3.

[4] Of course the similarity in both, *de Certeau*'s approach and our approach to law's normativity, mediated through the concept of practice, is no coincidence: because both approaches have foundations in *Wittgenstein*'s late philosophy. *See* only *above* Chap. 3, Sect. 3.2.3. and Chap. 2, Sect. 2.3.1.

of space and transfer some of its characteristics to law. The aim stays the same: to gain a perspective on law that allows us a conceptual description and delivers methodological tools for law's exploration.

In order to receive a conceptual description of law that is a bit easier to handle, we have to draw a new distinction here—a distinction that is not necessary and not qualitative,[5] but one that is to facilitate our capacity of imagination when we talk about legal spaces. Earlier, we grasped the law as a space, consisting in a set of interconnected events of performative law generation. Now we draw distinctions between three sub-spaces: one consisting in legal norms (*space of legal norms*), a second one consisting in judicial decisions (*space of legal decisions*), and a third one that integrates legal theory, principles, and doctrine (*space of legal thinking*). Of course it is very questionable whether we can add the *space of legal thinking* to what we call *legal spaces*. On the one hand it is not certain, and even not very probable, that the production of a legal theory, of a doctrinal idea, or of a legal principle that is not written in positive legal norms has the same normative quality as for instance a legal norm. On the other hand, it is at least uncontested that both legislators and courts refer to elements of this space of legal thinking in generating their legal acts. They become objects of normative perception, and they doubtlessly perceive elements of the other spaces, too, the only insecurity to which we are exposed being the question of the normative quality of this second form of perception. At least, hence, the space of legal thinking is a passive part[6] of the processes of the generation of law. This should be sufficient for the present study to accept this third space as part of the legal spaces. Of course, this has to be added here, we could also describe law as one legal space, comprising these three spaces, and we draw the three-fold distinction only for reasons of better imagination and of simplification.

According to this, we can now state the following: law consists in different constellations of elements that are to be identified with performative events of law generation. We call these constellations legal spaces, and of course these legal spaces are interconnected just as their elements are interconnected. The distinction of 'different' constellations is only an additional distinction, a terminological one, not a categorical one. We can describe these spaces as well as the picture of all three spaces together using their spatial characteristics: they are relational and they are dynamic, which means that they change in time; the change of one element, or the addition of one, has implications for the whole: for the affected legal space and for the constellation of all three spaces that we call 'law'. This impact is what we call 'transformation'. The instrument for changing a space or adding an element is a performative act of law generation that we can describe as an act of normative perception. Because it establishes a new relationship to one or more already

[5] *Qualitative* means here that it would differentiate different qualities of each element of the distinction.

[6] If it did not exceed the scope of the present study, we would argue even in favour of the elements of the space of legal thinking having the same normative status as the other two spaces here: along the notion of passive normativity that was a result of our theoretical considerations in Chap. 2, we would try to show here that this being a passive part of the generating processes is to be identified with the passive normativity of any legal norms or decisions that are perceived. Again, concerning this moment of description of law, it is all a question of the perspective we are taking.

existing elements of law by referring to them. The relationality of the legal spaces implies a possible multiplicity of simultaneous relationships taking different directions—this phenomenon corresponds to what in our presuppositions we called 'hybridity'. Thus, thinking law spatially means to identify law's hybridity, relationality, and dynamics with the spatial concepts of dimensionality, normative perception (as the space-producing practice), and transformation. This process of identification will open a series of questions we can ask with respect to law, and hence opens a new scope of possible insights into law. In the next section we shall undertake the adventure of formulating some of these new questions.

4.1.2 Characteristics of Legal Spaces

Following this modelling[7] of three legal spaces that together serve as a model of law, we can identify two general complexes of problems to be solved by a conceptual description of law: on the one hand the question how the inside structure of these spaces might be described. And on the other hand the question of how to describe the relationships in between these three spaces. Many of the questions that a spatial thinking of law could expose will be part of one of these two complexes of problems. Before we shall try to extract some of these questions in the following paragraphs, it is helpful to sketch the whole picture to the extent that we have outlined it so far.

Maybe a rudimentary outline of the processes of judging a legal case can give a first notion of how to think law spatially. In a civil law system, for example, a court usually finds out how to solve a legal problem of a specific case with the help of legal norms. But the question whether a certain legal norm is applicable to a certain case is quite often not answered concretely by the words of the norm text.[8] The reason for this difficulty is the tension between the generality of legal norms on the one hand and the specificity of legal cases on the other. To bridge this gap, a court typically has to resort to different strategies of interpretation. In doing so, a court refers to other legal norms and their relationship to the present norm,[9] or it refers to earlier interpretations of the same legal norm by the same or different courts

[7] We are in the sphere of modeling here, because we have already seen that it is impossible to grasp a 'real' total perspective on law understood as space, as the concept of space involves this impossibility.

[8] *See* only Hart, H. L. A. (1997). *The Concept of Law*. Oxford University Press: Oxford, p. 126: "In all fields of experience, not only that of rules, there is a limit, inherent in the nature of language, to the guidance which general language can provide. (...) Canons of 'interpretation' cannot eliminate, though they can diminish, these uncertainties; (...) They cannot, any more than other rules, provide for their own interpretation."

[9] This is the case with 'systematic interpretation', *see* e. g. Spaak, Torben (2008). Relativism in Legal Thinking: Stanley Fish and the Concept of an Interpretative Community. *Ratio Juris 21*/1, 157-171 (159).

(in other words: to different judicial decisions),[10] or else the court refers to theories, doctrine or principles that are assumed to form the backdrop for the legal norm. These different norms as well as decisions or theories/principles in turn require interpretation, because they, too, are expressed in language. To be noted in this description is that we (before a judgment) cannot exactly foresee or describe regularities as to what kind of reference, of normative perception a court will apply in a certain case.[11] The reason for this impossibility of prediction lies in the structure of any legal decision itself: in order to be a decision, it has to presuppose an undecidable constellation.[12] But the most important characteristic of such a legal decision, such a judgment in our context of considerations lies in the fact that every thus-made judgment becomes, as soon as it is made, itself an element of the set of judgments already passed that may be normatively perceived by future judicial decisions.

Having this in mind, we can now emphasize: if we apply law, we do not only establish a legal relationship between a norm and a case, but we simultaneously establish a relationship to other norms, decisions, or theories/principles—because they are normatively perceived by the moment of application, by the decision. At the same time, theories and doctrine, for instance, are developed further; they themselves perceive the decision normatively. The more acts of law generation we were to add here, the more we were to go into detail, the denser and the more confused the web of normative perceptions would become. Important for a spatial thinking of law is the observation that any act that is performed on any element of the legal spaces, any act that is connected to a legal norm, to a legal decision, or to legal theories contains at least one normative perception of any other such act. Drawn back to the notion of law consisting in three spaces—the space of legal norms, the space of legal decisions, and the space of legal thinking –, we can see now that any perception of one element of one space does not only transform this space from which it stems originally, but also at least one of the other two spaces. This is the case because in normatively perceiving an earlier interpretation of a legal norm (by interpreting a legal norm by way of a legal decision), we change the position of that decision in the web of the space of legal decisions. And because norms cannot be applied without interpretation, the addition of an interpretation of a certain norm by way of its normative perception through a legal decision also changes the position of this norm in the space of legal norms. The same would be

[10] *See* e. g. Schauer, Frederick (1987). Precedent. Stanford Law Review 39, pp. 571-606; Alexander, Larry (1989). Constrained by Precedent. Southern California Law Review 63/1, pp. 1-64.

[11] *See* also Müller-Mall, Sabine (2010). Interpretation *als* Rechtserzeugung, in: Groh, Thomas & Lorenz, Jörn (eds.). Interpretatio Mundi. Wie deuten die Wissenschaften ihre Welt?, pp.235-251.

[12] This is what *Derrida* calls the 'aporia of decision' (*see* Derrida, Jacques (1992). Force of Law: The "Mystical Foundation of Authority", in: Cornell, Drucilla & Rosenfeld, Michel & Carlson, David Gray (eds.). *Deconstruction and the Possibility of Justice*, New York: Routledge pp. 3-67 (pp. 24)) and what *Luhmann* calls the 'paradox of decision' (*see* Luhmann, Niklas (1995). *Das Recht der Gesellschaft*. Frankfurt am Main: Suhrkamp, p. 308 and Luhmann, Niklas (1993), Die Paradoxie des Entscheidens, *Verwaltungsarchiv 84*, pp. 287-310.).

true for the development of a specific theory, which up to the new decision was the main doctrinal argument for interpreting the norm—it would have implications for the space of legal norms as well.

Maybe these statements still seem a little complicated, not very familiar. For the moment, what we should keep in mind from this is the following: in this modelling, law consists of three spaces. Performative acts of law generation are normative perceptions of elements of at least one of these spaces. Any such perception transforms the positions of both, the perceived element of one space and the one of the (new) act of normative perception which directly becomes an element of another space. These transformations on their part can be described as changing relations between the legal spaces. And because the distinction of three spaces is only a terminological one, not a categorical one, we can also describe these relations as being relations between the elements of the legal space (understood as the whole relationality of law). The notion of the three legal spaces provides a structure in our imagination of law as a web of normative perception acts by classifying the elements into conventional sets: norms, decisions, and theories. This notion also involves a presupposition that is necessary for our intention of finding methods of taking a closer look at concrete constellations: the notion of a sub-space presupposes that we can pick constellations out of our relational space of law that themselves have the same (spatial) characteristics as the (entire) space of law. Before outlining such methods in Sect. 4.2 of this chapter, we shall now say more about these spatial characteristics that are central to our model. Most aspects have already been mentioned in one context or another. But it seems to be important to bring them together to refine the notion of thinking law spatially.

4.1.2.1 Dimensionality

Working out the concept of hybridity in order to describe certain characteristics of law in Chap. 2, we connected the concept to the notion of 'multi-dimensionality'. We said that the concept of hybridity (applied to law) "includes the multiplicity and the whole of law at the same time, and *both are not even separable*".[13] The important conclusion contained in this description was that from the point of view of a hybrid law it would be impossible to understand law as a linear and hierarchical normative order; neither would we be allowed to imagine law as a system arranged only vertically or horizontally.[14] Now, after having taken the path through the previous considerations, we can even lay out the reasons for these conceptual exclusions in a more precise way: law's relationality is constituted by performative events of law generation. These events refer to other, previous events of generation by perceiving them normatively. It is the case for every event that a

[13] *See above*, Chap. 2, Sect. 2.2.3.2.

[14] Again, *see above* Chap. 2, Sect. 2.2.3.

limitation to a defined number of normative perceptions is impossible. In making a legal judgment, for instance, a court might perceive a multiplicity of legal norms, legal theories, and other legal decisions, which in turn are to be understood as events of law generation, also including a multiplicity of normative perceptions. The relations that are constituted by the first event, by the judgment, therefore become more blurred the more precisely we look at them. One presupposition for thinking law spatially then lies in the assumption that every normative perception made in a performative event of law generation takes a different direction: and these directions for their part are what we in the context of spatial thinking can call *dimensions*. The term 'dimension' is but a name for the direction of extension that constitutes a space, in other words, for the spatial extent. Hence, the quality of having dimensions, dimensionality, is a presupposition for thinking something as a space—without dimensionality, spatiality is not thinkable.

If we understand law as constituted by a multiplicity of normative perceptions through events of law generation, we already include a notion of dimensionality—otherwise we could neither think the extended relationality of law nor the performative event of law generation as both generative and perceiving and thus establishing relations to other events. But in what sense could the concept of law's dimensionality now deliver insights?

At first, it excludes two kinds of conceptual description of legal constellations that are quite powerful in contemporary legal debates: the one of collision and the one of fragmentation.[15] As for 'fragmentation', "the suggestion is that where once was unity, there is now a splintered and fractured world".[16] But the dichotomy of unity and fragmentation—this is quite obvious—does not apply in our spatial modelling of law: because thinking law spatially means to presuppose a web of relations that are necessarily established by performative events of law generation. This, again, is contrary to any idea of unity for two reasons: one reason is linked to the spatial approach's characteristic of not being dependent on the concept of the meaning of a norm. The idea of unity in law, in particular, can be understood as an extension of the concept of the meaning of a norm. This is the case if we understand the notion of unity as a state of law in which law does not show any contradictions. The other reason for the conceptual incompatibility of the notion of unity with the spatial approach has to do with the dynamics and relationality of spatial law. Simultaneity and dimensionality are necessary characteristics of our spatial model of law—and as soon as we have simultaneous normative perceptions that might point to different directions of extension (dimensions), it is impossible to speak of unity.

Without the conception of unity, of course its counter-concept, 'fragmentation', is lost as well. Almost the same reasons exclude the notion of 'collisions' from a

[15] *See See* e. g. Fischer-Lescano, Andreas & Teubner, Gunther (2004). Regime-Collisions: The Vain Search for Legal Unitiy in the Fragmentation of Global Law. *Michigan Journal of International Law* 25, 999-1046.

[16] Koskenniemi, Martti (2005). Global Legal Pluralism: Multiple Regimes and Multiple Modes of Thought. http://www.helsinki.fi/eci/Publications/Koskenniemi/MKPluralism-Harvard-05d[1].pdf. Accessed 10 December 2012, p. 2.

spatial thinking of law: there are no requirements of coherence, because the core concept of law thought spatially is the one of normative perception, not the one of being bound. The constellation of being bound by two different laws that are contradictory, that are in collision, simply does not exist in the spatial model of law; there is no place to describe it.

But is this spatial approach to law not an idea of high losses, then, in terms of insights into questions that we have to pose to law? It is true that this approach does not answer some of the questions actual discussions ask—but its productivity has to be seen in the new questions it asks. For even scientific questions always depend on the perspective we are taking on the object of inquiry—as soon as we change the perspective, new questions will arise. Any comparison or reproach of not answering the questions of other perspectives is somewhat senseless, then. So what are some of the questions that thinking law spatially allows us to ask?

As for the aspect of dimensionality, the most important question we have to ask in order to find insights into law is: *if legal spaces necessarily have dimensions, how can we extract them and what can we do with them?*

The main problem included in this question is the problem of 'extracting dimensions'. What does it mean to extract dimensions, and how can we do that? This occurs as a *problem* because of the dynamics of law's spatiality. We have seen that a spatial thinking of law presupposes the idea of dynamics in its most developed form: that a space is only thinkable through dynamics and that the dynamics concern not only discrete events, but that their dynamic act always affects the whole. We therefore cannot think the space of law as still, not even at any single moment. As soon as we do so, we are in the sphere of place,[17] which means firstly that we can only think of it from a specific location. As we have seen before,[18] the consequence of defining a specific location departs from the spatial level of thinking. And secondly, this place-based approach presupposes a reference frame that allows for defining the specific location in the first place. We have already seen that any such reference frame necessarily has to be *added*, that it is artificial. The concept of dimensionality in space now opens a possibility: to bridge the perspectives of space and place by way of the notion of dimensions—because any reference frame can be thought of as a coordinate system, as a definition of dimensions. Extracting dimensions is thus a method of defining a reference frame. Of course this process of extracting cannot be a deductive one. This is the case because the spatial perspective forbids any deduction or any linear translation of the perspective of place. The concept of extracting dimensions, even if it is always already part of the perspective of place, only becomes meaningful if we imagine law spatially, because only then can we coherently speak of dimensions. Trying to extract dimensions from the space of law is therefore necessarily a method of the perspective of place, but one that finds its conceptual grounds in the spatial thinking

[17] *See above* Chap. 3, Sect. 3.3.1.

[18] Again, *see above* Chap. 3, Sect. 3.3.3.

of law. How it could be carried out, the extraction of dimension, is what we shall investigate and exemplify in Sect. 4.2 and also Sect. 4.3.2.

4.1.2.2 Normative Perception

As for the concept of 'normative perception', we have already developed it earlier,[19] and we have already seen that it describes the practical moment that produces space.[20] Similar to the concept of dimension and its connection to the notion of hybridity, 'normative perception' is linked to the concept of relationality: the way of acting in a performative event of law generation is what we call normative perception, and the perceiving operation establishes the relations that produce the space of law. Both concepts, the one of dimensionality and the one of normative perception, constitute different conditions for the possibility of thinking law spatially. Once again: what questions can we ask concerning spatial law that are only made thinkable by this concept—why do we need this concept for taking a perspective on law?

First, it indicates the necessity of a closer look at the establishment of relations, which means: a closer look at performative acts of law generation and their quality of referring to other such acts. As an example for such a closer look, we shall investigate legal judgment in Sect. 4.2.3. Second, and very much connected to this first version of a question, is the one of elements of law that are not perceived normatively. A conventional distinction, such as for example between an appropriate and an in-appropriate legal norm concerning a specific case, is then substituted in a spatial approach to law by a distinction between those elements that are perceived normatively and those that are not—which opens the perspective for reasons of perception or non-perception. This description might sound only like a different formulation of the same question—but it is not: because the perspective is turned around from a legal objectivity, where a norm is suitable or not, appropriate or not, to a subjective notion of legal decision. This allows us to extract reasons from decisions and then to evaluate them, rather than evaluating something that is presupposed as objective.

In general, the concept of normative perception as producing space opens up two strategies of legal investigation that are based on spatial thinking of law: A quantitative one and a qualitative one.

Quantitative Investigation of Law

Quantitative investigation in this context means—if we suppose normative perception as the moment of practice in law—to examine relative frequencies of normative perception of the different elements of law and thus to gain insights about the relationships between these elements. This way of quantitative investigation

[19] *See above* Chap. 2, Sect. 2.2.3.

[20] *See above* Chap. 3, Sect. 3.3.3.

presupposes that all elements of law can be qualified as being equal at the starting point. This means, for instance, not to differentiate legal norms or legal decisions on a scale of hierarchy. A quantitative description in this sense could be useful to answer the question of which legal norms, decisions or theories are more powerful than others. In a second step, then, it would be possible to include such differentiations by factorizing the relative frequencies observed in the first step: this could mean, for example, to ascribe to legal decisions of high courts a different value than to legal decisions of district courts. And if one integrated in such a quantitative investigation not only national courts or norms, but also European or international ones, one could as a result achieve an idea of how for instance European legal norms influence the decisions of German or French courts—at least with regard to quantity. Strictly speaking, in the perspective of place (where we are as soon as we look at concrete elements of law) we would thus add a geo-political dimension to the actual reference frame: the geopolitical origins of legal norms or decisions. This kind of quantitative investigation might be executed quite easily via statistics and databases (even if it can require quite an industrious commitment, depending on how far-reaching such a database will be)—and in some studies, this is already done.[21] But to qualify this, we have to note that concerning the object of 'law' any quantitative investigation has to be undertaken with caution; because the discovery of relative frequencies alone does not allow us to draw any conclusions towards qualitative statements. They only have a limited capacity of description. And still such quantitative studies are experiencing an upward trend.[22]

[21] *See* e.g. Merryman, John H. (1954). The authority of authority: What the California Supreme Court cited in 1950. *Stanford Law Review* 6, 613-673; Merryman, John H. (1977). Toward a Theory of Citations: An Empirical Study of the Citation Practice of the California Supreme Court in 1950, 1960, and *1970. Southern California Law Review 50*, 381-428; Friedman, Lawrence M. & Kagan, Robert A. & Cartwright, Bliss & Wheeler, Stanton (1981). State Supreme Courts: A Century of Style and Citation. *Stanford Law Review 33*, 773-818; Landes, William M. & Lessig, Lawrence & Solimine, Michael E. (1998). Judicial influence: A Citation Analysis of Federal Courts and Appeals Judges. *Journal of Legal Studies* 27, 271-332; Fowler, James H. & Jeon Sangick (2008). The Authority of Supreme Court Precedent. *Social networks 30*, 16-30; Chandler, Seth S. (2005). The Network Structure of Supreme Court Jurisprudence. *University of Houston Public Law and Legal Theory Series* 2005-W-01; Kosma, Montgomery N. (1998). Measuring the Influence of Supreme Court Justices. *Journal of Legal Studies 27*, 333-372; Caldeira, Gregory (1988). Legal Precedent: Structures of Communication Between State Supreme Courts. *Social networks 10*, 29-55; Caldeira, Gregory (1985). The Transmission of Legal Precedent: A Study of State Supreme Courts. *American Political Science Review 79*, 178-194; Johnson, Charles A. (1986). Follow-Up Citations in the U. S. Supreme Court. *Western Political Quarterly 39*, 538-547; Landes, William M. & Posner, Richard A. (1976). Legal Precedent: A Theoretical and Empirical Analysis. *Journal of Law & Economics 19*, 249-307; Sirico, Louis J. Jr. (2000). The Citing of Law Reviews by the Supreme Court: 1971-1999. *Indiana Law Journal 75*, 1009-1039 and Shapiro, Fred R. (1991). The Most-Cited Articles from The Yale Law Journal. *Yale Law Journal 100*, 1449-1514 ; *see* also above Chap. 2, Sect. 2.2.4.3.

[22] As the citations in the previous note might prove.

Qualitative Investigation of Law

More interesting from our perspective of a conceptual and descriptive approach to law seems to be a qualitative investigation—but it should also be more complex, because the parameters that might define any reference frame for observation are yet to be found and determined in a more precise way. We should therefore take into consideration legal criteria—but the difficulty lies in extracting them. Here again, we are concerned with the problem of extracting dimensions, which we have already exposed above[23] and which we shall negotiate again below.[24] The main problem of any such qualitative investigation based on parameters or dimensions that are extracted *from* law is that they have to be applied in a way that is free of presuppositions, free of presupposed evaluations. For the moment, we shall only try to give an example of what the procedure could be like. For instance we could think of some legal principles: democracy, liberty, and equality. In what follows, we will fall back upon our terminological distinction between three sub-spaces of law: the space of legal norms, the space of legal decisions, and the space of legal theories. The principles of which we are now thinking are elements of the space of legal theories. First they have to become parameters of the investigation as empty phrases: without any meaning, without any evaluation. We could roughly say that we are putting them into relation with each other as pure terms, so that they stretch a reference frame by constituting its dimensions. In a second step, we would further put them into relation with one another by connecting all decisions, norms, or theories that refer to the principle of democracy for instance with all those that refer to the principle of liberty or the one of equality. In doing so, we neglect that in the legal discourse these three legal principles are often understood as linked to each other—we are even obliged to neglect this because such a connection would only be established through a spatial investigation.[25] The next step we need to undertake now in order to get a spatial picture of this specific constellation is to scale these dimensions, which means here: to scale the principles of democracy, liberty, and equality. This scaling, again, can be aligned with different possible entities. If we take for the subject of scaling for instance a specific legal subject (not a concrete but a general one, which means: the notion of a legal subject), then for every norm, decision, or theory that is an element of our concrete constellation we should have to evaluate how strong or weak its infringement or its foundation of rights is concerning this legal subject with regard to its potential reference to democracy, liberty, or equality. One of the main difficulties in doing so would be to scale the dimensions without falling back upon known or common legal evaluations.

---

[23] *See above* Sect. 4.1.2.1.

[24] *See below* Sect. 4.2.

[25] Again, while extracting these principles as dimensions we are in the sphere of place, because any such concretization functions as a specific localization, which is only possible in the perspective of place.

In such a spatial constellation, a legal norm that for instance would infringe on equality and liberty in order to protect democracy, this legal norm would show a relatively high distance to a norm that would strengthen liberal rights in order to achieve the same objective.

If now we classified all legal norms, decisions, and theories of one or more normative systems in such a representation, and if we completed it with the relations established by normative perceptions, then we would receive a comprehensive picture. This picture of course remains one of a singular perspective; and the perspective is dependent on the criteria of scaling. On the one hand this confirms the impossibility of objectivity in the description of law; but on the other hand such a procedure makes it possible to take a perspective at law at all—in making the criteria of scaling explicit, it is then possible to describe a certain constellation of law under definable, and thereby also changeable, coordinates. The criteria of scaling, again, do not arise out of nowhere, but we take them from the legal spaces: for instance we could base a perspective on a certain notion of democratic theory (or: liberal, or: equality theory). And in this context *to base it* means to value this notion at 100 %. Then we could measure and value certain legal norms, decisions, or theories in relation to a 'scale of a democratic notion', wherein complete conformity with the democratic theory from which we are starting is put at 100 %, while norms or concepts that match only partly are put in more distant places on the scale. In case one changes the approach on which the whole scaling is based, the result should be the following: all relations in between all elements of law should be unaffected as relations of normative perceptions, whereas their distances, their spatial constellation, will experience quite a bit of alteration. Once the relations are registered empirically for the space of legal norms, the space of legal decisions, and the space of legal thinking, then thinking law spatially permits making these relations visible under different conditions that are to be defined anew each time. Of course it is not possible to register all relations of law, not even for one distinct point in time. We will discuss later on in Sect. 4.2.2 how it could be possible to do so for certain constellations of law, and what scaling will mean in such a procedure of describing law. For the moment, it is important to keep in mind the just-described picture of registering law's relations—it is not more than a first idea that can hopefully help illustrate what spatial thinking of law can mean. Its benefit for the description of law lies for instance in its capacity to make explicit the different approaches to law taken by each investigation, respectively. We can thereby make legal investigations connectable for both: other legal approaches as well as non-legal approaches to law, for instance political or sociological ones. And making this explicit in such a manner also allows us to reveal overlaps and simultaneity in hybrid, relational, and dynamic law. As we have already pointed out, these overlaps or simultaneities are not to be described as collisions or frictions that have to be resolved, but as necessary parts of spatial law. Strategies of escaping these overlaps or simultaneities in practical constellations (where we have to find unambiguous solutions for cases) may make use of the spatial thinking of law: by referring to such a thinking of law, they could find possibilities and methods of formulating different perspectives. We could think of spatial perspectives on law for instance that let any 'collision' appear in a different light. What this could look like in a more concrete sense is the topic of Sect. 4.2. For the moment, it is sufficient to recognize that thinking law spatially means most notably to accept a multiplicity of possible perspectives on law—it is a relativist approach in this sense. But before seeing more regarding the art of taking concrete perspectives on law, we have to glance at a second level of thinking law spatially: the notion of transformations.

4.1.2.3 Transformations

A good illustration of the concept of transformation in the spatial thinking of law can be found with regard to the three legal (sub-)spaces that we have already introduced above. The notion of transformation is very much linked to that of dynamics—if the concept of dynamics refers to the change of something in time, the one of transformation describes this change with regard to the changed object, which in our context is: the legal constellation. We have already outlined that any dynamics of law in our model are established by acts of normative perception—these acts are the moving part of law, constituting the space, or the three spaces. The concept of transformation, then, will grant us the capacity to analyse how a certain normative perception (e.g. the reference to a legal norm in a legal decision) might not only affect one single element of one legal space, but how it affects the entire constellation of law. The concept of transformation should also include an explanation of elements and constellations in law that are *not* affected by an act of normative perception—because any transformation may integrate both: changing and not-changing relations, both of which are meaningful to the description of a legal constellation. It is indicated in this expression of changing parts of the constellation and *not*-changing other parts of the constellation: the notion of transformation opens up the topological approach to law, which we have already brushed above.[26] While we will look deeper into possibilities of topological approaches to law in Sect. 4.3 of this chapter, for now we can state that the term 'transformation' denotes the functional component of individual acts of normative perception. The functional aspect is to be understood as the directedness of these acts towards either a special constellation of law or the entire constellation of the space of law (or the three legal spaces). Of course we can only talk about functionality in this sense from a certain perspective that includes ascribing different values to different dimensions, elements, and thus, constellations of law—it therefore presupposes taking special perspectives that lead us directly into the sphere of place. But at the same time, in including the dynamics of law as presupposition of the notion of transformation, this approach negotiating transformations of law integrates the conceptual spatial perspective. *The concept of transformation*

[26] *See above* Chap. 3, Sect. 3.3.3.

therefore connects the perspective of space to the one of place on the descriptive level, just as the notion 'topology' does on the conceptual level. Before having a closer look at and showing an example of this connection, we now have to describe more precisely what it means for the description of law to take a concrete perspective, or, in other words, to approach law from the sphere of place.

4.2 Placing: Taking Concrete Perspectives on Law

Taking concrete perspectives on law is a very prominent procedure among the epistemological strategies of exploring law—because any answering concrete legal questions presupposes a concrete perspective. The paradigmatical situation for a concrete question is certainly that of making judicial judgments: is it lawful to do this or that? Or: what is the legal situation concerning copyright? This could be another typical concrete question with respect to law. In a first step it becomes quite clear that such a question might not be answered by references to law's spatiality. Any reference to the hybridity, relationality, or dynamics of law will not help with concrete questions—because those are concepts for describing law as a whole. But even if they do not permit us to answer concrete questions, they are the theoretical grounds for a description of what it is that we do in taking concrete perspectives on law: we place ourselves as observers in law, or in other words: we *locate places in law*. In Chap. 3 we developed this method conceptually out of the distinction of space and place.[27] Taking place in law or taking a concrete place in law means—as we have outlined—looking at a single event of performative law generation through the lenses of a reference frame. Any reference frame is an artificial system, which we *attribute* to law at a certain point of action (which is the performative event) and its environment. Applying a reference frame, therefore, is always an act that is beyond law but that refers to and presupposes a spatial concept of law: because on theoretical grounds the locating of places is thinkable through the distinction of space and place (that grasps space as practiced place); and because on practical grounds the locating presupposes a reference frame that refers to dimensionality—a key concept of the spatial thinking of law. In this present section, now, we are going to refine these connections. We will therefore take a closer look first at the notion of a reference frame for locating places in law, or for taking concrete perspectives (Sect. 4.2.1); furthermore we shall expose what the idea of scaling or measuring signifies in this context (Sect. 4.2.2), before we will negotiate a central case of application for these tools: the legal judgment (Sect. 4.2.3).

[27] *See above* Chap. 3, Sect. 3.3.

4.2.1 Taking a Perspective: Reference Frames

4.2.1.1 How Reference Frames Are Embedded in Law's Spatiality

Because it is not possible to refer to a norm as a discrete (locatable) entity in law, exploring law concretely under this condition of spatiality means referring to single events of performative law generation.[28] And because, furthermore, looking at such a single act is not yet *locating* it (any location necessarily presupposes references), and because on the other hand locating is not possible under the condition of spatiality (because of the space/place-dichotomy[29]), we need an artificial system to establish the environment of such an act. This artificial system is what we shall call 'reference frame'. Such a reference frame has to be *added* to a certain element of law in order to open up a concrete perspective on it—it cannot simply be extracted. But by way of the concept of *dimensions*, as we have outlined above,[30] it is possible to bridge this gap of space and place, of conceptual description and concrete exploration: even if any reference frame is artificial, is not more than a fiction—it is still not completely invented out of nowhere. To the contrary, it conceptually refers to the dimensionality of space, to its directions of extension. Even if it is not possible to define these concretely in the sphere of space because of the latter's dynamics and hybridity that do not permit taking a perspective at any given moment—we can assume the space of law to have dimensions. Extracting some of these dimensions hence signifies analyizing the references that a concrete act of performative law generation draws up, and it signifies putting these references into an order—that is assumed to be a system of dimensions, like a coordinate system, a reference frame. Of importance in this description is especially that such an 'extraction' of dimensions is an assumption of a representation of space. This in turn means that such an 'extraction' is neither a real extraction, nor is its result a correct representation of a part of the space of law. Taking a place in law, taking a concrete perspective is therefore nothing but to *assume* a location or a reference frame. Recognizing this hypothetical character, of course, denies any idea of the (single) right decision, or of the correctness and incorrectness of a legal analysis. This is probably not a very surprising result if we describe law as a relationality of (subjective) normative perceptions. We cannot evade law's relative grounds. Nevertheless, making them explicit opens a variety of possibilities for negotiating this relativity. One of them lies in a method of making explicit the (still contingent) reference frame underlying any endeavour, including the search for concrete answers to concrete legal questions. For making it explicit allows us to compare its consistency, its advantages, or its gaps to those of different reference frames applied to the same act of performative law generation.

---

[28] *See above* Chap. 3, Sect. 3.3.1.

[29] *See above* Chap. 3, Sects. 3.2.3 and 3.3.1.

[30] *See above* Sect. 4.1.2.1 in this chapter.

4.2.1.2 What Reference Frames May Look Like

A reference frame that can establish a place in law and makes it possible to define a concrete perspective on an event of normative perception in law basically has two characteristics: first, it contains references—those established by the act of normative perception. These references might also contain second- or third-order references—those to which a different act of normative perception, referred to by the first, refers, and so on. However, the quality of references in our description of law is to consist in normative perception.[31] Second, a reference frame works as a *frame*, and in our context axes of dimension constitute the frame. These axes of dimension we apply to the references that we extract—they are interpretations of our analysis and they refer to the spatiality of law. Their number is not limited, but to receive a reference frame that displays a certain degree of clarity, we shall better confine the number. How such a reference frame may look in a concrete case—this we shall picture in detail at the end of this chapter. For the moment it is sufficient to remain at this dry level of characterization, because there is still one feature of reference frames left that could be interesting and maybe already is central for taking concrete perspectives on law: the one of measuring, or: scaling.

4.2.2 Scaling

The concept of scale, again,[32] emphasizes the contingency of any reference frame: not only can we choose different reference frames for localizing a single place in law, but we can also apply different scales to the axes of a reference frame. While the axes at first are not more than representations of certain dimensions, in applying scales to these axes we are introducing a second level of contingent proportionalization. Depending on how large or small a scale we choose, we look at law with a different resolution, respectively.

Scale is of course a very important concept in geography, treating natural spaces—because it is along scales that we can measure spaces. According to the turn towards the production of space with[33] and after *Henri Lefebvre*, the concept of scale entered the relative waters of also being the result of a production.[34] There are even some legal approaches that negotiate the concept—and arrive at the similar result of scale's relativity on the one hand, but on the other hand often accompany

---

[31] *See above* Chap. 2, Sect. 2.2.3.

[32] *See above* Chap. 3, Sect. 3.1.2.

[33] *See* e. g. Lefebvre, Henri (1976). De l'État. Vol. 2. Paris: Union Générale d'Éditions, p. 68.

[34] Among the extensive literature in human geography negotiating the concept of scale, *see* e.g. Smith, Neil (1993). Homeless/Global: Scaling Places, in: Bird, Jon & Curtis, Barry & Putnam, Tim & Robertson, George & Tickner, Lisa (eds.). *Mapping the Futures: Local Cultures, Global Change*. London: Routledge,, pp. 87-120; Brenner, Neil (2001). The limits to scale? Methodological Reflections on Scalar Structuration. *Progress in Human Geography* 25/4, 591-614; Marston, Sallie A. (2000). The Social Construction of Scale. *Progress in Human Geography* 24/2, 219-242.

"the move from theory to policy"[35]: because there is not much distance between the observation of the contingency of scale and the claim for multiscalar governance,[36] for example.[37]

But for our context it is sufficient first to accept the contingency of any scale. If we apply a scale to an examined dimension of law—whether for instance in investigating the legal situation in anti-discrimination law we decide to limit our scope of investigation to the positive rules of a certain anti-discrimination act or to all references on which we could rely in the field of liberty and equality theory makes quite a difference. But should we not admit at this point that it is law itself that provides the scales we might use for deciding a case, or for defining the legal situation with respect to a certain question? Of course, this is a very seductive idea, and a powerful one in legal positivism, too: law would provide scales and we would merely have to apply them. But, as is the case with many seductive ideas, this would not be very helpful for approaching our goal of finding a conceptual description and methods of exploring law on the basis of our presuppositions—because it contradicts our theoretical presuppositions: law is not a system of norms, of scales, that are ready to be applied to questions or cases—instead, law is a relational system of performative acts of law generation. In normatively perceiving other acts, we are constructing scales, not just applying existing scales. Therefore, we have to negotiate the concept of scale in law as one of construction—the legal construction of scale.

The construction of scale is even identical to what is often called 'proportionalization'—to put different norms, different legal principles into proportion with a concrete question. This description is illustrated best by having a closer look at the principal example for proportionalization in law: at the legal judgment, which can be understood as an application of scales to a reference frame that locates a place in law: the one of the judgment itself.

4.2.3 Legal Judgment: Application of Scales to Reference Frames

Like any judgment, *legal* judgment can be understood in a general sense as a proportionalization of a general and a special. Most typically (in theory), a legal judgment combines a legal norm or a legal rule and a factual case. On a very

---

35 Osofsky, Hari M. (2007). A Law and Geography Perspective on the New Haven School. *Yale Journal of International Law 32*, 422-453 (441).

36 Referring to 'multiscalar governance' as a solution to complex environmental problems, *see* e.g. Ruhl, J. B. & Salzman, James (2010). Climate Change, Dead Zones, and Massive Problems in the Administrative State: A Guide for Whittling Away, *California Law Review 98*, 59-120; Osofsky, Hari M. (2010). The Future of Environmental Law and Complexities of Scale: Federalism Experiments with Climate Change under the Clean Air Act. *Journal of Law & Policy 32*, 79-97.

37 Showing this for the New Haven School, *see* again Osofsky, Hari M. (2007). A Law and Geography Perspective on the New Haven School. *Yale Journal of International Law 32*, 422-453.

abstract level, the structure of such a legal judgment can be described as follows: this is just, that person A has to pay 1000 dollars to person B because of rule X. Even if the formula 'this is just' does not appear in most of courts' decisions, we still cannot imagine a legal judgment that is not oriented towards a predicate depending on the concept of justice: the aim of any judgment is to result in a proportion between a case and a norm that we can call *just*.

There is a long tradition in legal philosophy and theory of trying to give explanations of what the meaning of this concept of justice could or should be.[38] Of course we would transgress the scope of our investigation if we now tried to approach the concept of justice. But it is important to mention in this context of the present study, because I assume that a procedural component of the concept of justice is very much connected to the idea of scaling, the application of reference frames to law, and of *placing* in law: but we shall investigate this assumption step by step. First, we have to recapitulate what the problems of a traditional conception of legal judgment as proportionalization of norm and case were (Sect. 4.2.3.1). Following this, we shall approximate these problems from the other side, from the 'case' and its implications for legal judgment (Sect. 4.2.3.2). Third and finally, we shall try to reformulate the procedure of legal judgment in terms of the concepts of scaling, application of frames of reference, and placing in law (Sect. 4.2.3.3)—based on a spatial thinking of law we thus have the opportunity to describe legal judgment in a new perspective. And at the same time we might be able to extract from this description a method of making legal judgment; this of course not in the sense of instructions, but by providing conceptual tools that are derived from our spatial thinking of law and make possible at least a different description of method.

4.2.3.1 Problems of a Traditional Positivist Conception of Legal Judgment

In a traditional (positivist) description of legal judgment, as we have said, one would probably think of facts and norms, of cases and rules, whereas the application of the rule to a case would be what we call judgment. The rule in this sense works as a standard, or as a scale which is stable and well-defined, and which is to be applied to the case in order to read the result, which is then called judgment. The rule or the norm in this picture is to be understood as a measuring instrument that a judge can use to measure the case. A first observation of this description invites the remark that norm and case, normative and factual constellation, are independent entities here. This would not be very striking, had we not outlined the mutual dependence of *Sein* and *Sollen*, of the normative and the factual, in our recursive formulation of normativity before.[39] From this point of view we can already state that the traditional positivist conception of legal judgment cannot be true, granted that our presumptions are true.

[38] For a classical overview, *see* e. g. Raphael, D. D. (2003). Concepts of Justice. Oxford: Oxford University Press.

[39] *See above*, Chap. 2, Sect. 2.2.3.

But what I called the traditional positivist conception of judgment is not valid in an unrestricted sense even in the positivist tradition: it rather serves as an explanation for so-called 'soft cases'—cases in which a judge can easily see, without taking further steps, which legal norm is to be applied, and how. But 'soft cases' are only one side of a famous positivistic distinction—the one of hard and soft cases. So there are also hard cases for which the legal judgment has to be more complicated. In legal theory, this distinction of soft and hard cases is often traced back to *H. L. A. Hart*, who tried to illustrate with the help of this distinction that any legal rule shows a core and a penumbra on the level of meaning[40]: Cases that fall into the core of a legal rule are soft cases, then, according to *Hart*, while cases that fall into the penumbra are (and, by the way, these are less common) hard cases.[41] To find a solution for hard cases, then, the legal rules have to be subject to an interpretation in order to find out whether a certain case can be subsumed under the rule or not. And therefore, it is indicated in this description, the distinction of hard and soft cases is mostly treated as a question of interpretation of legal norms. Again, this sounds seductively convincing—especially because most lawyers have the experience that some cases are easier and some are more difficult to solve.

But, not only with regard to our theoretical presupposition of a mutual dependency of *Sein* and *Sollen*, of the normative and the factual, we have to admit that this distinction of hard and soft cases is not really helpful for answering the question of how legal judgments are made. If we have a closer look at the distinction of hard and soft cases we shall see that it is a distinction we can only make from a perspective taken *after* a legal judgment. Afterwards, we are able to admit whether or not a case was difficult to decide, whether or not we have undertaken interpretative operations towards the norm. To decide whether a case is hard or soft is not possible, in contrast, *before* a judgment, without any consideration of the normative situation. In the time *before* a judgment (or at least before its preparation), a case is nothing more than a narrative that might be connected to a normative question. It becomes difficult or easy due to our legal assessment: without any normative consideration, it is not possible to make an assumption about the easiness or hardness of a case, simply because no scaling comes into view—no relation between the case and the law. This relation that is the result of any legal judgment is identical to what we previously called 'proportion'. And recognizing a proportion without having undergone a procedure of proportionalization is simply not possible. Classifying a case as hard, which means realizing that it was or is difficult to find a proportion between the case and a legal norm—this is something one can only do after having at least started a procedure of proportionalization. For this reason, but also for the one referring to the mutual dependency of *Sein* and *Sollen*, the traditional positivistic description of legal judgment is not very helpful to our approach. And there is a third reason with the same tendency, at which we shall have a short look.

[40] Hart, H. L. A. (1997). *The Concept of Law*. Oxford: Oxford University Press, p. 124-154.

[41] Hart, H. L. A. (1958). Positivism and the Separation of Law and Morals. *Harvard Law Review* *71*/4, pp. 593-629 (607).

4.2.3.2 Why This Cannot Be "The Case"

As soon as we ask the question 'What is a case?' we will recognize similar problems that stem from the other side of the proportion: the case. In talking about the case, we are referring to the object of legal judgment; and like the measuring instrument for the case, the legal norm, the case itself as what is to be measured is not as easy to define as the traditional positivistic description suggests. To explain this we could imagine the situation of a court: someone comes along and brings a charge against someone else, e.g. his house neighbour. Let us imagine that the plaintiff tells quite an amount of stories about his neighbour: that he does not cut his apple trees, that his hedge is so high that he, the one who brings the charge no longer gets any sun in his garden; moreover the neighbour seems not to be too happy with his wife, and every night they scream their heads off so that the kids of the one bringing the charge can no longer sleep. And finally, he writes in his charge, he wants to stop all of this. In the hearing, then, he tells even more stories, e.g. that his neighbour sometimes makes faces to him and also imitates his gait. What is the case then? In order to make a legal judgment, the court would have to find out which elements of the stories brought up by this man are relevant, and which are not. And of course the question for the court is not which elements are relevant for the person's mental health, or the degree of happiness he might reach in his life, but only: which elements are relevant for a *legal* judgment. These, again, cannot be determined without any reference to legal norms—and here we find the reason for which I described this example: also to determine what the case is, we have to refer to the legal norm that is going to decide the same case. In other words, again in the perspective of the case, the factual and the normative are not independent of one another: what becomes part of the case, object of the legal judgment, can only be decided according to the normative situation. Again, we have a recursive formulation as the result: a case is the recursive formulation of a legal judgment, and the other way around.[42] If we want to describe legal judgment as a procedure of proportionalization, we therefore have to understand it as a procedure that approximates sides, the factual and the normative, until it reaches some degree of correspondence between the two. How, then, do we know the point at which we will manage to find this correspondence? And how can we describe the procedure of adaptation of both, the 'measuring instrument' and the object to be 'measured'? These are the questions we have to negotiate in order to get a description of legal judgment. And how this could be possible in terms of the concepts of space and place, of scale and of reference frame, this we are going to investigate now.

---

[42] *See* for more detail concerning this issue: Müller-Mall, Sabine (2013). Fall und Urteil. Zur Rekonstruktion des Falles im Juridischen, in: Döhl, Frédéric & Feige, Daniel M. & Hilgers, Thomas & McGovern, Fiona. *Konturen des Kunstwerks. Zur Frage von Relevanz und Kontingenz.* München: Fink., pp. 249-262.

4.2.3.3 Legal Judgment as the Application of Scales to Reference Frames

Let us begin this paragraph with its central hypothesis: legal judgment in a spatial perspective cannot be understood as building up a proportion between a general norm and a special case, but as a transformation of legal space. As we have seen before, the concept of transformation connects the perspective of space to the one of place on the descriptive level.[43] On the one hand, a transformation is not more than another act of normative perception that constitutes legal space—and at the same time the term 'transformation' refers to the changing moment of any such event: through the perceptions it takes, and through the ones it does not take, it changes the whole constellation of legal spaces. In this sense, a legal judgment has an impact on the spatial perspective. But on the other hand, making a legal judgment means answering a concrete legal question, and, as we have already seen, as soon as one is asking or answering a *concrete* legal question (we could also say: a material legal question), one enters into the sphere of taking a place in law.[44] At a first glance, taking a concrete place in law means to look at this act of normative perception not as a space-transforming moment, but *through the eyes of a reference frame.*

Such a reference frame can only be constructed as an artificial coordinate system that we attribute to law, or, more concretely: to the act of normative perception and its environment, as we have seen.[45] The application of a reference frame in a legal judgment then basically means two aspects: *extracting* the dimensions of law that seem to be useful for locating the concrete event one is investigating—with all the limitations the procedure of extracting is subject to.[46] And it also means *alignment* of these dimensions. This alignment is important to expose in order to see what making a legal judgment signifies for the spatial perspective on law.

Resuming what we have already stated about the legal judgment, we can see that: (a) it is itself an act of normative perception; (b) it is a procedure of proportionalization of a case to a normative situation; (c) the case as well as the normative situation have to be *constructed* out of both, factual and normative material; (d) this construction already is the procedure of proportionalization; (e) in doing so, one first has to extract dimensions of the normative situation, depending on the aspects that are normatively relevant aspects as well as those factually relevant; (f) the relevance of each depends on the relevance of the other, respectively; (g) one has to scale the chosen dimensional axis in order to find a comparable measure.

These are quite a lot of steps, and they are to quite an extent dependent on one another. Making a legal judgment is a completely recursive situation, even supplemented by the directedness of a judgment towards a predicate that is called justice. Illustrating this procedure of ad*just*ment with a metaphor is probably the best way to grasp it: let us imagine the situation of taking a photograph of a still life, e.g. a set of things on a table. We have certain dimensions of the camera we can

[43] *See above* Sect. 4.1.2.3 in this chapter.

[44] *See above* the beginning of Sect. 4.2 in this chapter.

[45] *See above* Sect. 4.2.1.

[46] *See* concerning the limitations of extracting dimensions *above* Sect. 4.1.2.1.

choose to adjust: we can zoom in and zoom out, and so change and choose the section of the table we integrate into our picture. We can also change the degree of light intensity, e.g. by applying a flash, or a specific type of flash. In addition, we can change the digital resolution of the picture, as well as the focus. And we can choose between different exposure times. Many different dimensions of taking a picture, and we can even apply scales to all these dimensions, e.g. a time scale for the exposure time, or a pixel scale for the digital resolution. We can change some of these aspects and keep others, we can change them all, and we will try and make these adjustments until we are convinced that the picture is well-adjusted. How we do know once it is well-adjusted—this question is difficult to answer, because it depends on experiences we have had with other pictures we have taken ourselves or only looked at; maybe it depends also on normative claims we have learned about how pictures are best adjusted, but most important, it depends on the concrete object of our picture—it is not possible to make explicit an abstract rule that would be applicable to every picture. What the object is in this case of taking our picture—what is part of it and what is not, in which light it appears or does not, whether it is very big or very small; this changes with every adjustment we make.

This whole constellation of taking a picture is very similar to placing in law, to taking a concrete perspective, and to making a legal judgment. The features of the camera are very similar to the dimensions we can extract from law and attribute to a reference frame—these features are artificially produced by us and the camera, they are in a way contingent because it is thinkable that a camera has very different features; and it is also a matter of our taste which ones we use. All our adjustment efforts are also directed—towards a proportionalization between the technical instrument's characteristics and the object to be taken as a picture. Any changing of the object requires a new adjustment of the camera, and the opposite is also probable. When through the lens of the camera we can see a fictional picture that matches, that is proportional to its object, then we press the button. In law, we cannot press a button, but we can state: 'this is just'. It is the end of a procedure of adjustment of the normative and the factual sides. Only after having said 'this is just' can we define what 'this' is exactly, what the elements of a case are, and also at what points of what normative scales we have placed them. And every judgment is contingent in the sense that it is not impossible for there to have been a very different kind of adjustment—a different constellation of the object and the normative situation that would also have led to a just judgment. In law, the one and only right decision does not exist. What we do in making a judgment is a procedure of constructing and adjusting a reference frame to a case which, too, is adjusted and constructed out of the factual material. But since we do not have a camera, do not have a technical instrument in our brain to offer the different possible dimensions of a possible reference frame, we have to find them ourselves: by exploring the space of law as a web of normative perceptions that can be thought to be in different orders along different dimensions of this space—we have to pick them out and to try an adjustment to the case. Of course it is possible that judges receive factual material, and directly see in front of their eyes which dimensions of law are relevant and which scaling is applicable in order to find a judgment. This constellation occurs perhaps in cases that are quite frequent, or if normative situations are involved that the judge has studied very well. We can call these constellations soft cases. Even if they are solved legally, in accordance with the normative situation, we probably would not call the solutions 'just'—because justice is the predicate we apply to judgments that have undergone a procedure of proportionalization as I have described.[47] Even if it refers to the normative situation, any legal judgment remains a subjective procedure, because the idea of the factual and the normative being adjusted, being in the 'right' proportion, can only be thought of as subjective, through the eyes of each observer, just as only the one looking through the camera's lens can decide that the picture is proportional.[48]

A legal judgment, to resume in other words, therefore *takes place* at a point zero of the reference frame we have found in this subjective procedure of proportionalization. The case, on the other side, like the recursive formulation of the judgment, can be understood as the negative of the reference frame, as its in-between-space.

4.3 Law's Topology

In the first two sections of this chapter we have dwelt on two types of aspects that are sequels to our considerations of thinking law as space: conceptual ones and methodological ones. The first negotiate the concept of law, while the latter concentrate on the question of how to take a concrete perspective on law. The relationship of the two types of aspects is characterized by an insurmountable gap: even if we have found certain conceptual bridges between the concepts of space and place (via dimensionality for example,[49] or the definition of space as practiced place[50]), on the level of perspective the gap still remains open. Either we are thinking law spatially, then it is impossible to take a concrete perspective on law at the same time; or we are taking a concrete perspective on law by defining a reference frame that is necessarily artificial, and therefore not part of the legal spaces but an interpretative extraction of them. In that case our perspective on law cannot transcend the reference frame, and thus the extra-legal scope.

The aim of this last section now is to indicate a possible strategy for transgressing the gap of space and place on the methodological level, too. Of course, due to the

[47] *Similarly* Derrida, who is differentiating 'calculation' and 'justice'—e. g. Derrida, Jacques (1992). Force of Law: The "Mystical Foundation of Authority", in: Cornell, Drucilla & Rosenfeld, Michel & Carlson, David Gray (eds.). *Deconstruction and the Possibility of Justice*, New York: Routledge pp. 3-67 (48).

[48] Of course any such judgment may contain the *claim* of being universally valid, of being objective in this sense, just as Kant exposes for reflective judgment in his *Critique of Judgment* (*see* Kant, Immanuel. *Critique of Judgment*, §§ 7,8). But the claim to universal validity has to be distinguished from universal validity itself.

[49] *See above* Sect. 4.1.2.1.

[50] *See above* Chap. 3, Sect. 3.3.3.

limits of this present study, we shall undertake only preliminary works in the following pages, trying to outline to which direction further investigations could possibly tend. These preliminary works, furthermore, connect to our previous considerations of topology.[51] As we have said before, a topological approach might be fruitful in this context, because it might be able to integrate the notion of constant transformation (which stems from a spatial thinking of law) *and* the technique of *locating places* in law by constructing and applying frames of reference. The strategy in doing so would be to build a meta-perspective on a series of concrete perspectives in law that presupposes the constant transformation of legal spaces.

4.3.1 Topological Observation: Combining the Perspectives of Space and Place

Considering the conceptual gap between space and place, such a combination of both, the perspective of space and the perspective of place, involves a necessity concerning the perspective to be gained: that it will be limited to the sphere of second-order observation and investigation. Its output allows us to construct theories that require translation into concrete perspectives in order to answer concrete questions. In any case, such a perspective belongs to the sphere of legal science, understood as the science of producing insights and knowledge about law.

How, then, could we undertake a topological observation of law? In order to do this, we shall illustrate the two conceptual bridges we have found between the perspective of space and that of place—an understanding of space as practised place and the concept of dimensionality. Concerning the first bridge, we have seen before that on the one hand the concept of space presupposes practised places, and on the other hand we cannot grasp concrete *practised* places, but are able to capture concrete places. Grasping concrete places, again, is only possible by applying artificial reference frames to concrete elements of law. Dimensions that are extracted from law constitute such a reference frame. Even if it is impossible to define a concrete location in legal spaces because of the latter's constant transformation,[52] we can still determine a reference frame quite exactly by naming its axes and scales. And thus it is possible to apply the same reference frame, which is defined referring to one element that builds its point zero, to other elements of law. Of course, these elements, as they are different from the first, then cannot be located at the same point, the point zero of the former reference frame. To the contrary, they are spread out over the reference frame. Interesting for the notion of topological observation, now, is the fact that this distribution over the reference frame can be understood as a geometrical one. The distribution is not *only* to be understood, but *also* to be described as a geometrical one, which means in terms of lengths,

---

[51] *See above* Chap. 3, Sect. 3.3.3.

[52] *See above* Sect. 4.1.2.

distances, and possibly angles. A legal topological examination, then, would have to distinguish different distributions and to find ways to describe distributions that show continuities and such that show fractions, just like the spherical shape and the doughnut.[53] Of course, these considerations are in a way quite abstract, and therefore it seems best to illustrate them using an example. In this example, I will allow myself to go into a bit more detail in order to make the idea explicit.

4.3.2 *Example: European Administrative Law II*[54]

Again, the example is settled around the problem of subjective (public) rights in German and European Administrative Law: this time I am going to examine a concrete question of legal protection that refers to the Air Quality Directive (96/62/EC).[55,56] As do many of the concrete questions in law, this one, too, requires some elaboration. The directive in question contained in its Art. 7 (3)—it expired on 10 June 2010—an obligation for the member states to draw up action plans that identify measures to be taken in the short term in case of a risk of exceeding the air quality limit values.[57,58] This obligation was transposed as obligatory in Germany into § 47 (2) Bundesimmissionsschutzgesetz,[59] now old version.[60] Subsequent to this transposition of the European directive, many residents of highly-frequented roads tried to get such action plans to be drawn

---

[53] *See above* Chap. 3, Sect. 3.3.2.

[54] This analysis has been already published in a very similar version (in German): Müller-Mall, Sabine (2011). Verwaltungsrechtsraum Europa – Zur Möglichkeit seiner rechtswissenschaftlichen Erschließung, in: Debus et. al.(eds.). Verwaltungsrechtsraum Europa, Baden-Baden: Nomos, pp. 9-31.

[55] Framework directive from 27 September 1996 on ambient air quality assessment and management (OJ EC L 296/55).

[56] On the one hand this example, as an in the meantime classical problem of European Administrative Law (*see* e.g. Ruffert, Matthias (2007). Anmerkung zu BVerwG Beschl. v. 29.3.2007. *Juristenzeitung*, pp. 1102-1104)) seems to be clear enough for making visible the specifics of a spatial/topological perspective; and on the other hand it shows a sufficient degree of complexity for being examined in such a perspective in a profitable way.

[57] Concerning these air quality limit values, *see* daughter directive 99/30/EC of 22 April 1999 (OJ EC L 163/41).

[58] Directive 96/62/EC, Art. 7 (3): "Member States shall draw up action plans indicating the measures to be taken in the short term where there is a risk of the limit values and/or alert thresholds being exceeded, in order to reduce that risk and to limit the duration of such an occurrence. Such plans may, depending on the individual case, provide for measures to control and, where necessary, suspend activities, including motor-vehicle traffic, which contribute to the limit values being exceeded."

[59] Federal Emission Protection Act.

[60] From 6 August 2010 on a new version of § 47 Federal Emission Protection Act entered into force that leaves in the discretion of the competent authority only whether to draw up action plans for the case of risk of exceeding air quality limit values, cf. § 47 (2) Federal Emission Protection Act.

up.[61] For reasons of clarity, I will confine myself to a presentation of a series of decisions that are interlinked by the different levels of review. This series consists in different judicial decisions in the case of *Janacek vs. Free State of Bavaria*, and within this series I will concentrate only on the principal proceedings.[62]

The plaintiff was a resident of an area in which the air quality limit values were exceeded 36 times in the year 2005. He sued—among other things—for the immediate drawing-up of an action plan for air quality that indicates measures to be taken in the short term; these measures should be suitable for minimizing the period during which the air quality limit values concerning dust particles are exceeded.

For a topological examination of this series we now have to undertake more or less three steps: first to define a reference frame[63]; second, to locate the different judicial decisions contained in this reference frame[64]; and third, to draw conclusions from the topological constellation of the different placings.[65]

4.3.2.1 Definition of a Suitable Reference Frame

The reference frame that I choose for the examination of this case integrates three axes that correspond to dimensions of a spatial legal observation. The first axis is oriented towards the question of which concept of subjective-public law is normatively perceived in the respective decision.[66] We can choose a scaling for this axis whose spectrum spans from a very weak concept that requires only a collective interest for the establishment of a subjective right on the one hand to a concept based on interests that show at least the capacity to be individualized on the other hand. And at the far end of this scale there might be a concept of subjective rights that requires a concrete subjective legal position to be touched. A second axis, then, will be constructed on the question about the system of legal protection: in which cases and to what end should there be legal protection because of subjective rights? Here,

---

[61] Cf. e.g. Administrative Court (VG) of Munich, Neue Zeitschrift für Verwaltungsrecht 2005, pp. 839; Administrative Court (VG) of Stuttgart, Neue Zeitschrift für Verwaltungsrecht 2005, pp. 971 (; High Administrative Court of Munich (VGH), Neue Zeitschrift für VerwaltungsrechtNeue Zeitschrift für Verwaltungsrecht 2005, pp. 1094; Administrative Court of Munich (VG), Neue Zeitschrift für VerwaltungsrechtNeue Zeitschrift für Verwaltungsrecht 2005, pp. 1219; High Administrative Court of Munich (VGH), Neue Zeitschrift für Verwaltungsrecht 2007, pp. 233; Federal Administrative Court (BVerwG), Neue Zeitschrift für Verwaltungsrecht 2007, pp. 695; ECJ, Neue Zeitschrift für Verwaltungsrecht 2008, pp. 984 (Janacek ECJ C-237/07).

[62] Those are published in: Administrative Court of Munich (VG), Neue Zeitschrift für Verwaltungsrecht 2005, pp. 1219; High Administrative Court of Munich (VGH), Neue Zeitschrift für Verwaltungsrecht 2007, pp. 233; Federal Administrative Court (BVerwG), Neue Zeitschrift für Verwaltungsrecht 2007, pp. 695; ECJ, Neue Zeitschrift für Verwaltungsrecht 2008, pp. 984 (Janacek ECJ C-237/07).

[63] *See below* Sect. 4.3.2.1.

[64] *See below* Sect. 4.3.2.2.

[65] *See below* Sect. 4.3.2.3.

[66] For a better understanding *see* already in Chap. 3, Sect. 3.1.3.

the scaling ranges from an objective comprehension not requiring any existing subjective rights for the enforcement of objective law through an understanding that grants subjective rights for the purpose of enforcing objective law, up to a radically subjective comprehension that demands legal protection to be granted *solely because of* subjective rights and exclusively for the purpose of enforcing these subjective rights, but not for the purpose of enforcing objective law.[67] A third axis, finally, might be constituted by time, which is necessary to make visible the chronological order of the decisions. This way, if time is not the only benchmark of investigation, it will also be possible to disclose simultaneities, in contrast to a continuous sequence.

4.3.2.2 The Various Judicial Decisions to Be Investigated

Administrative Court of Munich of 26 July 2005

In its judgment of 26 July 2005, the Administrative Court of Munich rejected an entitlement to the drawing-up of an action plan in this case on the grounds that the sole purpose of the German legal norm transposing the Air Quality Directive, § 47 (2) of the Federal Emission Protection Act, is to protect the general interest, but not to protect individual rights of third parties[68]; Any other interpretation, so the Court, would be alien to German administrative law.[69] Art. 7 (3) of the Air Quality Directive would not allow any different interpretation either, even if this norm were designed to grant subjective rights to citizens affected by emissions; because, nonetheless, action plans according to Art. 7 (3) would be only one means among others to achieve the aim of health protection—therefore it would not be sufficiently precise to derive a subjective right from it.[70]

---

[67] These scales are a matter of choice, just as for instance a linear measure does not *necessarily* have to be expressed in meters and centimeters or in inches and feet, because scalings—in contrast to the axes that constitute any frame of reference—are arbitrary, while the axes are subject to and expression of an internal perspective. As I have termed it before: the dimension or the axes are *extracted* of the legal space, even if this extraction cannot be understood as a deductive procedure, as we have seen above (this chapter, Sects. 4.1.2 and 4.2.1). But despite the arbitrariness of scales, it is reasonable to adjust the scale to the particular research question—we probably would not measure a mile's distance using a scale of millimeters.

[68] To have the character of protecting individual rights of so-called third parties, which means not only and not necessarily to protect a general interest, but also individual rights of an at least definable person or constellation; for an important theoretical line of German administrative law this is a necessary precondition for assuming the existence of a (public) subjective right—this approach is called, in short, "Schutznormtheorie", i.e. in a literal translation "theory of standard protection".

[69] Administrative Court (VG) of Munich, *Neue Zeitschrift für Verwaltungsrecht* 2005, pp. 1219 (1221).

[70] Administrative Court (VG) of Munich, *Neue Zeitschrift für Verwaltungsrecht* 2005, pp. 1219 (1222).

High Administrative Court of Munich of 18 May 2006

In its judgment of 18 May 2006,[71] the High Court of Munich, however, affirmed a citizen's entitlement to the drawing-up of an action plan that is derived from § 47 (2) of the Federal Emission Protection Act as well as from Art. 7 (3) of the Directive 96/62/EC. The Court justifies this result by means of systematic legal and teleological interpretation[72]: the drawing-up of an action plan serves the protection of residents, and in this respect it shows the necessary character of protecting third parties; because the means of achieving the aim of health protection was the compliance with the values set in § 4 (2) of the 22nd Federal Emission Protection Regulation, which themselves were unquestionably protecting third parties. The case-law of the European Court of Justice has established, furthermore, that in cases such as endangerment of human health, affected persons should be able to rely on mandatory rules in order to claim their rights.[73] Moreover, the European regulation concerning the action plan in Art. 7 (3) of the Directive 96/62/EC was sufficiently precise in this context.[74]

Federal Administrative Court of 29 March 2007

The Federal Administrative Court, in turn, stayed the proceedings in its order for reference of 29 March 2007[75] in order to refer to the ECJ among others the question of whether Art. 7 (3) of the Directive 96/62/EC would force the national legislator to a design of the governmental obligation to draw up an action plan in a way that protects third parties. The Federal Administrative Court stated, nevertheless, that a third person that is affected in health by the exceedance of the limit value would not have an entitlement to having an action plan drawn up within the meaning of § 47 (2) of the Federal Emission Protection Act under national law. In addition, the Court states that it is inclined to the interpretation that even European law would not force the national legislator to a design of the governmental obligation to draw up an action plan in a way that protects third parties.

§ 47 (2) of the Federal Emission Protection Act would not serve the protection of third parties, and to derive such an effect from the protection of health (to which the compliance with the limit value aims) would confuse the effects of the protection of third parties with its preconditions. The drawing-up of an action plan would neither lead to an immediate improvement of air quality, nor would it lead to the compliance

[71] High Administrative Court of Munich (VGH), *Neue Zeitschrift für Verwaltungsrecht* 2007, pp. 233.

[72] High Administrative Court of Munich (VGH), *Neue Zeitschrift für Verwaltungsrecht* 2007, pp. 233 (233, 235).

[73] High Administrative Court of Munich (VGH), *Neue Zeitschrift für Verwaltungsrecht* 2007, pp. 233 (pp.235).

[74] High Administrative Court of Munich (VGH), *Neue Zeitschrift für Verwaltungsrecht* 2007, pp. 233 (236).

[75] Federal Administrative Court (BVerwG), *Neue Zeitschrift für Verwaltungsrecht* 2007, pp. 695.

with the limit value, so that any effect of protecting third parties could not be justified with the limit value's character of being a protection norm.[76] Rather, an action plan would not be required for the enforcement of a defensive claim that is derived from the limit value, because the latter could also be enforced by measures that are independent of action plans.[77] The court is also inclined to the opinion that a subjective right cannot be derived from Art. 7 (3) of the Directive, because it would not include such a subjective right expressly and because it could not be derived from the aim of the limit value to protect third parties that the only possible measure is to draw up an action plan.[78] Moreover, the court states that to fulfill the European legal requirements it would be sufficient to design the modalities of procedure no less advantageous than in corresponding domestic procedures. This would be particularly important in order not to render practically impossible or excessively difficult the exercise of rights that are granted by European Law.

European Court of Justice of 25 July 2008

Finally, the European Court of Justice stated in its judgment of 25 July 2008 that Art. 7 (3) of the Directive has to be interpreted as meaning that a subjective right has to be granted to immediately-affected persons that allows them to enforce the drawing-up of an action plan in court, even if they might have other possibilities of action under national law.[79] Furthermore, any general exclusion of the possibility of affected persons to enforce obligations that are imposed by the Directive would be incompatible with the mandatory character of ex Art. 249 TEC.[80] The obligation to draw up action plans would result clearly and unequivocally from Art. 7 (3) of the Directive.[81]

4.3.2.3 Towards Topological Observations/Legal Conclusions

If we try now to classify these judgments into the before-defined reference frame, we can first recognize some congruencies of the three German judgments: all three normatively perceive the concept of a 'Schutznormtheorie (theory of standard protection)'[82] in qualifying a norm's characteristic of protecting third parties as

[76] Federal Administrative Court (BVerwG), *Neue Zeitschrift für Verwaltungsrecht* 2007, pp. 695 (697).

[77] Federal Administrative Court (BVerwG), *Neue Zeitschrift für Verwaltungsrecht* 2007, pp. 695 (pp. 697).

[78] Federal Administrative Court (BVerwG), *Neue Zeitschrift für Verwaltungsrecht* 2007, pp. 695 (699).

[79] ECJ, *Neue Zeitschrift für Verwaltungsrecht* 2008, pp. 984 (Janacek ECJ C-237/07).

[80] EuGH, *Neue Zeitschrift für Verwaltungsrecht* 2008, pp. 984 (985) (Janacek ECJ C-237/07).

[81] EuGH, *Neue Zeitschrift für Verwaltungsrecht* 2008, pp. 984 (985) (Janacek ECJ C-237/07).

[82] Similarly to this evaluation Couzinet, Daniel (2008). Die Schutznormtheorie in Zeiten des Feinstaubs. *Deutsche Verwaltungsblätter*, pp. 754-762 (pp.754).

the critical point for the question, whether a subjective right is established by this norm or not. In the context of German administrative law, this normative perception is not very surprising, since this precondition is very close to the German concept of subjective-public rights in the following of *Bühler*'s definition: the existence of a subjective (public) right requires a legal norm that is mandatory, that protects an individual interest, and that establishes a claim.[83] On the first axis of the present reference frame, the one that is oriented towards the question of which concept of subjective-public law is normatively perceived in the respective decision,[84] these three decisions are placed on the scale in relative proximity to each other. Even the (at least in their result) different interpretations of § 47 (2) of the Federal Emission Protection Act will not change this: while the High Court of Munich derives from the capacity of the limit values to protect a third party the same capacity for § 47 (2) of the Federal Emission Protection Act, the Administrative Court of Munich as well as the Federal Administrative Court both interpret the same legal norm as one that protects general interest only. But this does not challenge the relative proximity of the three decisions on our scale, because the High Administrative Court of Munich, too, does not deviate from the principle of requiring the quality of a norm to protect a third party for a subjective right to be established. The constellation is very similar concerning the question whether the decisive legal norm is a mandatory norm—the High Administrative Court of Munich considers the obligation to draw up an action plan in Art. 7 (3) as mandatory, while the Administrative Court as well as the Federal Administrative Court do not. But still, all three Courts normatively perceive a comparable conception of a subjective-public right that presupposes the characteristic of the norm's decisive element to be mandatory. Precisely this characteristic is also presupposed in the judgment of the ECJ[85]; but the ECJ, in contrast to the German Courts, does not require for the concrete norm (here Art. 7 (3) of the Directive) to protect third parties in order to recognize such a subjective right—the ECJ considers it to be sufficient if the Directive as a whole pursues the aim of granting rights to individuals.[86] According to the ECJ, this would be true especially for the sphere of health protection[87]—thus the ECJ connects merely typecast interests of a collectivity to a possible endangerment of health[88] and considers this to be sufficient for establishing subjective rights. In this respect we can see that

---

[83] *See* already Chap. 3, Sect. 3.1.3 with further references, and also Bühler, Ottmar (1914). Die subjektiven öffentlichen Rechte und ihr Schutz in der deutschen Verwaltungsrechtsprechung. Stuttgart: Kohlhammer, p. 224.

[84] *See above* Sect. 4.3.2.1.

[85] ECJ, Neue Zeitschrift für Verwaltungsrecht 2008, pp. 984 (985) (Janacek ECJ C-237/07) in reference to ECJ C-361/88 [1991] ECR I -2567 and ECJ C-59/89 [1991] ECR I-2607.

[86] *See* Calliess, Christian (2006). Feinstaub im Rechtsschutz deutscher Verwaltungsgerichte. *Neue Zeitschrift für Verwaltungsrecht*, pp. 1-7 (3); Murswiek, Dietrich (2009). Anmerkung. *Juristische Schulung*, pp. 74-76 (75).

[87] ECJ, Neue Zeitschrift für Verwaltungsrecht 2008, pp. 984 (985).

[88] *Similarly* Murswiek, Dietrich (2009). Anmerkung. *Juristische Schulung*, pp. 74-76 (75).

already with regard to the concept of a subjective right there is a relative distance between the ECJ-decision and the three German decisions on our scale.

If we now add the second axis of our reference frame to the picture, the one along the question of granting legal protection, then the situation is altered a little. There we can begin by stating a clear proximity between the judgment of the Administrative Court of Munich and that of the Federal Administrative Court: both normatively perceive an approach which is to be qualified as strictly subjective-right-oriented. According to this approach, legal protection can only be granted on the basis and for the purpose of the enforcement of subjective rights. Correspondingly, the Administrative Court for instance considers an approach as 'alien' ("wesensfremd")[89] that in the present case grants the plaintiff a subjective claim, just because the drawing-up of an action plan (concerning the aspect of a possible charge of badly definable third parties) would show a quasi-legally-objective character. The Federal Administrative Court argues that a subjective-public right could only be derived from the limit value.[90] The obligation to draw up an action plan, being an obligation for the public administration, does not include such a subjective right according to the Federal Administrative Court[91]; and the Court argues further that it is only possible to deduce this obligation's character of protecting third parties if and only if it can be connected immediately to the value limit, that is if it is the only possible measure to achieve compliance with the limit. This argumentation permits the conclusion that the decision is based on a similarly strict approach to the granting of legal protection: legal protection will only be granted in order to enforce subjective rights. In the sphere of German administrative law, one can identify this approach with a normative perception of § 42 (2) of the German Administrative Procedure Code and Art. 19 (4) of the German Grundgesetz. It is certainly true that the decision of the High Administrative Court of Munich also refers to these two norms. But in justifying the subjectification of the imperative of drawing up an action plan, the High Administrative Court of Munich considers (in the course of interpreting national law in accordance with the directives) the normative perception of the ECJ's jurisdiction as sufficient justification for the acceptance of the imperative of drawing up an action plan as being of third-parties-protecting character.[92] According to this jurisdiction, in cases of the endangerment of health, affected

---

[89] Administrative Court of Munich, Neue Zeitschrift für Verwaltungsrecht 2005, pp. 1219 (1221).

[90] Federal Administrative Court (BVerwG), Neue Zeitschrift für Verwaltungsrecht 2007, pp. 695 (pp.697).

[91] Federal Administrative Court (BVerwG), Neue Zeitschrift für Verwaltungsrecht 2007, pp. 695 (pp.697). A claim for the drawing-up of an action plan would insofar be a foreign object to German administrative law; similarly also Faßbender, Kurt (2009). Neues zum Anspruch des Bürgers auf Einhaltung des europäischen Umweltrechts, *Europarecht*, pp. 400-409 (403), who argues still for the acceptance of the establishment of a claim, and Sparwasser, Reinhard (2006). Luftqualitätsplanung zur Einhaltung der EU-Grenzwerte – Vollzugsdefizite und ihre Rechtsfolgen, *Neue Zeitschrift für Verwaltungsrecht*, pp. 369-377.

[92] High Administrative Court of Munich, *Neue Zeitschrift für Verwaltungsrecht* 2007, pp. 233 (236).

persons have to be able to invoke mandatory rules in order to assert their rights.[93] But actually, we have to read this argument as one that does not *justify* the normative aim of protecting third parties by the normative perception of this ECJ jurisdiction, but as one that argues for granting legal protection independently of the subjective or objective substance of the actual obligation to draw up an action plan, if only the directive in general pursues a certain goal.[94] In the German system, subjective-public rights provide access to legal protection, but the reverse is not always true: from the acceptance of a possibility of legal protection we cannot derive subjective-public rights.[95] Therefore, in this case the interpretation of national law in accordance with the directives leads to a certain systematic contradiction. Even if in a very wide approach one considers the Schutznormtheorie (theory of standard protection) as a generic term for the rules and methods of making accessible the subjective substance of legal norms, in this normative perception of the ECJ jurisdiction one concludes the character of a norm to be protecting third parties from the granting of legal protection. Further, one concludes the existence of a subjective-public right from the character of a norm to protect third parties (via the theory of protection standard). This conclusion, however, is not possible, seen from the point of view of the subjective-public right. This contradiction finally necessitates considering the judgment of the High Administrative Court as acknowledgment of a different basic decision concerning the system of administrative law, by the back door as it were: in other words, it implicates the conception that legal protection cannot only be granted for the purpose of enforcing subjective rights, but also for the purpose of enforcing objective law, provided that it is in a however broad relation to any defense of interests. Even if we do not consider the Schutznormtheorie (theory of standard protection) to be entirely inaccessible for such further development,[96] it would substantially change the concept of protection standards as well as the systematic constellation of administrative law.[97]

---

[93] ECJ, *Neue Zeitschrift für Verwaltungsrecht* 1991, pp. 866 (867); Sparwasser, Reinhard (2006). Luftqualitätsplanung zur Einhaltung der EU-Grenzwerte – Vollzugsdefizite und ihre Rechtsfolgen, *Neue Zeitschrift für Verwaltungsrecht* 1997, pp. 369-377 (370).

[94] Cf. concerning this still Schoch, Friedrich (1999). Individualrechtsschutz im deutschen Umweltrecht unter dem Einfluss des Gemeinschaftsrecht. *Neue Zeitschrift für Verwaltungsrecht*, 457 -467 (463).

[95] Wahl, Rainer (2010). Vorbemerkungen § 42 Abs. 2, in: Schoch, Friedrich & Schmidt-Aßmann, Eberhard &. Pietzner, Rainer. *Verwaltungsgerichtsordnung. Kommentar*. München: CH. Beck. 20th ed, no. 45; Scherzberg, Arno (1988). Grundlagen und Typologie des subjektiv-öffentlichen Rechts. *Deutsche Verwaltungsblaetter*, pp.129-134 (132).

[96] *See* for example Schoch, Friedrich (1999). Individualrechtsschutz im deutschen Umweltrecht unter dem Einfluss des Gemeinschaftsrecht. *Neue Zeitschrift für Verwaltungsrecht*, 457-467 (465); Calliess, Christian (2006). Feinstaub im Rechtsschutz deutscher Verwaltungsgerichte. *Neue Zeitschrift für Verwaltungsrecht*, pp. 1-7 (4); Couzinet, Daniel (2008). Die Schutznormtheorie in Zeiten des Feinstaubs. *Deutsche Verwaltungsblätter*, pp. 754-762 (761).

[97] Of course one could thoroughly doubt whether it is still meaningful to call cases in which legal protection is granted for reasons of European rules but not for these rules' character of protecting

The ECJ, for its part, argues clearly according to an objective law conception[98]: the Court argues exclusively by referring to the mandatory character of the directive and does not even ask whether the norms serve as protection for third parties. We can therefore admit a wide distance from the judgment of the ECJ to those of Administrative Court and Federal Administrative Court on this axis, while there is only a relative distance from the decision of the High Administrative Court to those of Administrative Court and Federal Administrative Court in one direction, and to that of the ECJ in the other.

On the third axis of our reference frame, the one of time, the four decisions are of course put in chronological order.

4.3.3 Conclusions for the Topological Examination of Law

But what is the advantage of such a description, referring to proximities and distances? At first, even if the reference frame we applied is necessarily arbitrary and contingent, it helps us get a clearer picture of a legal constellation under the condition of this arbitrariness: concerning the concept of subjective rights we have seen that the three German judgments apply similar presuppositions, take similar normative perceptions referring to the mandatory character of the decisive legal norms, and also referring to a certain theoretical concept, the Schutznormtheorie (theory of standard protection)—although they draw different conclusions. The ECJ instead does not perceive the Schutznormtheorie (theory of standard protection) and considers well-defined collective interests being an objective of the concrete norm's systematic surroundings as sufficient for the establishment of individual rights. In this presentation, the judgment of the High Administrative Court of Munich receives a specific position that is to be emphasized: all at once, the decision refers to the Schutznormtheorie (theory of standard protection) *and* justifies the subjectification of the obligation to draw up an action plan with a reasoning that is based on an objective-law approach. Since the Schutznormtheorie (theory of standard protection) is a basically subjective approach, we have seen that in this decision two approaches that contradict each other are normatively perceived in spite of this contradiction. On a purely time-based reference frame, we could have stated not more than a *development* of the Schutznormtheorie (theory of standard protection). Along the way of a legal investigation, then, the question arises how this development has to be assessed—in a very short step the whole investigation arrives at a question of policy. In a topological approach, in contrast, we can describe the development as a contradiction in a more precise manner—and differentiate its criteria.

Of course we could generate a drawing of the reference frame, set the points at the placings of the different judgments as we have described them on the three axes.

---

third parties—whether it is meaningful to call such cases 'applications of the Schutznormtheorie (theory of standard protection)'.

[98] Similarly Murswiek, Dietrich (2009). Anmerkung. *Juristische Schulung*, pp. 74-76 (75).

In this drawing, we could further recognize a figure of three dimensions—just as our chosen reference frame. This figure we can call a (concrete) 'topology', just as the doughnut we have mentioned above can be called a (concrete) 'topology'.[99] Then this topology would make the contradiction visible as a connection of some points, which looks to the other connections in a transverse direction. The geometrical representation of such a phenomenon is not the necessary core of a topological approach to law, nor is what we developed here as topological approach the only method of achieving such visibility or evaluation. And still, as we have seen, the notion of topology that we have developed here from the spatial thinking of law was able to help us generate a method for finding a perspective on a legal question. And the conceptual derivation from such an approach to a concrete legal question (that is in this sense: a topological approach can remind us of the meta-observational sphere we are operating here: we have applied an artificial reference frame that is only definable for one single place in law to different normative perceptions, to different legal decisions. Such a proceeding in itself already transgresses the sphere of taking a place in law, the sphere of taking a concrete perspective as we have described it above.[100] In addition, by receiving a geometrical figure, a topology, we re-enter the sphere of space: out of the dynamics of any constellation of different normative perceptions, that are by definition dynamic elements of law, that are proceedings rather than entities—out of these dynamics we imagine the configuration of different decisions in our artificial reference frame as geometrical. And this idea presupposes a notion of law as space. Although, as we have seen, thinking law spatially presupposes the dynamics of law (otherwise we could not explain the relationality that constitutes the spatiality of law), the geometrical imagination itself no longer shows these dynamics. But because it is not thinkable without these dynamics as it is not thinkable without the notion of space, we can understand such a topological approach to law as a fictitious bridge over the space/place dichotomy that can only be explored at a meta-sphere of observation. On the level of legal investigation, this bridge makes it possible to describe certain configurations of law in terms of well-defined coordinates. The topological approach is not a necessary condition for such descriptions, but a helpful tool to get there.

For the moment, this remains quite a rough outline of what legal topology could make possible in terms of legal investigations. After having outlined how a spatial thinking of law indicates a conceptual approach to law, and after having outlined how the notion of taking a place in law in terms of applying a reference frame might blaze the trail for a descriptive approach to law, the present topological sketch might now give us a clue as to how the perspectives of space and place could be connected to integrate a conceptual and descriptive approach to law in order to answer concrete questions. A topological approach that tries to describe different configurations of elements of law, of normative perceptions, in one single reference frame might thus allow us to jump over the gap of space and place without constructing a stone bridge—at least for a short moment of time.

---

[99] See *above* Chap. 3, Sect. 3.3.2 and in the present chapter, Sect. 4.3.1.

[100] See *above* Sect. 4.2 of this chapter.

References

Alexander, Larry (1989). Constrained by Precedent. Southern California Law Review 63/1, pp. 1-64.

Bird, Jon & Curtis, Barry & Putnam, Tim & Robertson, George & Tickner, Lisa (eds.) (1993). Mapping the Futures: Local Cultures, Global Change. London: Routledge.

Brenner, Neil (2001). The limits to scale? Methodological Reflections on Scalar Structuration. Progress in Human Geography 25/4, pp. 591-614.

Bühler, Ottmar (1914). Die subjektiven öffentlichen Rechte und ihr Schutz in der deutschen Verwaltungsrechtsprechung. Stuttgart: Kohlhammer.

Caldeira, Gregory (1988). Legal Precedent: Structures of Communication Between State Supreme Courts. Social networks 10, pp. 29-55.

Caldeira, Gregory (1985). The Transmission of Legal Precedent: A Study of State Supreme Courts. American Political Science Review 79, pp. 178-194.

Calliess, Christian (2006). Feinstaub im Rechtsschutz deutscher Verwaltungsgerichte. Neue Zeitschrift für Verwaltungsrecht, pp. 1-7.

Chandler, Seth S. (2005). The Network Structure of Supreme Court Jurisprudence. University of Houston Public Law and Legal Theory Series 2005-W-01.

Cornell, Drucilla & Rosenfeld, Michel & Carlson, David Gray (eds.)(1992). Deconstruction and the Possibility of Justice, New York: Routledge.

Couzinet, Daniel (2008). Die Schutznormtheorie in Zeiten des Feinstaubs. Deutsche Verwaltungsblätter, pp. 754-762.

Debus et. al.(eds.)(2011). Verwaltungsrechtsraum Europa, Baden-Baden: Nomos.

Derrida, Jacques (1992). Force of Law: The "Mystical Foundation of Authority", in: Cornell, Drucilla & Rosenfeld, Michel & Carlson, David Gray (eds.). Deconstruction and the Possibility of Justice, New York: Routledge, pp. 3-67.

Döhl, Frédéric & Feige, Daniel M. & Hilgers, Thomas & McGovern, Fiona (2013). Konturen des Kunstwerks. Zur Frage von Relevanz und Kontingenz. München: Fink.

Faßbender, Kurt (2009). Neues zum Anspruch des Bürgers auf Einhaltung des europäischen Umweltrechts, Europarecht, pp. 400-409.

Fischer-Lescano, Andreas & Teubner, Gunther (2004). Regime-Collisions: The Vain Search for Legal Unitiy in the Fragmentation of Global Law. Michigan Journal of International Law 25, pp. 999-1046.

Fowler, James H. & Jeon Sangick (2008). The Authority of Supreme Court Precedent. Social networks 30, pp. 16-30.

Friedman, Lawrence M. & Kagan, Robert A. & Cartwright, Bliss & Wheeler, Stanton (1981). State Supreme Courts: A Century of Style and Citation. Stanford Law Review 33, 773-818.

Hart, H. L. A. (1958). Positivism and the Separation of Law and Morals. Harvard Law Review 71/4, pp. 593-629.

Hart, H. L. A. (1997). The Concept of Law. Oxford University Press: Oxford.

Johnson, Charles A. (1986). Follow-Up Citations in the U. S. Supreme Court. Western Political Quarterly 39, pp. 538-547.

Koskenniemi, Martti (2005). Global Legal Pluralism: Multiple Regimes and Multiple Modes of Thought. http://www.helsinki.fi/eci/Publications/Koskenniemi/MKPluralism-Harvard-05d[1].pdf. Accessed 10 December 2012.

Kosma, Montgomery N. (1998). Measuring the Influence of Supreme Court Justices. Journal of Legal Studies 27, pp. 333-372.

Landes, William M. & Lessig, Lawrence & Solimine, Michael E. (1998). Judicial influence: A Citation Analysis of Federal Courts and Appeals Judges. Journal of Legal Studies 27, pp. 271-332.

Landes, William M. & Posner, Richard A. (1976). Legal Precedent: A Theoretical and Empirical Analysis. Journal of Law & Economics 19, pp. 249-307.

Law, John (2002). Objects and Spaces. Theory Culture Society 19, pp. 91-105.

Luhmann, Niklas (1993), Die Paradoxie des Entscheidens, Verwaltungsarchiv 84, pp. 287-310.

Luhmann, Niklas (1995). Das Recht der Gesellschaft. Frankfurt am Main: Suhrkamp.

Marston, Sallie A. (2000). The Social Construction of Scale. Progress in Human Geography 24/2, pp. 219-242.
Merryman, John H. (1954). The authority of authority: What the California Supreme Court cited in 1950. Stanford Law Review 6, pp. 613-673.
Merryman, John H. (1977). Toward a Theory of Citations: An Empirical Study of the Citation Practice of the California Supreme Court in 1950, 1960, and 1970. Southern California Law Review 50, pp. 381-428.
Müller-Mall, Sabine (2010). Interpretation als Rechtserzeugung, in: Groh, Thomas & Lorenz, Jörn (eds.). Interpretatio Mundi. Wie deuten die Wissenschaften ihre Welt? Dresden: Thelem, pp. 235-251.
Müller-Mall, Sabine (2011). Verwaltungsrechtsraum Europa – Zur Möglichkeit seiner rechtswissenschaftlichen Erschließung, in: Debus et. al.(eds.). Verwaltungsrechtsraum Europa, Baden-Baden: Nomos, pp. 9-31.
Müller-Mall, Sabine (2013). Fall und Urteil. Zur Rekonstruktion des Falles im Juridischen, in: Döhl, Frédéric & Feige, Daniel M. & Hilgers, Thomas & McGovern, Fiona. Konturen des Kunstwerks. Zur Frage von Relevanz und Kontingenz. München: Fink, pp. 249-262.
Murswiek, Dietrich (2009). Anmerkung. Juristische Schulung, pp. 74-76.
Osofsky, Hari M. (2007). A Law and Geography Perspective on the New Haven School. Yale Journal of International Law 32, pp. 422-453.
Osofsky, Hari M. (2010). The Future of Environmental Law and Complexities of Scale: Federalism Experiments with Climate Change under the Clean Air Act. Journal of Law & Policy 32, pp. 79-97.
Raphael, D. D. (2003). Concepts of Justice. Oxford: Oxford University Press.
Ruffert, Matthias (2007). Anmerkung zu BVerwG Beschl. v. 29.3.2007. Juristenzeitung, pp. 1102-1104.
Ruhl, J. B. & Salzman, James (2010). Climate Change, Dead Zones, and Massive Problems in the Administrative State: A Guide for Whittling Away. California Law Review 98, pp. 59-120.
Schauer, Frederick (1987). Precedent. Stanford Law Review 39, pp. 571-606.
Scherzberg, Arno (1988). Grundlagen und Typologie des subjektiv-öffentlichen Rechts. Deutsche Verwaltungsblaetter, pp.129-134.
Schoch, Friedrich (1999). Individualrechtsschutz im deutschen Umweltrecht unter dem Einfluss des Gemeinschaftsrecht. Neue Zeitschrift für Verwaltungsrecht, pp. 457-467.
Schoch, Friedrich & Schmidt-Aßmann, Eberhard & Pietzner,Rainer. Verwaltungsgerichtsordnung. Kommentar. München: CH. Beck. 20th ed.
Shapiro, Fred R. (1991). The Most-Cited Articles from The Yale Law Journal. Yale Law Journal 100, pp. 1449-1514.
Sirico, Louis J. Jr. (2000). The Citing of Law Reviews by the Supreme Court: 1971-1999. *Indiana Law Journal 75*, pp. 1009-1039.
Smith, Neil (1993). Homeless/Global: Scaling Places, in: Bird, Jon & Curtis, Barry & Putnam, Tim & Robertson, George & Tickner, Lisa (eds.). *Mapping the Futures: Local Cultures, Global Change*. London: Routledge, pp. 87-120.
Sparwasser, Reinhard (2006). Luftqualitätsplanung zur Einhaltung der EU-Grenzwerte – Vollzugsdefizite und ihre Rechtsfolgen, *Neue Zeitschrift für Verwaltungsrecht*, pp. 369-377.
Wahl, Rainer (2010). Vorbemerkungen § 42 Abs. 2, in: Schoch, Friedrich & Schmidt-Aßmann, Eberhard & Pietzner,Rainer. *Verwaltungsgerichtsordnung. Kommentar*. München: CH. Beck. 20th ed.

Chapter 5
Epilogue

The aim of this study was to find and propose a theoretical approach to contemporary law. This approach was to include two features that were to be differentiated and yet connected to one another: *the conceptual description* of contemporary law on the one hand, and *methods of taking concrete perspectives* on law on the other hand. While the conceptual description of law usually belongs to the field of legal theory, the procedure of taking concrete perspectives on law seems to be a typical part of what we might call 'legal practice' or 'legal doctrine'. It is a widely shared opinion in the legal world, that it is possible to generate knowledge of law without having a (theoretical) concept of law. The present study does not provide any arguments to prove this opinion wrong. And still, it makes a theoretical proposal that shows the constructive contrary of proving that a certain hypothesis is wrong: it gives a perspective or an idea of how things could be explained differently.

The perspective is built upon several presuppositions concerning the complexity and normativity of law. According to these presuppositions, law is hybrid, relational and dynamic on the one hand, and on the other hand its normativity is generated by way of performativity (Chap. 2). The so-described law can be grasped through a concept of *space* that is developed in Chap. 3 as corresponding to the presupposed characteristics of contemporary law. Finally, such a concept of space does not only make possible a conceptual description of contemporary law, but it also indicates how concrete perspectives could be taken on law: methods of exploring law are developed from its conceptual description (Chap. 4). And thus, the present approach can be seen as an example of how the concept of law on which we fall back might be connected to the methods we apply to explore law and find concrete answers to concrete legal questions.

Fortunately, this aspect is not the only potentially fruitful one in the present approach: the suggestion of thinking law spatially as developed here offers an integrated concept of contemporary law as hybrid, dynamic, and relational law, whose normativity is generated in a performative way. This law can be described through a concept of space that refers to the idea of a relationality that is generated performatively and that is always and already dynamic. The elements that constitute such a legal space can be conceptually described as normative perceptions, as a

S. Müller-Mall, *Legal Spaces*, DOI 10.1007/978-3-642-36730-4_5,

practice. When we think of thus-described law, we are not thinking of a norm system defined along a certain hierarchy that depends on (stable) contents of legal norms, but we think of many practices of normatively perceiving other elements of law (again: normative perceptions). The concept of space therefore allows us to think law as a practice rather than as a textual system.

At the same time and in addition to the theoretical implications of *thinking law spatially*, the concept of space—referring to a long tradition of spatial thinking throughout different disciplines such as physics, mathematics, human geography—leads us to some methodological considerations of how to explore concrete configurations of law. One of these, for instance, is the application of reference frames to concrete places in law; another refers to complex legal configurations and possible topological investigations thereof. Chapter 4 of this study cannot but outline such methods that are derived from the concept of space. They need further development—as does the idea of thinking law spatially.

This study, therefore, can hopefully exhibit the promising conceptual possibilities of a spatial approach to law. In any case, it can be read as a contribution to one of the main problems of contemporary legal theory: the question of how to conceptually describe law in a globalized (legal) world.